"This book is a Gonzo Gita – a Gone-so Song of Goa; a soaring, rampaging, loving outpouring of Unmanifest Source displayed in manifest consciousness, playing a complex spiritual melody through the hollow bamboo flute of a Vermont farmer/carpenter/building contractor who was all but ignorant of the non-dual tradition before a disorienting full enlightenment struck and he realized 'there's nobody home.'

"The melody is at once intimate, vulnerable, informal, passionate, and rigorously rational in savaging the smug mind that uses language to seek security in concepts. Each time the self tries to survive by seizing upon some truth and running to safety, the Understanding always stands there blocking the way, producing a perpetual Zen koan throughout the book that just might stop the mind for long enough to...

"In the meantime, while you are still in the apparent realm of experience, if you want to read about the complete Understanding of What Is, and its aftershocks – the gaga phase of trying to communicate how it is that there is no choice or free will, no acting or doing, that there is not even any you – and if you want to know how life looks when no longer seen upside down and backwards, how the empty Void fills with mysterious Love, then this book's for you.

"Beyond St. Augustine, who invented the literary genre of the autobiography and wrote a spiritual autobiography of the peak experiences of a separate self, comes this account of the No-Self, continuing and updating the tradition of the great mystics and sages."

– Robert Gussner PhD,
Professor Emeritus
University of Vermont Dept. of Religion

# Perfect Brilliant Stillness

*beyond the individual self*

david carse

*This book, and the thoughts and concepts expressed here,
are not copyrighted. They are not 'mine.'
Understanding or misunderstanding,
interpreting or misinterpreting, quoting or misquoting,
using or misusing, appropriating or misappropriating,
may or may not occur.
All is Presence, Awareness, in which
all apparent thoughts and concepts, events and actions,
arise spontaneously.*

david carse
2006

Printed in the United States of America
first printing 2006
second printing 2007

ISBN: 0-9765783-0-1

Library of Congress Card Number: 2005902191

published by:

Paragaté Publishing
PO Box 925
Shelburne, VT 05482
2006

*The fine print:*

There are many books out there that will help you to live a better life, become a better person, and evolve and grow to realize your full potential as a spiritual being.

This is not one of them.

At the time of this writing, almost every popular spiritual teacher in America and Europe is teaching that ultimate spiritual enlightenment, once attained only by certain yogis, gurus and other extraordinary beings, can now be yours; and that reading their book or attending their seminar will help you toward that end.

This book will tell you that these ideas are absurd, because it's quite obvious that neither you nor anything else has ever existed.

In fact, notwithstanding the enthusiastic blurbs on the cover, I would actually encourage any reasonably normal person not to buy this book. I say this because there's no point in spending good money on yet another 'spiritual' book only to have it turn out to be of no use to you. The subject matter is such that only a very few will be interested in it. What is written about here, if it is really understood, is so genuinely strange that it is on the far edge of what the normal human brain can comprehend or accept. I wouldn't have understood it myself, or found it interesting, before what happened in the jungle.

In addition, if you do find yourself interested, and are able to see past the words to understand at least some of what they point to, you are likely to find it quite disturbing. Few people buy books on spirituality to be deeply disturbed, so consider yourself forewarned.

And finally, if you read it anyway, and what is hinted at here resonates and is by some remote chance followed to its end, then that will likely also be the end of you. So again, a warning. With any luck, you will not come back from this with a life you can call your own; 'you' will not come back at all.

There's no way to know what the chances are of this happening, but the Upanishads say that "only once in a thousand thousand years does a soul wake up," so there's probably no need for concern. Probably.

*That said, enjoy.*

*From the beginning, this life never made sense.
For forty-six years, life was experienced as
arbitrary, chaotic, and painful.*

*There have been many:
parents, brothers and sisters,
teachers, classmates, friends,
girlfriends, wives,
co-workers and business associates,
advisors and counselors,
shamans, priests and prophets,
doctors, therapists, healers of all kinds,
and more than a few relatively innocent bystanders;*

*who, each in your own way, gave
solace and support, aid and comfort,
wisdom and guidance
to a fragmented soul
as it flailed about in the dark,
until no longer.*

*This book is dedicated to all of you,
with eternal gratitude.*

*Now it is seen so simply:
you are all mySelf.*

Cover painting (untitled) by Bianca Nixdorf,
who lives and works in Bombay.
("It's all words, no? – Words and concepts.
And the truth is beyond.
So it's better to forget all the concepts
and all that I have heard here... ")
Used with permission.

*"When you are very quiet,
you have arrived at the basis of everything.
That is the deep, dark blue state
in which there are millions of stars and planets.
When you are in that state,
you have no awareness of your existence."*

— *Nisargadatta Maharaj*

---

Heartfelt thanks to those whose
comments, questions and proofreading
all had a part in shaping and birthing this work:
Cindy, Annie, Bill, Jina, Anima, Michael, Kara, Marcey,
Diana, Dave, Anna, Claudine, and Koshen.

---

And for Ramesh, with deep affection and appreciation.

Be still.

And know.

I Am.

God.


- Psalm 46:10

# Contents

## One

1. Outpouring ..................................................................... 3
2. A Thread ....................................................................... 7
3. Telling the Story ........................................................... 11
4. Prologue ....................................................................... 27

## Two

5. The Jungle, Part I ........................................................ 39
6. Surrender ..................................................................... 47
7. The Jungle, Part II ....................................................... 51
8. Words Fail ................................................................... 57
9. The Jungle, Part III ...................................................... 67
10. Gone Beyond .............................................................. 73
11. The Jungle, Postscript ................................................ 81
12. The Dr. Bronner's Bottle ............................................ 87
13. Deliverance ................................................................ 95
14. Spinning Out ............................................................ 103

## Three

15. No Guru, No Method, No Teacher ........................... 113
16. Free Fall ................................................................... 127
17. Love ......................................................................... 133
18. Morning Talks ......................................................... 137
19. Teaching Truth ........................................................ 143
20. Not Taxi .................................................................. 149
21. Don't Know ............................................................. 155

## Four

22. Question/Answer ................................................. 169
23. Perspective ..................................................... 181
24. Incredibly Simple ............................................... 191
25. Never Interfere ................................................. 195
26. Dream Machine ................................................... 199
27. Confused Thinking ............................................... 209

## Five

28. Surrender Revisited ............................................. 219
29. Too Many Words .................................................. 225
30. Stop ............................................................ 229
31. Explode Your Brain .............................................. 233
32. Exemplary Behavior .............................................. 241
33. Natraj .......................................................... 247
34. Metanoesis ...................................................... 261
35. The Difference .................................................. 267

## Six

36. Time ............................................................ 275
37. Subject/Object .................................................. 281
38. An Impossible Weight ............................................ 287
39. A Splinter... ................................................... 297
40. Still Expanse ................................................... 305
41. Peripheral Vision ............................................... 307
42. Dreams Within Dreams ............................................ 319
43. Trinity ......................................................... 323

# Seven

44. How Can This Be Said? ................................................. 333
45. Most Peculiar ................................................................ 341
46. Eternal Unborn ............................................................. 349
47. Magical World .............................................................. 355
48. All Is Well ..................................................................... 359
49. A Parable: Wake Up! ................................................... 363

Epilogue: An Eckhartian Ontology ............................... 381

Notes ................................................................................. 393
Readings ........................................................................... 397

―――――

"The essential Understanding is that
in reality nothing is.
This is so obvious that it is not perceived."

―――――

- Wei Wu Wei

# One

*the Brilliance
within
where the
Heart
opens
and there is
Nothing*

# 1.

## OUTPOURING

*"Whoever brought me here
will have to take me home."*
*- Rumi*

AND SO
there is only One
all else is illusion
   construction in mind
there is nothing happening here
there is only
One Being Awareness

stillness silence perfection
and in the stillness
   a breathing perhaps
   as if
there is only One
breathing

and all this is that breathing
all this is That
we are That
we are that One
yet not –

   not even we are One
   because there is no we
only One

nothing happening here
despite what it seems
nothing matters

still
the One breathing
is an Outpouring of
   pure blazing compassion
   love forgiveness beauty gift

and I find that I am not
who I thought I was
what I have called 'myself'
is nothing – is an idea is
an accretion of memories
   attributes patterns thoughts
   inheritances habits ideas
which I can look at and say

not I
I am not this

## 1. Outpouring

as myself I simply
   am not
no self no me has ever existed –
   illusion
   fabrication

there is nothing happening
   nobody here
there is only One
   breathing
That is what I – is

I Am That
And That is All

and That is the Brilliance
which all this is –
   life death love anguish
   compassion understanding healing
   light

the Brilliance within
where the Heart opens and there is
Nothing
no self no one
only aching beauty
   and overwhelming gratitude

Outpouring

# 2.

# A Thread

*"Let yourself be silently drawn
by the stronger pull
of what you truly love."*
*- Rumi*

*"Wisdom can be learned -
but it can't be taught."*
*- Anthony DeMello*

There is only One. There is not ever in any sense many, or even two. All perception of distinction and separation, of duality, and therefore of what is known as physical reality, is a mind-created illusion, of the nature of a dream. What you think you are, a separate individual entity, is part of this illusion. You are not the doer of any action or the thinker of any thought. Events happen, but there is no doer. All there is, is Consciousness. That is what You truly are.

In the study or practice of philosophy, religion or spirituality, one comes across a recurring set of ideas and statements such as these, which attempt to point to the true nature of reality: a continuous thread of understanding spanning nearly all cultures and all of history and which has been referred to as 'the perennial wisdom.'

In terms of sheer numbers, relatively few people have been interested in discovering or learning about this thread of insight, and far fewer have understood it fully. Hence there is something of an aura of secret or mystery about it; an aura which, according to human nature, has been exploited and capitalized on throughout history, by mystery schools and secret cults and all kinds of teachers who claim to have special, exclusive knowledge about the nature of What Is.

But truly it is and always has been an open secret; passed on, offered and made available both within and outside of all the major spiritual traditions. Although pursued and understood by so few, this thread of Understanding, this perennial wisdom, has endured because it offers no less than everything: the answers to life's questions, the true nature of all that is, ultimate meaning and purpose, and the end of suffering.

Since it offers so much, it might seem peculiar that the Understanding of this, and the elements of what is simply referred to as the Teaching, have been discovered by so few. There is actually a basic reason for this, inherent in the Understanding itself. But the immediate, functional reason as viewed from human experience and understanding is this: the Teaching, the perennial wisdom, cannot be directly expressed. Teachers who have come to understand it can point to it, talk around it, suggest ways and means for others to approach it; but cannot directly and clearly

## 2. A Thread

state it. This leads many to believe it is not real or not worth pursuing, while to others who are drawn to it this characteristic of the Teaching is the source of much frustration and exasperation.

Albert Einstein once said that a problem cannot be solved by the same mind that created it. In a similar way, any answers to the questions concerning human existence which arise from within that human experience will themselves be part of the problem, conditioned by and arising from the same situation which they seek to explain. It stands to reason that any true answer or ultimate understanding must in a sense come from outside of, must be other than, the condition it understands.

Such is the case with the Understanding. It is not of this human condition; it comes from 'outside,' it is completely other than or prior to all of human experience and comprehending. But of course as such, it is inherently incomprehensible; since it arises outside of human thought and experience, it cannot be put into, limited to, or captured by human concepts and words. While it can be learned, it cannot be taught. While it can in itself be in-seen, apperceived, or if you will intuited, it cannot be directly talked about or even for that matter thought of in linguistically structured thoughts or ideas or concepts. Does exist. Cannot be expressed.

Naturally, this is enough to put off most of the human race, to lead them to look for whatever meaning may be found in something a little more tangible. And it is enough to spark and hold the interest of the few who find themselves drawn, or driven, into that ineffable flame. These are the ones called 'spiritual seekers.' They know, and are haunted by the knowledge, that the ultimate answer is there, just beyond their perception. And they spend their lives following and listening to the seers and sages, masters and elders, trying to learn what cannot be taught.

And then, inexplicably, there are those who are surprised by grace, in whom the true nature of What Is becomes obvious. Perhaps after long years of following and listening and learning, or perhaps even more incongruously with little or no overt seeking. If it seems peculiar that so few should awaken from the dream of everyday life to see things as they are, consider that it is stranger yet, given the parameters of the dream, that any should awaken at all.

And of these in whom the Understanding of What Is does occur, what can be said? They are the inverse; awake to what the world is asleep to and asleep to what the world is awake to. Little about them will make sense to the regular person, even to those well versed in spiritual things.

> "The awakened mind is turned upside down and does not accord even with the Buddha-wisdom." (Hui Hai)

Of these, there will be some through whom will come, just as inexplicably, an attempt to communicate the incommunicable; thus keeping alive the continuous thread of the perennial wisdom.

Does exist. Cannot be expressed.

# 3.

## TELLING THE STORY

*"I have lived on the lip of insanity,
wanting to know reasons, knocking on a door.
It opens.
I've been knocking from the inside!"*
*- Rumi*

### I

RECENTLY, I WAS ONCE AGAIN ASKED to share my story... and once again declined. Good reasons: you see, it is precisely this constant creating and maintaining, telling and retelling, polishing and honing of the personal story which maintains the sense of individual self. The ego is only the story it constantly tells of itself, the experiences and difficulties it has had, the path it has followed, the wounds it carries.

The invitation here is precisely to stop telling the story. When the sense of individual self disappears, this intensely important and deeply cherished story that makes us who we think we are is seen as the really rather shallow and poorly told pulp fiction it is, and it is left without polishing, without retelling, to crumble into the thin air whence it came. This is the invitation to spiritual awakening: to let drop this constant propping up of the belief in yourself as a separate individual self, and in so doing to emerge from endarkenment.

And so, of course, divine justice, or at least divine irony; circumstances dictate that the story is to be told after all. So be it. Let it be done this once, and it will be enough.

There are other reasons for the reluctance, perhaps not so noble: deep resistance in the mind/body, laid down in the fabric of its conditioning. There was a running away from 'the holy man gig' once before, leaving behind the Roman Catholic priesthood; a deep distrust of anything that would call attention here, that might reinforce a deadly sense of specialness. Down that path lay certain destruction, and I ran like hell and kept running, constantly shirking the leadership roles that were continuously offered, until I learned to avoid the situations that offered them. Working as a carpenter, hammering nails and sawing two-by-fours, was safe... while the mind, propped up by therapies and medications, teetered on the edge of chaos. Twenty-five years pass, and two failed marriages. Consciousness thinks nothing of time.

Then, goaded by some force unknown at the time (shit, I thought it was 'my' idea) the rediscovery and exploration of Native American roots (back when there was thinking that a personal history mattered) gives rise to pottering around with native elders, medicine men and shamans.

## 3. Telling the Story

One thing leads to another and the david thing, despite finding travel uncomfortable and unpleasant, harboring in particular a secret fear of the (myopically perceived) dark continent of South America, and possessed of a severe allergy to anything involving being part of a group, finds itself nevertheless with four other delightful characters undertaking several days of travel by bus, small plane, canoe and foot, south and eastward from Quito: first down off the Andean plateau, through the cloud forest and then down various tributaries into the upper Amazon basin.

The time spent with the medicine men and shamans of the Shuar people deep in the rainforest is the stuff of great stories filled with wonderful drama. And all of it irrelevant, and signifying nothing, except as an elaborate setup in Consciousness for the rather heavy-handed measures that would have to be taken if the david thing was to be cracked open. Why Consciousness would bother, when there are thousands of deserving and ripe devotees out there just waiting to be popped, is beyond comprehension.

## II

"What happened in the jungle." Tony Parsons speaks of "walking across the park." For Suzanne Segal it was "the bus stop." U.G. Krishnamurti refers to an event he calls "the whole calamity." In Douglas Harding's case it was "the so-called Himalayan experience." Here, it is "what happened in the jungle." Nothing happened in the jungle. What happened is everything, the only thing that has ever happened any'where' to any'one.' What happened is unspeakable. Nothing happened.

What happened in the jungle would fill many conversations, if the conditioning here was not so allergic to the idea of what that might lead to. So it is being written here instead, coming clean, and it will inevitably lead to the same damn thing.

And ultimately, so what? "Settles forevermore the ponderous equator to its line…" All things find their balance. The shreds and remnants of david's conditioning, flapping noisily in the wind, fret dire warnings of the ego trap here, wanting to run away, to find the anchorite's proverbial cave to live in, at least metaphorically.

But it's silliness. There is no ego, no trap; this too is illusion, thin as a summer morning mist on a hay field. The aversion is there in the conditioning of this mind/body apparatus, like the aversion to certain foods or to loud music. This is seen, but it no longer holds any significance. One Consciousness streams through all these billions of forms and what happens in which, including this one, truly is of no significance. There is no choice here, only the pure and choiceless awareness of Consciousness streaming. Tony DeMello called it, "wholehearted cooperation with the inevitable." So here goes.

Much of what happened in the jungle was experiential, and so could be thought about, remembered, talked about. Deep, transformative experience. Nice stuff. Transcendent stuff. Beautiful. Major peak experience type stuff. You know well what I mean. Enough to burn the livin' be'jesus out of the david thing. Preparatory, could be said of it now. This can be talked about, however haltingly and with much abuse of the rules of grammar and the intended meaning of words.

## 3. Telling the Story

But there then came a time when all that stopped, when the experiencing stopped, and here it gets dicey. Because david also stopped. But of course that's silly. david never was.

Looking at the journal entries from shortly after, it's gibberish. Pointing toward the unspeakable and going, "gagaga." It all goes to show the infinite but from this perspective rather twisted sense of humor possessed by the Brilliance beyond light we call Consciousness. "Hey look, we've tried all the other combinations: many years of preparation and then awakening; many years of preparation and then no awakening; many years of preparation and then almost awakening but whoops, sorry, not quite. Here's one we don't do so often: how about complete realization, total consciousness, pow, without any preparation at all! Take some schmuck, renegade part-Indian, renegade couldn't-quite-make-it priest, tortured psyche, carpenter from the hills of Vermont, poor bastard won't know what the fuck hit him. Great entertainment!"

You have to understand, I knew absolutely zippo about any of this shit. Didn't know there was any such animal as a 'seeker,' let alone the whole seeker subculture. Never heard any of the jargon, didn't know any of the concepts. Never heard of *saddhana* or *moksha* or *lila* or *samadhi* and if I had I'd probably have thought they were salad dressings. No categories or thoughts with which to think about this. Absolute, pure, utter, appalling Grace which makes absolutely no sense whatever.

There is some writing slightly less garbled, augmenting those first journal entries, months later, after Consciousness got merciful and set a plate of Advaita ideas in front of what was left of the david thing. These I share with you, in the pages that follow. That snap, that pop, the instantaneous out-of-time in which it is obvious that there is a simple 'watching' (not yet knowing that the correct Advaita term is 'witnessing') of that david thing, of what I had thought was 'me;' not just the body but all of it, the so-called body-mind-soul-personality-spirit; and realizing instantly that there is none such; there is nobody home. Nothing there. Obviously no 'me,' no thing to be a 'me.' And it is even more obviously not 'me' watching, witnessing. The witnessing fills the universe and there is not a thing any where, there is no where and no things, no beings, no entities. There is only this, this thisness, Awareness, and that is what 'I' is.

"A shift of perception" is the neat phrase, but... sweet mother! Not seeing differently or seeing different things, but no seer to see. As near as can be said: the perception now is not as from this mind/body thing.

And of course at the same time all of the above is pure bullshit, negated by the equal realization that nothing at all happened. Near as can be said there's a sort of retroactive sense to the whole calamity. Nothing changes because it is seen that it has always been so: a misconception stops, a misperception ceases. What has happened? Nothing. There has always been nobody home. This thisness is always what 'I' is. Funny that there should have been that little misunderstanding, that there at one time were these funny ideas about 'time' and 'things' and ideas and persons and beings and david and jungle and Source and all...

Nisargadatta Maharaj called it Understanding, but it has nothing to do with comprehension. A knowing, which has nothing to do with knowledge.

## 3. Telling the Story

Listen, this is important. There are words and concepts being used here descriptively. But whether or not what happened in the jungle corresponds to what various teachers, sages or traditions might have been referring to with their words or concepts, I do not know, and ultimately do not care. Of its essence this nothing that happened is completely self-validating. It relativizes everything and is relativized by nothing.

On the one hand there is everything; everything known, felt, thought, believed, everything that exists or doesn't exist, everything possible and impossible. Everything that was, is, or ever will be, or never will be. And on the other hand there is this. And everything is not. And this is.

Whether another soul in the known or unknown universe ever recognizes this or not has been forever irrelevant since that out-of-time in the jungle. I cannot explain this, because I am otherwise somewhat rational. Not only is there no doubt. The very concept of doubt does not exist.

The word that comes frequently is that it is 'obvious,' but evidently that is an abuse of a good word because when it is used in conversations it usually draws blanks. Nevertheless. What is right in front of you, more than that, what you actually are, what all *this* is, what cannot be escaped from, what cannot be otherwise, is obvious, even if in most cases apparently there is not seeing.

So anywhat, it could have ended there. Tried to express it to a few people ("gagaga") but they thought I was crazy, so gave up. Watching of the david thing going back to hammering nails. Bathed in Brilliance, which no one saw. Astonishing, breathtaking gratitude. Tears most of the time, spontaneous and unstoppable. david has lost his marbles, but he seems a happy idiot so what the hey. Always everywhere perfect Brilliant Stillness, and no-thing, which has no name (love and compassion and bliss are pathetic shadows) outpouring constantly seen now always not as from this mind/body thing.

## III

*I*T COULD HAVE ENDED THERE. But then Consciousness got merciful again, or brutal again, same difference; brutally merciful; and, totally out of character, signed the david thing up for a course, which led to exposure to a certain dynamic duo of self-styled teachers of Advaita. In time, they turned out to be almost entirely ego, way off the mark as spiritual teachers go. But, quite brilliant and with a good intellectual grasp of the teaching, so obviously, coming from zippo in that regard, I could learn a lot there. Odd experience, because some of what she talked about tingled, like maybe she knew... but then obviously she didn't.

Gradually learned and pieced together that there's a whole culture out there of the blind leading the blind, that there has been enough of a sprinkling through the eons of occasions when seeing happened, and the eyes through which was seeing, knew they were not. Enough writings by Buddha-things, Rumi-things, Seng-Ts'an-things and Ramana-things, that other things who thought they were things but it was not them thinking, who didn't see, (but it's all a joke because 'they' is the I-ness that is the Is-ness of all seeing) could read and think they comprehended; and in the interim between the occasions when seeing happened, there would be the developing of whole structures

## 3. Telling the Story

and systems around a theory of seeing, and some would get many others to follow them and worship them because nobody knew the difference. Nobody knew the bloody difference, so they are so easy to fool!

So that was odd. And meanwhile of course always everywhere perfect Brilliant Stillness, outpouring constantly.

It is said that when you need a teacher you will find one. Of course, this assumes that you need teachers at all, which is a highly dubious assertion. The universe is on a need-to-know basis, and for the most part, we don't need to know. But when, in the overall grand picture, it is necessary for a body/mind to know something, then they will hear it, and in a way that it can be taken in. This may take the form of finding a teacher; or, it may be that a conversation is overheard, or a taxi driver makes a comment, or, simply, a thought occurs. How can it be otherwise? Consciousness is all.

In the jungle, everything stopped; david stopped; the world stopped. And for a time there was being in this and this only, without concepts or thoughts in which to frame it. Then, there was coming across those first two, and finding that the ideas they talked about corresponded somewhat with the unspoken knowing that occurred in the jungle. There is simply following the natural trail that emerges, seeing only the next step. Which, after all, is all we get to see.

In any case, just about the time there was figuring out that some basic intellectual framework was about all that could be learned from these two, one day in a talk she mentions the name 'Ramesh,' who she refers to as one of her teachers.

## IV

*L*ONG STORY SHORT: INTERNET SEARCH, *The Final Truth* from Amazon.com, and the rest is story. Devouring everything Ramesh Balsekar had written up to that date, and finding it more helpful than anything I had encountered since the jungle. These early works by the retired Bombay banker ring with clarity. The writing is highly metaphysical, reflecting influence from his own teacher Nisargadatta Maharaj, and from an earlier writer known as Wei Wu Wei. Everything available by these gentlemen is read as well, and also what can be found by and about Ramana Maharshi, the mystic sage teacher saint of southern India.

With this reading and reflecting there is the realization that although this no-thing that happened in the jungle could not be recognized or explained by anyone in the immediate context when it occurred, nevertheless there does exist a context, a tradition in which such occurrence is known and recognized. In a world of spiritual mumbo-jumbo and garbled third-hand tales, there are some, a handful, in whom there is clear thinking and writing about What Is. Provided of course that you already know what they are talking about and can sense where their words point. Taken literally or at face value, most of their talk is all but incomprehensible. Necessarily so, given the deficiencies of language.

Thus I was introduced to the timeless thread of the Teaching, the perennial wisdom. And at some point in the midst of this, there is the thought: sometimes it's a good idea, when you're new in a place, to maybe go see and talk to, listen to, someone who's been here a while. Of the four I had so far found as reliable sources, Ramesh is the only

## 3. Telling the Story

one still alive, and in fairly good health for a lifelong resident of Bombay in his mid-eighties.

The first few meetings are remarkably helpful. The story is asked for, and the story is told; the david thing tells what happened in the jungle. Haltingly, hesitantly, using words and concepts that arise spontaneously from the context of this life, to attempt to describe what is known to be indescribable. And there is recognition, confirmation, from Ramesh, that what occurred in the jungle corresponds with what (echoing Wei Wu Wei and Maharaj) he calls the complete Understanding, what in his tradition is known as awakening or enlightenment. During one visit, he does allow as how it is a little odd, the way of this happening; no guru, no teacher... but then there was always the Maharshi with his mountain, so... the slightest shrug, the biggest smile. He's quite sure of his-not-self.

It takes some convincing. The first response to this is an instinctive recoiling; that old fear of specialness stirring again. And whatever vague preconceived ideas there may have been of what 'enlightenment' might be, they had not included the obliteration of that night in the jungle, and this vast outpouring in Presence. Yet at the same time there is also a sense that this is what is. There is no one home. There is recognition, and yet it is of no consequence and changes nothing. Whatever anyone (including Indian gurus) may have to think or say about this, and however helpful that is, there is no labelling the unspeakable. There can be no owning, no taking on of a label, of a concept, of a tradition.

Over the next weeks, years, more visits, more talks. Awkward at first; that great hesitancy in the conditioning, still flapping in the wind. Some visits, when Ramesh is heard to reiterate, as he does on several occasions, that the complete Understanding is here, I am hounded afterwards by others in the group of seekers who come to the morning talks; or the opposite, avoided. So there is often a hanging back, incognito among the miserable seekers, happy in the wider and deeper always Brilliance outpouring.

If there is a 'purpose' in these visits, it is something of what I can only call a 'backwards process:' in the jungle, the answer was given before there were questions, so this time was spent filling in the questions to the answer, the framework to understand the Understanding after the fact.

## V

So; THAT'S WHAT HAPPENED IN THE JUNGLE. And in Bombay. Nothing happened.

What is seen cannot ever be un-seen. It is all so perfectly simple. Always and everywhere perfect Brilliant Stillness. And no-thing, which has no name: Outpouring, constantly. Seen now, always, not as from this mind/body thing. And the talking about it, when it arises, cannot not be, and the writing about it, it would appear, cannot not be. And I am very acutely, keenly aware of the difficulty this presents.

It was Wayne Liquorman, in his preface to Ramesh's *Consciousness Speaks,* who made the thoroughly pithy observation that "The mere incident of enlightenment does not necessarily confer an ability to communicate the concomitant understanding."

## 3. Telling the Story

He got that right. I am not a teacher. There is no interest in teaching, and the mind/body thing does not have the skill or qualification. From the perspective of anyone with knowledge of these things, what you have here is one very coarse renegade part-Indian (wrong kind of Indian) carpenter from the hills on your hands, notably and thoroughly lacking in any kind of 'skillful means' and having only a limited intellectual comprehension of the subject, and lacking the training or discipline that could have been instilled by years of meditation or service. Saying that the david thing is seriously flawed and not cut out for what is happening here is being unnecessarily kind. Except of course that the david thing has been designed and cut out and conditioned for exactly this. Consciousness has a sick sense of humor.

There is only this. And this would be a preposterous claim if there were any'one' here to claim it, which there is not. There is only this, and this is clear. I know absolutely nothing about anything except this: knowing, seeing, understanding; the knowing, seeing, understanding that is not, that is beyond human understanding, has occurred here, is here. Seen now always not as from this mind/body. Unearned, unsought, even unasked for, at least overtly. It is unspeakable, cannot be expressed, cannot be thought.

Rumi was right:
> "As salt dissolves in the ocean,
> I was swallowed up in You
> Beyond doubt or being sure.
>
> Suddenly, here in my chest
> A star
> Comes out so clear
> It draws all stars to it."

And Ramesh is right: it's got to be what he calls 'divine hypnosis.' How else can you explain it? All these mind/bodies are staring at it, are bathed in it, *are* it, and can't see it. How can you show someone something they are already, especially when it is no-thing and they are no-one? It is all so incredibly simple. There is obviously no one home. All-That-Is, is Love beyond love, Light beyond light, Peace beyond peace, Freedom beyond any concept of freedom… throw capital letters on words and shout them, cry them, weep them.

And folks scratch their heads, say they don't get it, "Well, that's kind of philosophical…" they say; or, "But I like my story, I like my drama;" or, "Gee, aren't we sounding Advaitically correct today." All defended, in various ways, from seeing What Is. Even devout seekers, when they hear, "this is a dream," say "Uh huh," and keep talking. No one *stops,* to see, to be. Pardon the crude david thing if it exhibits a marked lack of interest in these discussions.

And Hafiz was right too:
> "Dear ones, you who are trying to learn the miracle of love through the use of reason, I am terribly afraid you will never see the point."

Or, through the use of experience or thought or language or emotion, I might add. It simply has to be in-seen.

Ultimately, there is truly nothing to say. The dream continues; and there is re-entering the dream (not by choice but because that, apparently, is what is to occur in this dream character) with the full knowledge that it is a dream… But you just can't expect I-I to take any of it seriously.

### 3. Telling the Story

And that hermit's cave still looks awfully good. Nothing is needed. It is so completely not important that anything happen, that anything come of this. No need, no requirement, no mandate, no role. Simple. Utterly simple.

# 4.

---

# *Prologue*

*"I can assure you there is no such thing as God.
There's no such thing as creation,
and there's no such thing as the universe.
So there's no such thing as the world,
and there's no such thing as you.
There's no such thing as 'I.'
What is left? Silence!"*
*- Robert Adams*

## I

ONE COULD SAY THAT reality is not at all what it seems or how it appears to be, and that nearly the whole human race is operating under a mass hallucination. One could say this, but it would be greatly inaccurate because the idea that there is a human race, and the idea that there is 'one' to say so, are both actually part of the hallucination. These things we call 'persons' or 'human beings', along with everything else we can either think of or perceive with our senses, are actually only illusory appearances in one infinite Consciousness, which is all there is.

How are we doing so far? Sounds almost like the ultimate paranoid conspiracy theory, doesn't it? In fact, it sounds so far-fetched and so at odds with everyday perception and common sense that most people if they were to hear it would be inclined to call it crazy raving; laugh, or shrug, and go back to their daily lives.

And yet our histories as well as our religious and philosophical traditions tell us that as far back as they go, there are accounts of the occasional 'human being' becoming convinced that this fantastic-sounding scenario is in fact the truth; and accounts also of them trying to communicate this conviction to others. In fact, such visionaries and such 'raving' are at the foundation of most of the world's great religious and philosophical traditions. Few of these traditions still explicitly claim such ideas as part of their overt teachings or practices, but a little research reveals that they were there at the beginning, in the ideas or experience or vision of the person around whom the tradition formed or in its foundational writings.

Which again is an inaccurate statement, since again the idea that there was a 'person' as an individual entity whose individual ideas or experience were the beginning of a tradition is itself part of the illusion. So you can see that there is something of a communication problem here.

Look at it this way: if you were to grant for the moment, for the sake of argument, that it might be possible for someone to see, come to know, become convinced beyond doubt, that everything that we think of as 'reality' is in fact a mind-generated fantasy, and that this illusion includes all ideas

## 4. Prologue

and words and experiences and perceptions as well as the things we think are the 'human beings' having such ideas or perceptions; and granting also for the moment that such a person is not simply insane but may somehow, just possibly, be seeing something others do not see; then in such a case how could such a person communicate to others what he or she sees, when she knows that she herself, all others, and any ideas or words that might be used to communicate are all themselves part of the illusion and therefore quite ineffective?

What analogies, what metaphors or word-tricks might then be used to try to convey what is beyond what can be conveyed? Such things as, "it's like light but it's not light, so completely beyond light it can't be seen," or "it is everywhere and nowhere at the same time," or "it is the fullness of what everything is, which is complete emptiness; it is what you already are though you can't see it," or simply, "I-Am-That."

And of course if you've delved at all into the mystical or esoteric traditions of the world's religions you will recognize that this is exactly the kind of thing that Gautama Buddha, Jesus of Nazareth, Rabbi Bal Shem Tov, Jalaluddin Rumi, Adi Shankara, Meister Eckhart, Seng-Ts'an, Ramana Maharshi and various other Zen, Christian, Hasidic, Sufi, Taoist, Advaitin and other 'spiritual teachers' are recorded as saying.

Please listen carefully; this next bit is important. It is the opposite of what you have always been told, and what you have been told is not true. What is at issue here is extremely simple. It is not complexity or difficulty which makes this so hard to communicate or to understand. It is very simple and very easy. It is just that it is so completely at odds with what is believed, and with how experience is commonly interpreted, that the mind cannot comprehend it.

There is an agreed upon, consensus reality which almost the entire human race shares. The world has been around a long time; it is ancient. Into this world, you are born as an individual; you grow, learn, experience life, and die. There is some disagreement concerning what happens after that, except that for everyone else, life will go on – until they also die. Everybody thinks they know this – or some local variation of this. But in fact when you were 'born' you did not know this. You *learned* this. Everyone else learned it too and so it is an almost universally shared idea. But everybody believing something doesn't make it true.

From eternity, without time, I Am, the unborn. Just as a dream begins at some point during sleep, so 'at some point' That which I Am appears as Consciousness here, and this world comes into being. I open my eyes: there is experiencing of life in this apparent body/mind. After a certain span of experiencing, I close my eyes: the world ceases to be, and from eternity I Am, the unborn.

What could be simpler, or more obvious?

Every once in a while someone will come along and try to tell folks this, but a consensus reality is tough to crack. It is self-reinforcing and has built-in ways to deal with cognitive dissonance. One way is to call the offenders 'crazy.' Another, just as effective, is to call them 'mystics.' Either way the illusion of separation, the consensus reality, is maintained.

4. *Prologue*

So the teacher works in strange stories, parables, metaphors, actions; statements pronounced one day and directly contradicted the next. Trying to work around the defenses. If you take any one of the teacher's statements literally, you'll be off looking where that statement seems to point, at something within the consensus reality, which is not what was intended. Which is why the time-honored way of learning from these characters, if one is so inclined, is to sit with them for some time: months, years, enduring their contradictions and reversals and *non sequiturs* and apparent craziness until enough of these divergent vectors have been absorbed that one can make something of an average of them, to look out beyond them as it were, to a point where they might converge, beyond anything that can be comprehended or imagined.

## II

THERE ARE THOSE WHO SPEND their lives thus, at the feet of such a teacher, but that's not what occurred in this case. Nevertheless, the pages that follow are an account of what happens when 'What Is,' that which cannot be taught, which is beyond the consensus reality of things, ideas, thoughts, experiences, and sense perceptions, is suddenly and spontaneously seen or apperceived; and when all of this so-called reality is seen and clearly understood to be illusion, of the nature of a dream.

Convention would suggest that I refer to what follows as a 'first person' account, but you see here we are again, with that little problem with words and ideas and communication. This 'first person' who would be relating this account is clearly seen as part of the illusion, a mere character in the dream, and not in any way as an actually existing individual to whom these events could have occurred or who could be experiencing or thinking or relating anything. After all, if you fall asleep at night and have a dream in which you dream of flying over the mountains, would you, when you awaken, say that anyone actually flew over the mountains last night? No matter how vivid the dream was, the characters, the story, the events, the 'doing,' were, in terms of waking reality, all fictitious.

This analogy of a dream, and waking up from a dream, is one that we will be coming back to frequently. It is an image used by many of those who try to teach or convey or just talk about this, and it is one of the best analogies available, but of course it is only an analogy. It is used for illustrative purposes only; if you get to taking it literally it'll all come apart and make no sense.

When there is a ceasing of the misperceiving of the illusion as real, there is a sudden, complete and irrevocable seeing that there exists not a separate person, but only an appearance in the play of Consciousness which functions in that play or dream as a so-called human mind/body organism. This organism is an appearance only, existing as an illusory, dream-like construct within that which is beyond or prior to this illusion.

This 'That Which Is' can be referred to from within the illusion as Consciousness, or Presence, or All That Is, or even perhaps (with some qualification) as 'God;' and it is understood that this Presence (to pick one term) is all there is, so that anything which is perceived is always and only Presence *being perceived as* some (illusory) thing. This Presence is what streams or flows, to use the image, through the mind/body apparatus, animating it, rendering it conscious; so conscious that it actually thinks, as most others like it also think, that it is an individual autonomous entity, a separate being which is conscious.

But it is not. That is the illusion. There are no separate beings. There is nobody home. There is always only Presence streaming through these apparent forms thus creating this illusion. 'Me,' 'myself,' 'david,' does not actually exist except as a mistaken idea, a misguided and totally conceptual and never 'real' separating off of Consciousness into an illusory separate self. And what is realized is that this Consciousness, Presence, All That Is, is what 'I' truly *is*.

## III

*T*RYING TO EXPLAIN WHAT IS, within what is not (which is to say, trying to explain or describe Truth with terms and concepts provided by illusion) is doomed from the start to be particularly fruitless. All there is, is seeing, Understanding, in What Is, in thoughtless, wordless stillness. It is simply impossible to communicate.

Why bother trying? Good question. All I can say is, like the Understanding itself, like 'life' itself, the attempts at communication come unsought, unasked for, unwilled, and there is no trying nor any doing.

What follows is a conglomeration of odd bits of scribbled verse, journal entries, emails, letters, answers to questions, conversations reconstructed loosely from memory, and sometimes just sitting down at the computer and typing. Most of it is quite raw and unpolished. And all of it is simply

Consciousness streaming through a mind/body apparatus completely empty of any individual self.

By which there is no special claim being made: the same is true of Consciousness streaming through the mind/body you think of as 'yourself.' You probably think you are reading this. I assure you, you are not. Reading is happening, but there is in no sense a 'you' doing it, and the 'you' you think you are most certainly does not exist. Welcome to All That Is.

I am fully aware that what follows may in places be quite difficult to read and make sense of. The word processor's spelling and grammar-checking functions choked on this document. Basic rules of language: grammar, capitalization, punctuation, syntax, have all been stretched and mutilated in this attempt to get words to point away from their common usage and toward the decidedly uncommon.

Not much can be done about this. There is no intention to be obtuse: words are used in odd ways for a reason; because that's as near as can be said. At this point, the text has been proof-read and spell-checked many times by many readers. If there are odd spellings, punctuations, or usages, these are most likely used intentionally, to convey a meaning; and the meaning would be (perhaps subtly) different if it were done 'correctly.'

Often the text does not flow smoothly; it is frequently chopped up with unconventional words and phrasing when more familiar language would read more fluidly. This is unavoidable. You may find occasions where the language seems to contradict itself or what was said earlier. Given the limitations of language, this too is necessary.

## 4. Prologue

Many of the themes are revisited, and so some of it may seem to be repetitive. See the repetition as an invitation to go deeper, to look through and beyond. Remember, these words are being used to point beyond themselves, and what is understood the first time they are read is rarely the deepest or the fullest understanding.

And please remember: none of the images or ideas or concepts presented here are themselves true or even directly indicate the Truth. All are only vectors pointing somewhere toward the general direction.

The reason nothing expressed here can be the Truth is that concepts, thought, and language are all inherently dualistic, and what they are trying to express is not. In duality, for every object there is a subject; for every better there is a worse; for each truth a falsehood; as much clarity as confusion; both love and hate, stillness and motion, perfect and imperfect, complete and incomplete.

This is why the masters were, and are, so fond of remarking, *"Neti, Neti."* Neither this nor that, neither one side nor the other. In duality, and therefore in language, there's always the flip side, the opposite that completes or complements and which is equally untrue.

Inherently dualistic language is used here in a peculiar way, to point to what transcends duality: 'Love' which is beyond love and hate; 'Stillness' that is not the opposite of movement; 'Perfection' which has nothing to do with perfect versus imperfect.

Traditionally, the teaching about this has been referred to as a set of 'pointers' rather than a set of 'truths' for this very reason; and also for this reason, there is a preference for pointers which indicate what 'All That Is' is *not,* rather than pointers which attempt to define what it is. *Neti, Neti.*

All these things, and everything written in the pages that follow, are just concepts, thought bubbles created here in this mind-generated illusion, and as such are severely limited and inherently flawed.

In fact, quite frankly, it's all crap. Eventually all ideas, all experiences, all words, all books, all teachings are beside the point. Eventually all there is, is complete letting go and going beyond; going, completed, beyond. Then everything will cease, everything will have never been, and there is only Understanding, and the Peace that passes all understanding.

When you learn that there is nothing you can do to accomplish this or bring it about, there will be a moment of frustration. But this, like every thing, thought, or experience, will only be temporary. Fortunately, it has never been up to 'you' anyway.

# Two

*Abruptly,
instantly.
Effortlessly,
out of stillness.
A dream.
A stirring.
Waking to the
Real.*

# 5.

## THE JUNGLE, PART I

*"Open your hidden eye and come,
return to the root of the root
of your own Self!"*
— Rumi

### I

A FINAL DISCLAIMER, A NECESSARY ONE, before we get on with the story already. The task here is to tell the story of what happened in the jungle. There is no reason to do this, no 'point' to the story. The Understanding itself cannot be talked about, can only be pointed to, and that is all that can be done now, is what everything that happens through this mind/body thing is. Talking about the experiential events in the dream that led up to and surrounded the 'pop' of perception, the realization, the waking out of the dream, is meaningless; it is just more dream story.

There are those who have asked for this story to be told, perhaps to be able to evaluate for themselves. Fair enough;

here are the circumstances surrounding that event. Ultimately it is only the Understanding itself which is of value, not the story of the mind/body thing. But the story is asked for, so here it is. This is what happened in this mind/body. So what? Who cares?

When Ramesh Balsekar's book *Who Cares?* was published, I found that in typing the title, these fingers (creatures of habit) would inevitably misspell it by inverting two letters and typing *Who Carse?* It brings a smile every time, a little gift in Consciousness. The title of Ramesh's book is not meant dismissively or rhetorically but rather, in the tradition of Ramana Maharshi's "Who am I?" as a question to be investigated: "Who is it that cares?" So too this: "Who is this 'carse'?" Who indeed. No one at all, and what does it matter? The accepted social norm is to emphasize the individual: the individual character, the individual effort, the individual experience, the individual story. In fact, nothing could be further from having any significance.

So please do not make the mistake of reading this to find out something about this so-called life, some pattern or path or some chain of causation. The perfect unfolding, the infinite expression in Consciousness is indeed perfect, is indeed infinite. There is no path, except in hindsight; and then there are infinite paths. If you read this story and add it to your collection of stories of pathways to enlightenment, and study the similarities and chart the differences, the story will be of no help and may actually be a massive hindrance.

Like any practice, any work, any trying, any thinking, any book; the only possible help it can be is if you spend your whole life doing it and finally realize it is of no value,

## 5. The Jungle, Part I

doesn't get you anywhere. Forget it. The Tao that can be spoken is not the Tao. The story that can be told is just more noise. Be still. Who is the 'I' that Is, in stillness? That is what you want. Not this. Read this for entertainment in the dream, if you must, but don't be sidetracked.

The story is thoroughly saturated with language making use of the words 'I,' 'me,' and 'my.' See how silly this story thing is? This is pure fiction. There is no such entity. 'Me' is a mythological idea. The story is told of events happening to someone; but there is no one here, no one to whom events can happen. The personal pronouns are used as necessary conventions of language, but they refer only to this body/mind organism, which is empty of any personal self or entity to refer to. See how vacuous this whole thing is? So what? Who carse?

This cannot be emphasized enough: the first parts of what happened in the jungle consisted of a series of experiences, and so can be thought about, remembered, talked about. In this case there were what could perhaps be called deep, transformative, even dramatic experiences. But it must be remembered that this part of what happened in the jungle, the preparatory part, however deep and wonderful, was still only experience, experience occurring in or through this mind/body thing. As such it is essentially without any particular significance. Dream events in the dream life of a dream character have no lasting significance.

Spiritual teachers sometimes remark that you can consider yourself fortunate if you have not had dramatic spiritual or mystical experiences. Perhaps I have not been as lucky; there have been experiences, some of which are related here. Such is the script for this dream character.

But with them, the clear seeing that experience is neither understanding nor wisdom, but only the circumstances under which these may or may not occur. An experience of awakening is not Awakening.

And so the story about these experiential parts of what happened in the jungle has nothing directly to do with what came later, with what we call Awakening or the Understanding. The first parts, the experience parts, the parts that don't matter, (although of course, like everything else, they play their part in the infinite unfolding) can be described more or less as they happened. The last part, an instantaneous event out of time and out of experience, can only be pointed to more obliquely.

## II

We had been in the jungle for several days; living in the Shuar village, going for treks in the forest, working mostly with a village elder and one of their *vegestalistas*; a medicine man, herbalist. The experience of traveling through Ecuador, coming into the rainforest itself, and living with and getting to know the people of this little village had all been pervaded by a sense of quiet well-being. Although of course it was all very different and strange, in another sense the jungle also seemed very familiar and welcoming, as if I was coming back to a home I'd forgotten.

But after a few days there came a time when this feeling of well-being abruptly wore off. Between midday and early evening of one day, my internal state went from open acceptance and trust to a growing unease, which escalated rapidly to serious fear and then to outright panic. I became

## 5. The Jungle, Part I

convinced that I was going to die if I didn't get out of there immediately.

In the context, there was some rational basis for the fear. There had been some incidents: a close encounter with a small but extremely poisonous jungle creature; a minor accident on one of the treks; misunderstandings with the shaman about the ingestion of certain plants. Clearly, slight missteps could have grave consequences.

When I had informed family and friends about going on this journey most had simply wished me well, but I had almost immediately received two phone calls with a different response. A family member and an acquaintance, who did not know each other and who called completely independently of each other, were each extremely concerned and tried to convince me not to go. The two women both have intuitional senses that I had appreciated and respected in the past; now, one had had a dream and the other simply a strong intuition that they could see me going on the trip but not returning. They felt that the trip posed extreme danger for me and tried to convince me to reconsider. I had taken their concerns to heart but on balance had decided to make the trip. Now, remembering their warnings only fed the thought that I was not going to make it out of there alive.

The mind took all of this and ran with it far beyond any rational basis, as the mind is so good at doing. What had been an adventure of exploration now seemed, like the fecund jungle around me, to have grown wildly out of control. I was in way over my head, and there appeared no way out. There was a quiet talk with the trip leader in which I was assured there was no possibility of leaving for at least several days, as the weather would not permit the

Cessna to land at the grass strip up river. Of course, the alternative was to withdraw from activities and try to keep to myself in the bamboo hut that had been assigned to me. But something prevented my taking that option.

In the midst of the fear that was growing in my gut, the certainty that I was going to die if things continued as they were, there was also a deep sense that what was being offered here was a once-in-a-lifetime opportunity for what at the time I thought of as "wholeness." The awareness was imprecise, in fact quite confused, but nevertheless very strong that whatever spiritual force had brought me here to the jungle had done so with the purpose of offering an opportunity for deep transformation and healing of what I saw then as my self: body soul and spirit. To retreat to safety would be to miss that opportunity and leave the jungle as I had come, a conflicted, restless and anguished soul. That option reeked of failure and meaninglessness: what would be the point of safety if achieved at that cost?

The conflict reached its most intense point in the early evening. I skipped the evening meal and was sitting in the communal thatched longhouse, staring out past the fire smoldering in the center and out the opening in the bamboo wall of the other side. The jungle began immediately outside, and the rain was falling through the leaves, its sound blending with that of the millions of insects as the rainforest slipped quickly into the evening darkness. The fear was intense, physically and mentally. The mind was running scenarios of various disgusting deaths in the jungle, the pulse was hard and rapid, and it was not only the increasing darkness that was causing my tunnel vision. I wanted to run, but the only place to run to was back to my hut and dismal defeat. So I sat and stared into the jungle.

## 5. The Jungle, Part I

Presently the mind went quiet, the scenarios stopped running, and a new thought appeared. It was quite calm amid the panic, and it went like this: "Well, if I'm going to die, (and I am going to die, if not here than somewhere, if not now then sometime) then if that's what is needed, if that's what it takes, then this is a good place to die, and this is a good time to die."

A good place. I had felt very at home in the jungle. Familiar, welcoming, nurturing. So obvious in its cycle of life and death and rebirth; a very appropriate place to leave a body. And, a good time. There were fewer loose ends in my life than usual; business deals and projects had been wrapped up and accounted for, and new ones not yet started. There was no relationship and no unresolved personal issues or responsibilities. Prompted in part by the concern of my sister and friend, I had even made out a will and left it on my desk when I left home. If I am going to die (and of course I am), then to an amazing degree this actually is a very good time and place in this life for that to happen.

Once this thought occurred, both the body and the mind went quite still, and there was a feeling as if someone very strong and gentle had walked up behind me and placed their hands on my shoulders. "Good," I thought, "this is very good." And I completely let go and relaxed into this new awareness that for this body to die here and now was a very good, appropriate thing, that this was why I was here. This was not resignation to something unwanted, but wholehearted acceptance and surrender in joy into what was known to be right and perfect. In mere moments the entire thought and feeling and physical symptoms of extreme fear for my life dissolved and gave way to pure joyful acceptance which even the certainty of death could not take away.

But the most remarkable thing about this transformation was that it was quite clear to me that I had not done it or caused it or earned it. One moment the fear was there, intense and graphic; the next moment there was only its complete opposite; peace and joy and clarity, and appreciation of being so well cared for by the unknown force of 'Spirit' that even death would be arranged and carried out in an appropriate and 'perfect' manner.

Yet it was clear that I had not worked the fear through, I had not resolved anything. To suggest or argue that I had somehow faced my fear and by some psychological process broken through it to the other side would have, in context, been a fabrication.

This new state of mind and body, surrender and acceptance, had simply landed in my lap without any accomplishment on my part. It seemed clear that left to my own devices, I could just as easily still be in that agonizing state of paralyzing fear and anguish. That I was not, but was instead sitting there in pure gratitude and joy and acceptance, was obviously pure gift. It was astonishing.

It would only be much later that I would realize that my sister, my friend, and that intuitive sense of panic all turned out to have been right. In fact, no 'me' made it out of there alive. As it turned out, no individual named 'david' would ever return from the jungle.

# 6.

## SURRENDER

*"What can you take from here?
You come into the world with your fists closed,
and you go out of this world
with your palms open."*
*- Kabir*

A CRUCIAL ELEMENT HERE is the idea, the concept, of surrender; and the inexpressible Truth that lies behind, prior to this idea. Most other spiritual traditions, methods of self-improvement, or paths of work treat this as a process, something you work at; working at letting go or at uncovering your stuff so that it can fall away or be purified. But of course here as always the truth is radical; since awakening is the realization that there is no one here to awaken, then the letting go, the surrender, is of one's entire individual existence.

This is where I discover how much *bhakti* (the spiritual path of devotion) is running in my blood, when it is Rumi and his Sufi way of surrender to the Beloved that resonates so truly, when it is realized that this is what I had been trying to do, in blind futility of course, all my life. The root of the name 'david' is a Hebrew word which means, 'the beloved;' I should have known; I have always known. And yes, *jnana* (the spiritual way of knowledge) is the other part of what is in the blood, that drive toward understanding and wisdom; but still it seems more natural to describe the Understanding as an essential intuitive seeing and inward knowing. It is understanding, to be sure, but one which has little to do with comprehending anything.

Teachers of pure non-duality frequently emphasize that there are no prerequisites, nothing that has to come before the Understanding happens. Here's living proof of that. Yet, at the same time, here also is this surrender. Essential, it seems; necessary. Back in the jungle, at that point where all this happened, when nothing happened, surrender also happened. Like the Understanding later, it was total gift, unearned, undeserved, unsought. And I see now, for this mind/body at least, necessary in order for the rest to happen.

How can there be understanding that one is not, without surrendering that one is?

Finally, ultimately, the surrender and the Understanding are the same, even if they are apparently, in perception or experience, separated chronologically. The very concept of 'the total Understanding' necessarily includes surrender, for it begins with the willingness, "Thy will be done;" and ends in seeing that one is not.

Thus there is a sensed rightness in the idea that humility in some form is a mark of a true sage; an intuitive sense that if one doesn't have a sense of humor about themselves

## 6. Surrender

and about what is happening, it is highly unlikely that awakening has occurred. Taking oneself too seriously may be a fairly good sign that there has not been the giving up, the surrendering, of the false idea that one actually exists. Doubts about the authenticity of certain teachers often boil down to this: that while they may have an excellent understanding of the teachings, it is the complete surrender of the sense of individual self that has perhaps not occurred.

In this phenomenality of duality, there is always the flip side, the complementary opposite that completes. Male–female, *Shiva–Shakti*, *jnana–bhakti*, understanding–surrender. Disdaining one or the other misses truth. Despite traditions to the contrary, there simply cannot be true *jnana* without true *bhakti*, there cannot be the ultimate understanding without the ultimate surrender. Certain personalities will try to avoid one or the other under the guise of some higher wisdom, but always at the cost of wholeness.

There is a tradition that *jnana* is the higher path because the *bhakta* relies on a belief in someone or something to be devoted to, whereas the *jnani* knows there is neither. But true *bhakti* is pure devotion with no object; and the true *jnani* knows nothing.

*Jnana* and *bhakti*, knowledge and devotion, understanding and surrender, inseeing and outpouring, mind and heart, cannot be divided or opposed; because they are the same.

> "The essential basis of self realization is the total rejection of the individual as an independent entity, whether it comes as a spontaneous understanding or through an utter surrender of one's individual existence." (Ramesh)

It can be seen that the path of the *bhakta* in devotion leading to surrender, and that of the *jnani* in knowledge leading to understanding, meet when each takes the final step. The ultimate surrender *is* the total Understanding; the complete Understanding *is* the utter surrender unto death of the individual self.

Jesus: "Only he who loses his life will find it." Again, "Not my will, but Thine be done," because it is understood that there is no 'mine,' no 'me' to will. It is the surrender of all vestiges of the sense of the individual person, including, ironic as it may seem, all those hopes and dreams and prayers of ever becoming a good or better person or a person other people might love or like or be drawn to. It is the complete surrender into 'This Is All That Is.'

And yes, that final surrender, that total Understanding is sudden and happens once. And that once is now. And that now is eternal.

# 7.

## THE JUNGLE, PART II

*"Light
will someday split you open;
even if your life is now a cage...
Love will surely burst you wide open
into an unfettered, blooming new galaxy."*
- Hafiz

LATER THAT NIGHT, IN THE DARK, lying on a mat on the floor of the bamboo hut, the rain pours down on the rainforest and the insects are an interweaving of a million sounds and rhythms. Lying there in the quiet peace of the surrender that had come a few hours before. Not knowing or caring at what time or in what manner the inevitable death would come.

There is a tearing, a searing physical pain in the chest that feels like my rib cage is being torn open; at the same time there is a tingling at the top of my head and the sensation is that the top is peeled off my skull like a tight cap being removed. There is peace, consent, no fear. The sensation is that there is an immense surge or explosion or expansion, which the body cannot contain. Something surges, spins up out of the top of the head to I know not where, to infinity; while my heart expands up and out of my chest, outward, until it fills first the forest, then the world, then the galaxy.

The surge out the top of the head is noticed, but not followed. What is followed with the attention is the expansion of the heart, because with the heart's expansion the 'I' sense also expands. And I find myself in what in my ignorance, without language or categories, I call Presence: expressing as Brilliance, like light but clearer and brighter, beyond light. Not white or gold, just absolute Brilliance. Brilliantly Alive, radiantly Being All That Is.

And there is an awareness, quite amusing, that Presence has been aware of 'david' forever, and is 'enjoying' that 'david' has woken up enough to perceive It. And there is a profound realization that nothing, absolutely nothing matters. Anything I had ever thought, or experienced, or ever would think, or experience, was nothing, a dream; absolutely did not matter. It was all really quite funny. I laughed and cried alternately for many hours, all night in the rain.

In this part of that experience in the jungle, I knew three things about this Presence, about All That Is. Three things, and later, a fourth. The three words I used at the time were:

First, that it is Alive. Not an inanimate cloud or energy field of some sort; nor even a thing which is alive: it is pure Life, Aliveness, Existence.

## 7. The Jungle, Part II

Second, that this Presence is Intelligence. It is alert, awake and Aware; it is Knowing. Not some*thing* that knows; rather it is the Knowing.

Third, that its nature, its essence, is pure, unfathomable, endless, unconditional Love, Compassion, beauty, outpouring. In this Presence, I find myself in a state of overwhelming gratitude, bliss, unfathomable Peace, Love.

Months later, I read about three Sanskrit words traditionally used together to try to express this brilliant Presence, this All That Is: *Sat, Chit,* and *Ananda.*

*Sat*: Being. Not being *something*, nor *something* being; but simply pure Being in itself; Am-ness. I Am who Am. What I called 'Alive.'

*Chit*: Consciousness. Not consciousness *of* anything, just simple, pure Consciousness itself; Awareness. What I called 'Intelligence,' knowing.

*Ananda*: Bliss, Peace, Outpouring.

I lay in this Presence for many hours. There was an intense experience of what I would call 'processing.' I felt that I was taken back through my whole life, stopping at the places where there were unresolved issues or unfinished business. Issues from childhood, from relationships; old pain, loss, grief, many of which I had dealt with extensively in many years of therapy. They were intensely re-lived, re-experienced, completed, and let go. When one was finished, another would arise. That night there was final resolution and closure on many old wounds that had never before been able to heal.

The Presence that was first experienced that night has, ever since then, never not been experienced. This life is lived in the Light of Presence, always: it cannot now not be. The sense of Presence is all pervading, this awareness of *Sat Chit Ananda*, which is Brilliance. The moment the heart seemed to expand out of the chest to fill the galaxy, Presence which is All That Is was first perceived as immense Brilliance, Light beyond light.

My eyes were closed when this happened, and the Brilliance was infinite. When I opened my eyes, the jungle was dark, black as only the deep rainforest can be, far from any lights and sheltered under the dense canopy of great trees from even the light of the moon and stars. With the eyes open, the Brilliance receded to the background, still there and still ultimately bright toward the back of the head, but allowing the eyes to see darkness in front of them. When my eyes closed, it was as if the Brilliance filled my head, or more as if there were no head, no bamboo hut, no jungle, no earth, nothing to contain this Brilliance which itself contains all and is all.

For the first few days and weeks, this was distracting and a little disconcerting. Whenever the eyes are closed, it is far brighter than when they are open, even in daylight. It took some adjustment to be able to sleep bathed in this Brilliance; darkness comes only with the eyes open, and even then the light is still there in the back. And the Brilliance is not inert light; it is *Sat Chit Ananda*, living, breathing, aware, love compassion bliss outpouring.

I have not talked with many people about the Brilliance. If it had been all that happened that night, more may have been made of it. But in view of what happened a few hours

## 7. The Jungle, Part II

later, it is simply what it is, no more. It has been suggested to me, by those who know about such things, that it has to do with release of *Kundalini* energy. I don't know much about *Kundalini*; and beyond reading enough to confirm that it does seem to fit the description, it really isn't important. All of this; surges of energy, *Sat Chit Ananda*, the Brilliance, the processing and healing of old wounds, was and is all experience. Wonderful, beautiful experience, but nevertheless experience and therefore dream stuff, dream experiences of a dream character, part of the 'everything' that is not.

There is a deep gratitude for this experience, for the Brilliance. It is a constant reminder and a deep comfort. It has made it impossible for the david body/mind to ever make the conceptual mistake of separating the world of mystical experience and *Sat Chit Ananda* from the world of body and mind and sense and objects. The Brilliance is not in some other realm accessible only under certain conditions: it is here, always, exploding in this head, affecting the visual functioning of this organism. It is a beautiful and astonishing gift: once again unsought, unearned, undeserved.

But all this is still dream stuff, and has nothing to do with the Understanding.

# 8.

# WORDS FAIL

*"Come out of the circle of time
and into the circle of love."*
- *Rumi*

WHAT WOULD YOU GIVE TO KNOW, absolutely know beyond any doubt, that everything really is all right, that there is no reason to fear. That there is no need to feel despair or loss or uncertainty. That all the pain and hurt and evil we have seen truly is only an illusion, and that the most beautiful things we have experienced are only a glimpse, a small taste, of what is truly 'real,' and truly ours. That everything is all right; that everything is perfect as it is; that all is well. This is what I see, and what I know.

No, none of that says it well at all, none of that is right. The words are slaves to the illusion. It is not "truly ours", not something we posses, but rather what we *are;* yet not even that because there is no 'we.' Of course, 'I' know nothing whatever, and there is no 'me' to see anything, nor is there any 'thing' to see. What is known, it is all but impossible to express or communicate. And ultimately it is not known or seen by 'I', it is what 'I' *is*.

Language, and the concepts on which language is based, fail. By definition this Truth, this Beauty is Beyond. (Beyond in the sense of being inaccessible by human thought and experience, although of course it is obvious that there is no literal 'beyond,' no 'other.') In Itself it cannot be experienced; it can only be 'known.' And even this knowing is not knowledge, not intellectual; this has nothing to do with mental comprehension.

The mystics and poets, saints and awakened masters who have glimpsed or seen or known all agree that what is seen and known is ineffable, inexpressible. Putting it into words and concepts misses it completely. It is described as that which "eye has not seen nor has ear heard nor has the human heart conceived..." And yet, the human heart cannot contain it and so it spills over in fumbling attempts at expression of what is beyond expression, always qualified by the caveat that any such expression, any description however awesome, cannot encompass it.

At the end of human vision lies the final, ultimate Truth, inasmuch as such can be at all within our vision even at its extreme limit. It cannot be experienced or thought of or spoken of because it cannot be conceptualized. Our language, and the thoughts and concepts which structure our language, are essentially dualistic, based on the relationship of subject and object. There is no way to think or speak of anything without thereby making it the object of the supposed individual self which thinks or speaks as 'subject.' Thus as soon as there is linguistically structured thought there is a deviation from Truth, a basic inversion

## 8. Words Fail

of true subject/object relationship. No individual self exists as subject: apparent individuals exist only as objects. And ultimate Truth exists not as object at all; it is original, pure Subjectivity, and to refer to it as an object, as one must necessarily do to think of it, to refer to it as "it" as this sentence does, is extreme absurdity.

Nevertheless. The knowing cannot be contained, and overflows. That which lies at the end of human vision is spontaneously described by many who have seen, by using three concepts, three words. They are only concepts, only words, and as such miss it completely. Nevertheless. Being; Consciousness; Bliss. Known in Sanskrit as *Sat Chit Ananda*. As Wei Wu Wei observed, "We can see no further and no path leads beyond;" and Nisargadatta Maharaj, "You can take it that *Sat Chit Ananda* is the limit which your mind can describe of that state which cannot be described."

This is the closest that mind and concepts can come to Self, Whole Mind, Pure Subjectivity, Consciousness, All-That-Is, Presence, ultimate Truth, I Am. It is not an entity, a person, a thing, an 'it.' It is pure B*eing*; absolute, fully aware Conscious-ness; overwhelming outpouring Love-Compassion-Bliss.

As it is beyond thought and concepts and language it is also beyond experience. Experience is determined by the illusory concepts, the constructs of space and time; every experience is determined by our sensory perceptions and has a beginning, a middle, and an end. This is true of physical, mental, and even of spiritual experiences. All experiences are structured by, and contained within, our conceptual framework of space and time. Self, Presence, ultimate Truth, is Beyond, outside of the structure of space and time, and therefore cannot be experienced. However, it can be known, Understood, in a way that transcends both time and space, transcends experience.

This is why awakening or enlightenment, the occurrence of this knowing or Understanding, is said by masters and teachers to be always instantaneous, not gradual or by degrees. Gradual or by degrees infers duration in time; to think of awakening as happening gradually is to still be thinking of this as happening to an individual who is experiencing in time. Awakening brings with it the awareness that there is no individual, and no time. The Understanding by its nature is outside of time, and occurs outside of time and thus always appears, from the vantage point of time-bound consciousness, as occurring instantaneously, that is, not taking any time.

However, the basic functioning of human mind/body organisms is experiencing. That is the basic operational process, what the programming calls for, what naturally happens: experiencing is what occurs in these mind/body organisms. Thus when the Understanding happens in a human mind/body, experiencing will occur; that mind/body will appear to 'have' an experience, an experience will be constructed, around that occurrence. Thus there will be what can be called an 'awakening experience,' or the experience of understanding or enlightenment.

This awakening experience is not the awakening. The experience of understanding is not the Understanding. It is merely a human experience created in the mind/body around the occurrence of the awakening, of the Understanding.

## 8. Words Fail

The Understanding, the knowing of Self, Presence, ultimate Truth, lies outside human experience as it lies outside time and space. The experience of the occurrence of this Understanding, the 'awakening experience,' is not the awakening, is not the Truth; it is only an experience created in the mind/body, similar to any other human experience. For this reason the masters and teachers discount even great and wondrous spiritual experiences as being essentially worthless and something to be disregarded; fixation on the experience will only draw the attention away from the true Understanding.

Nevertheless. The knowing cannot be contained, and overflows. In the attempt to express the knowing, language and concepts are used even though they are only words and ideas and miss it completely. In the attempt to express the seeing, aspects of the experience are described even though the experience of the seeing is only an experience, is not the seeing, is not the Truth. As Self, Presence, What Is is described in concepts by using the ideas of *Sat Chit Ananda*, Being-Consciousness-Bliss; so also it is often described in experiential terms by using the image of light. The experience of light, or something like light, often appears as part of the experience occurring around awakening or Understanding; hence it is called, en-light-enment.

Self, Presence, What Is, is said to be...

> "...like the sun shining in the blue sky – clear and bright, unmovable and immutable... illuminating all." (Tsung Kao)

> "...the blinding radiance of the great white light which has been called *Sat Chit Ananda* and which is also not at all..." (Wei Wu Wei)

"Pure it is, the light of lights. This is what the knowers of the Self know. The sun shines not there, nor the moon and stars, there lightning shines not; where then could this fire be? This shining illumines all this world." (*Mundaka Upanishad*)

"One day the sun admitted, I am just a shadow: I wish to show you the infinite incandescence!" (Hafiz)

"There was this light that became brighter and brighter and brighter, the light of a thousand suns... This brilliant light, of which I was the center and also the circumference, expanded through the universe, and... this light shone so bright, yet it was beautiful, it was bliss, it was ineffable, indescribable." (Robert Adams)

In this case it is understood, seen, known, as all-encompassing Presence, experienced as Light beyond light, clear Brilliance beyond any conceivable light or brilliance, which is every'where' and fills and suffuses all because simply it is All-That-Is; there is nothing that It is not. It is understood and experienced as Presence because it is the ultimate Aliveness of pure Being, and the ultimate Awareness of pure Consciousness, and it is 'Here,' it is what 'Here' is, it is What Is Here, What Is Present.

And of its nature it is limitless and uncontained. This ultimate Being and ultimate Consciousness overflows constantly in the Outpouring of its essence, its nature, which is pure absolute love beyond our conceptions of love: complete compassion, total truth, ultimate beauty, Outpouring. This is what is described as 'bliss;' not some great orgasmic physiological or psychological pleasure but all-encompassing unconditional unrestricted love, compassion, gratitude, Outpouring.

## 8. Words Fail

This overwhelming Beauty-Love-Compassion-Bliss is the very nature, the essence, of the Brilliance that is *Sat Chit Ananda*; and its constant Outpouring is This; all of this, what is known as the manifestation, the created universe, phenomena. This ultimate Truth at the end of human vision is not something far away, not something 'beyond' in the sense of being something other:

> "On no account make a distinction between the Absolute and the sentient world. Whatever Consciousness Is, so also are phenomena." (Huang Po)

Consciousness, Presence, All That Is, is not static; it is the infinite field of pure potentiality, the possibility of everything; spilling over, pouring itself out in pure Being, the beingness of everything; in pure Love, the Love which everything is.

Words fail; one must use words and then extrapolate from them, attempt to use them to transcend themselves. 'Love' is a word that stands for an idea, a concept, which in this context is inadequate to the extreme. In the culture by which these mind/bodies are conditioned, love is held up as the highest value, but we seldom examine what we mean by it. Like most of our thoughts and values, it is surrounded, protected by fuzzy thinking to avoid the clarity which leads to self-examination which can lead to awakening, to seeing through the mist of this world which has been pulled over our eyes to blind us to the Truth.

In fact, our ideas of love are much more tainted than we care to admit with concepts and feelings of involvement, specialness, ownership, exclusion, need, caring, guilt. We think of caring as something important, something of the heart. But caring is only involvement, anxiety, attachment to outcome. It is a misperception that we need to care about this illusory existence, this dream, or that things need to matter. This only generates worry, anxiety, confusion and feelings of separation and guilt. It does no good to the person we 'care' for, only perpetuates their own involvement in the dream. This is not love. Our claim to love only limits ourselves and those we try to love.

Love is not a basis for involvement. Love is neutrality; it is the true absence of judgments, censorship, desires, worry. It is our True Nature, All That Is, Presence. It is a reminder that nothing matters. When there is awareness of being always the Presence of this Perfect, uninvolved, neutral Love, there is "the Peace that passes all understanding."

> Meister Eckhart, the Christian mystic, said that
> > "You may call God love, you may call God goodness; but the best name for God is compassion."

Even the concept 'compassion' can carry meanings of pity, caring. But the Buddhist tradition has used the word to mean uninvolved, unattached openness to the best for 'all sentient forms' without any thought of anything in return. When there is no experience of separation, love 'for another' disappears along with hate 'for another.' There can be only being-in-love: being inside love, the Beloved. And when it is understood that All This unfolds as the perfect dream in Consciousness, the Outpouring of *Sat Chit Ananda*, there is no need for anything to be other than it is. Love then becomes something like the neutral holding of What Is, in Gratitude, in Compassion, in Presence.

The overwhelming sense is that 'all this' just is. What we

## 8. Words Fail

see as the phenomenal manifestation and life as we know it, with all its ups and downs and pleasure and pain and beauty and craziness; the perfect unfolding of the dream of Consciousness; the constant Outpouring of the Brilliance which is *Sat Chit Ananda*, Beauty-Love-Compassion-Bliss: it all just is. In Love.

You are not that mind/body, just as I am not this mind/body. What Is, (what You are) is *Sat Chit Ananda*, Consciousness, in whose dream appear these mind/bodies. When this is seen, there is awakening from identification as one of the mind/bodies in the dream. When there is not this identification, how can there be doubt, fear, despair, loss, uncertainty? The dream is unfolding Perfectly. And the beauty and wonder of the dream are astonishing, dazzling, cannot be contained. What happens to this mind/body in the dream cannot be determined by this mind/body, by the character in the dream. What happens to this mind/body in the dream cannot in any way alter or affect the dreamer, What I Am, Presence, All That Is.

It all just is. All there is, is for life, the dream, to continue to happen while it continues to happen, and for there to be acceptance of what is, in an attitude of overwhelming outpouring Gratitude. To be in Compassionate openness in the *Sat Chit Ananda*, to the Being-Compassion-Outpouring-Bliss. To rave with Rumi and Hafiz and Eckhart. To be in-love, in the Beloved. There is nothing else. What else can there be?

# 9.

## THE JUNGLE, PART III

*"The Great Way has no gate.
There are a thousand paths to it.
If you pass through the barrier
you walk the universe alone."*
— Wu Men

THE ANCIENT TEACHINGS FROM INDIA, the teachings of Advaita, of pure non-duality, of not-two-ness, make perfect sense. They make sense because at night, in the jungle, in a bamboo hut in a native village in the Amazon rainforest hundreds of miles from any road, in the dark, in the torrential tropical downpour, amid teachings and teachers very different but exactly the same, I wake up from a dream. I lie naked in the naked Presence and there is nothing else. There is not even me lying naked.

There appears to be this illusion, this dream, but it is only a wave that arises for a time on the surface of the ocean of the One, a dream that flickers in Awareness. And nothing is the same. Once aware of the dream, I cannot be unaware. Not a 'peak experience,' which comes and passes and you forever search to regain it. An awakening; a seeing with different eyes from a different vantage, and there is no going back. At the same time, nothing has happened. There has been no 'awakening,' because the sleep was only part of the dream.

The funny part is, I was never overtly a seeker. When I was younger, in my twenties, I spent many years in seminary, studying philosophy and theology, working my way up through the ranks of ordination to Roman Catholic priesthood. But as soon as I was there I turned my back on it, appalled by the misuse of power and control. For a time I explored the other world religions, spending time in Zen and Taoism (but, ironically, avoiding what had always appeared as the far-out weirdness of the *Yogis* and *Maharaj's* and *Sri*-this and *Ram*-that of India), before finally chucking it all, professing agnosticism and hedonism and going to work building houses for twenty years.

For a couple of years or so before the jungle, curiosity and a rediscovery of my own native roots had me poking around in indigenous cultures learning from shamans. It was fun questioning assumptions about what is 'real,' but I didn't know much about 'seeking' or 'awakening' or 'enlightenment' beyond a hazy memory of having read D.T. Suzuki twenty years before. And even that was academic, 'comparative religion,' nothing I had identified with or been attracted to personally. So there were no conscious expectations, no categories or concepts with which to frame or express what spontaneously 'happened' when it happened. Nothing happened.

## 9. The Jungle, Part III

Still later that night in the jungle, toward morning, lying there in Presence, there was a point when all the experiencing stopped. The thinking and the feeling and the processing that had been happening all completely ceased. I was not aware of it 'at the time,' because there was no thought and no awareness of time or indeed of anything; only in hindsight is there a looking back and realizing that there was a 'period of time,' out of time, when there was no thought, no experience, no thing, nothing.

It may have been hours, it may have been an instant; it was not of time. Only in retrospect can it be called a place or a time of stillness or emptiness, because when it was occurring there was no time and no place and no sense or awareness of anything happening. I was not asleep. It was a condition of complete stillness and completely alert awareness. But there was nothing there to be aware of, no sense even of self to be self-aware. It could be called a completely empty stillness and awareness. I have no idea how long this lasted.

Eventually, at some point, in this place of no time, no thought, no place, no self, there gradually began to creep in an awareness that there was a simple watching of something. As this awareness distilled out of the emptiness, attention focused; and the realization was that what was being watched, what there was awareness of, was a guy lying in a bamboo hut in the jungle. This continued to focus until there was awareness, a kind of recognition, of what had always been thought of as myself, 'david,' lying there on a mat in the middle of the rainforest. And there was an abrupt realization: "my god, there's nobody home."

This was the moment at which nothing happened. Like a 'pop' of a bubble bursting, a shift in understanding. I am not 'david:' there has never been a 'david:' the idea of 'david' is part of a thought, something like a dream, that doesn't matter. The individual 'self,' the one I thought resided in that body, looking out through those eyes, the one I thought a few hours ago had woken up enough to perceive Presence, is not there, does not exist, never has. There is nobody home.

This was not an 'out of body' experience. I have had these, in which 'me,' my'self,' experienced being out of this body rather than inside it, and experienced looking at the body from outside instead of looking out through the body's eyes. This was not like that at all. What was being watched here was not only the body, but the whole 'david' apparatus; body, mind, self, soul, personality. What is watching is All that is. The watching, what I came to know as 'witnessing,' is neither *other than* the body or mind or the whole 'david' thing, nor *not other*. It does not originate from here, from the body/mind; but also It does not stand apart from it, because It is inclusive of it. The witnessing is clearly not being done by 'me,' even a disembodied 'me.' This witnessing is not being done by anyone, any entity. That's the point: there are no entities; there is nobody home. There is only the witnessing.

Abruptly, instantly. Effortlessly, out of stillness.

A moment, an instant, of radical, severe disorientation, discontinuity; then a stepping through that into perfect clarity, not at all unlike the experience of waking up.

A dream, seemingly real, lasting all one's apparent life.

## 9. The Jungle, Part III

A stirring, and the sleep dropping effortlessly away.

A moment of disorientation as the dream is recognized as dream and there is waking to the Real.

Immediately, the dream falls away and it is known that the dream was never real, that one never was what one had been dreaming. There is no 'before and after,' no moment when I was 'no longer' david. This is the 'gateless gate:' only the seeing that david never was. As near as can be said: the perception now is that there is no 'me,' no 'david;' and 'I' is that which has never not been All That Is. Always everywhere perfect Brilliant Stillness, and no-thing which has no name continually outpouring, seen now always not as from this mind/body thing.

# 10.

# Gone Beyond

*"Gaté. Gaté. Paragaté. Parasamgaté. Bodhi. Svaha!"*
*"Gone. Gone. Gone beyond. Gone, completed, beyond.
Awakening: Svaha!"*
– *The Heart Sutra*

TELLING THE STORY IS PROBLEMATIC. In particular, like so much else in the teaching, it can fall prey to what I call the prescriptive/descriptive fallacy. The Understanding, Truth, what is apperceived, cannot be expressed. 'The Tao that can be spoken is not the Tao.' What is expressed is conceptual only, a translation into terms available in the dream; the reflection of the moon in a puddle of water, not the moon itself. And between the moon and its reflection, between Truth and its translation into dream concepts and terms, lies a conceptual chasm crossable only by the occurrence of the Understanding itself. Many are interested in crossing the chasm; they are the spiritual seekers, and they are hungry, insatiably so, for any shred of evidence, or guidance, or advice, or indication of what that chasm, and its crossing, and the other side, are like.

Essentially, the truth is that the other side is not like anything, and you can't get there from here. Rather, this already is the other side; all is 'here,' there is no 'there.' End of story. This is the true nature of things, always everywhere right before your eyes. But who can see it? Once seen, it is obvious that 'beyond' is this, here. But say that to an ardent seeker and you're likely to get a groan of frustration.

There is a recurring archetypal image that appears often in dreams and myths, in fantasy and science fiction stories. A traveler arrives at a great wall. After much searching he finds a door, a gate in the wall. When he opens the gate and steps through, he finds himself in a world, a universe, which is different from the one he came from but somehow familiar; the same universe, but somehow very different. When he turns around to look back through the gate at the place he came from, he sees that not only is there no gate, there is no wall. Not only is there no going back, but he has not come from anywhere. Thus it is with awakening: there is no wall, no separation between a 'here' and a 'there.' In a sense there has been a going beyond, yet that beyond is not other than here already. This is 'the gateless gate,' and 'I' has always been here. Where else?

Nevertheless, seekers are a persistent lot, driven or drawn by a force they do not understand; and those who they know, or believe, or at least suspect to have 'gone, completed, beyond' are watched, and examined, and plied with questions, and even imitated, in the hope that some of what they seek might wear off. But despite long tradition, the Understanding is not a contact high, nor is it known to be contagious. Whatever can be learned by observation of or contact with a known sage, or from direct answers to questions posed, is descriptive only; an attempt, however

## 10. Gone Beyond

apparently feeble or skillful, to translate the inexpressible into terms available in the dream. The story, the description, of how the Understanding occurred in a certain body/mind organism, and descriptions of the ongoing experiencing in that body/mind organism are only that, descriptions, and cannot be taken as prescriptions of how another body/mind organism might 'get there from here.' But of course, they usually are taken as prescriptive: that's how you get religion out of spiritual experience, how you get teaching about various practices, various paths, yogas, mantras, diets; advice on ways of thinking, ways of acting: the four applications, the five precepts, the six powers, the seven virtues, the eight impediments, the nine stages... the ten commandments.

One in whom awakening has occurred is observed to have no attachment to the outcome of actions, so this is taught as a prescription; you must work hard to somehow no longer be attached to outcome! One in whom the Understanding has happened is seen to sit quietly in deep stillness and silence for periods of time, and when asked what he is thinking, replies that there is no thought: so it is taught that you should try to sit quietly and have no thoughts! The teacher lives a celibate life, alone; so the students become renunciates. The teacher is married, so the disciples go out and get married. The teacher eats meat, or does not eat meat, and the devotees follow suit. Nisargadatta Maharaj smoked cigarettes, and a startling number of his followers took up smoking.

But what is happening in the awakened is happening spontaneously, without trying: either as a consequence of the natural programming and conditioning of that body/mind, in which case it has nothing whatever to do with awakening; or as a spontaneous outcome, a natural side effect of awakening in that particular body/mind organism. There is no one to try. This is what I mean by saying it comes naturally 'from the other side' and cannot in any way be achieved by working at it 'from this side.' This is another miserable metaphor and of course there is no this side and other side, but can you see what is trying to be said? If awakening, the Understanding, is to happen, it will happen, but I absolutely assure you it will not happen as a 'result' of a dream character performing some practice. A practice may happen. Awakening may happen. But there is not a linear causal relationship between the two.

Put another way. When you are asleep and dreaming, what does a character in your dream 'do' to cause that character to wake up? It is the dreamer, not the character, who 'wakes up,' and waking up happens when it happens, for reasons well and thoroughly outside the control of any of the characters in the dream, including the character which in the dream you think is you.

Gathering stories about awakening can serve as a huge impediment, keeping the seeker running in circles. I have had sincere seekers at Ramesh's morning talks in Bombay, when they heard some of my story, come and ask me how to book a trip to the Amazon jungle, and how to gain access to the tribe I was staying with. This is crazy. Forget it. It will not happen that way for you.

Two illustrations. One, a Zen saying, hence rather brief:

> Once a master has used a ladder to climb to the top of the wall, that ladder is thrown away forever and never used again.

## 10. Gone Beyond

Find your own damn ladder. Better yet, know that it will find you; that it already has; that your feet are already on the rungs!

The other, a rabbinical tale, hence somewhat more verbose:

A woman came to the rabbi complaining that she could not conceive a child, and asking for the rabbi's advice and help. "Ah," said the rabbi, "that is difficult. But you know, it was the same for my mother. For many years she could not conceive, and so she went to see the great rabbi, the Bal Shem Tov. He asked her only this: 'What are you willing to give, and what are you willing to do?' She thought about it; she was a poor woman and did not have many possessions. Finally she went home and got her most valuable possession, the shawl she wore at her wedding, a family heirloom which had also been her mother's and her grandmother's. Then she returned with it to the rabbi: however, since she was poor she had to walk, and by the time she returned the itinerant rabbi had left for another town. For six weeks she walked from town to town, always arriving just after the Bal Shem Tov had left. Finally, she caught up with him. He accepted the gift and gave it to the local synagogue. My mother walked all the way home," the rabbi concluded, "and a year later I was born."

"How wonderful," cried out the woman, truly relieved. "I have my wedding shawl at home. I will bring it to you, you can give it to the synagogue, and surely I will be given a child!"

"Ah," said the rabbi, shaking his head sadly, "unfortunately, that will not work. The difference, you see, is that now you have heard this story, while my mother had no story to go by."

Descriptive, not prescriptive.

This is why the Teaching has traditionally been called "a finger pointing toward the moon." Take your dog outside some evening. Say, "Hey, look!" and point dramatically at the moon. Your dog will most likely stare expectantly at your finger. It shows great devotion and is quite endearing, but demonstrates a basic lack of understanding, of any ability to see beyond. Fixating on the story, or elements of the Teaching, or practices, or a guru or teacher, or spiritual experiences, is staring at the finger, unable to realize that these are only pointers. None of these things have any importance in themselves. Look past these, beyond them to what is being pointed toward.

Once this is understood, descriptions and stories can perhaps be useful or at least interesting *as pointers*. There have always been texts, *sutras*, stories of the ancient masters and how it was that the Understanding occurred in the case of the Buddha, or Hui-Neng, or Shankara, or Ramana Maharshi. And there is no reason that the telling of these stories should stop there. As Suzanne Segal introduces her own account, *Collision with the Infinite*, "The story that follows is my contribution to the modern version of the ancient texts."

Yet ultimately, in Ramana Maharshi's summation,
> "There is neither creation nor destruction,
> neither destiny nor free will,
> neither path nor achievement.
> This is the final truth."

There really are no stories, as there is nothing happening here. The stories are only what the dream characters tell to

## 10. Gone Beyond

themselves and to each other over and over, and in so doing keep the dream going. As my friend Koshen would say with great irony, "It's something to do until Jesus comes!"

The story-telling is the dreaming, and the dreaming is desire – the desire to be. And more than that: the desire to be some *one;* someone separate, someone special; someone with his or her own story. The dream character is completely caught in this spinning of a personal web, building and maintaining the personal story, driven by that unknown, unexamined wanting to assert and continually reconfirm the individual *self.*

Awakening does not occur while pursuing a story, desire fueling desire, need fueling want, all of it constantly strengthening the sense of a separate self that does not exist. Awakening occurs when this desiring is irrevocably seen to be misguided, seen to be futile. Then the story telling stops. Then the story stops. That is the going beyond.

# 11.

## *The Jungle, Postscript*

*"Don't pretend to be what you are not,
don't refuse to be what you are."*
  *- Nisargadatta Maharaj*

*"The eye through which I see God
is the same eye through which God sees me:
my eye and God's eye are one eye,
one seeing, one knowing, one love."*
  *- Meister Eckhart*

Because I was not a 'seeker,' did not have preconceptions about what to look for or what might 'happen,' what did happen was almost as spontaneous, as innocent, as waking up from sleep and getting up and going about your day. Everything was completely different, but it had always been. Everything had shifted, but it just was. Some time passed and some learning before intellectual understanding caught up with, filled in the implications of, the shift in perception that had occurred.

Along with *Sat, Chit, Ananda,* (Alive, Intelligence, Outpouring: Being, Consciousness, Bliss) there was a fourth thing that I knew about Presence, about the Brilliance. I felt it, knew it at the time on a level beyond the mind, but my thoughts and categories wouldn't let me go there with conceptual understanding until somewhat later. In fact looking back on it, it's rather odd that, having realized that there is no 'david,' that there is nobody home, that the obvious implication of this was not understood conceptually until some time later. But then, there wasn't exactly a lot of conceptual basis or preparation going into this. Presence was persistent: it was not an experience that came and went. Once 'here,' 'It' never left; 'I' never left.

Days later I left the jungle, but Presence continued and I very soon came upon people and words and concepts that let me understand what my heart knew but my mind hadn't immediately had words for: that it is Presence Itself looking out through david's eyes, through all eyes. It always has been. There is nothing else. Presence is the 'I' that knows 'I Am.' Presence is not other, outside. Presence, *Sat Chit Ananda*, is my own heart, filling the galaxy; my own Self. This has always been here, and It Is What I Am. While what I thought I was, my own self, is not.

This 'I', this Self, is All That Is. It is the only Is-ness that Is. It is all that exists; the individual who thinks he is experiencing it, understanding it, does not. You can be told this forever and think, yeah, okay, I get that. But you don't. When this finally sinks in, hits home, explodes, nothing can any longer be the same. Nothing ever was.

And yet in another sense there was no 'awakening.' Because there is no one to awaken. 'david' has never existed,

## 11. The Jungle, Postscript

is a dream character, part of the cosmic joke. And Who I really Am is All That Is, which has never been asleep, has no need to awaken from or to anything.

'I Am That' is the other half, the completion, of the seeing 'there is no one home.'

> "Love says, 'I am everything.'
> Wisdom says, 'I am nothing.'
> Between these two my life flows."
> (Nisargadatta Maharaj)

The Understanding here will be forever colored by the fact that the awareness that 'I am not' came first, and as such is the basis, the essential pivotal breakthrough insight into awareness of What Is. Thus the Understanding that universal infinite Presence Awareness Brilliance is what 'I' is, is always in the context of that complete emptiness, the knowing that the separate self simply is not. Who is infinite Presence? Not 'me!' No 'who' at all. Only the 'I' which is All That Is.

There are cases where the realization 'I Am,' or perhaps a glimpse of it, comes first, without the surrender and the profound seeing that as any kind of an individual to be anything, 'I am not.' The result then may be something quite different.

So then, various sporadic practices – praying, shamanic journeying, some meditation – they were part of the conditioned routine of this dream character, and for a time they continue to be done but I see they are part of the dream. Pray to whom? Journey to where? There is no other, no two. These become gateways to where I already am: *Sat, Chit,*

*Ananda*, I Am That. There is no place to go, nothing to do: all is Awareness, around and through and as 'us.' This life is lived, in and around and through this mind/body thing, but not by a 'me.'

Spiritual practices and efforts, once motivated by a sense of separation or a need to connect, a need for meaning or purpose, fall away and cease naturally, with no intent or effort to stop them or continue them: they simply do not arise. What happens, happens spontaneously. Sometimes, quite often, there is sitting quietly, in stillness, in the Brilliance, in profound peace. But this can hardly be called praying or meditating. It is no thing, it is emptiness. It is Being. It is Consciousness. It is Bliss.

Life is, quite suddenly, marvelously, utterly, simple.

Ego, the sense of an individual self and all its misperceptions, is seen as itself a mistaken perception, as having never existed. The dream character goes on being the dream character: brushes its teeth, trims its beard, still likes the same foods, still has poor social skills and finds many things that are said and done confusing or disorienting. As it always did. But the character has been gutted, hollowed. It used to take itself seriously, think it was someone. Now when it looks within it knows there is nobody home. The character is a sham. Only the deep sense 'I Am' remains, and this is known not to belong to the character, but to Presence, which is always everywhere perfect Brilliance.

Like the electric fan which keeps spinning after the plug is pulled, like the bicycle that rolls on for awhile after the rider has jumped off, forty six years of conditioning had worn a path that this mind/body thing, creature of habit,

## 11. The Jungle, Postscript

could follow in its sleep. Which of course is exactly what it had been doing, following the script of the dream. Now it winds down. Took a lifetime of dreaming to write its story, to accumulate, accrete, build up these thoughts and feelings and memories and experiences into this personality. Now, with no intent or effort to either stop or continue, it may take a lifetime to fall away. Or a moment. Or not. While there is watching, witnessing. It doesn't matter. It just does not make the slightest difference.

# 12.

## THE DR. BRONNER'S BOTTLE

> *"It is all the mind can do –*
> *discover the unreal as unreal.*
> *The problem is only mental.*
> *Abandon false ideas, that is all.*
> *There is no need of true ideas.*
> *There aren't any."*
> *– Nisargadatta Maharaj*

So what then, after all, is there to say? Very little. The seeker community is daft about teachers and teachings and seeking and awakening, but from here quite obviously there is nothing to seek and nothing to teach. The whole grand show goes on, and even while this body/mind is very much part of the show, there is now a seeing it all from a very different perspective. It is clear that it is not the body/minds that are seeing.

There is no 'point,' no 'purpose.' Dream characters, characters in a movie, in this soap opera, spend their lives in anguish trying to discover their purpose. Take themselves so seriously! There is a witnessing, and a knowing that all the suffering, all the anguish, the yearning, the loss, the pain, the confusion, the hurt, the trying so damn hard, is all dreamstuff, all created by us in our attempts to get ourselves out of what we are not in.

Self-improvement, spiritual practice, seeking, attempts to walk the path, to follow the way; all attempts to dig ourselves out of a hole we create by the trying. It's like quicksand; the struggling is instinctive, and we think it helps, but actually it is itself the problem. The struggling, the seeking, is the sense of individual self trying to keep telling its story. There is nothing to seek. Separation is the illusion; there is nothing to be separate, no-thing. There is only One, not-two, and That Is. All else is not. And That not-two that Is is what is 'I,' here. All there Is is no-thing, This This-ness, This I-ness, which 'I' is, which is All That Is.

"I trust I make myself obscure?" It's really not the intention, but do you see why I prefer to go about my work and not talk about this much, why so much of what everyone is involved in makes so little sense; why it is so difficult even to understand questions and sometimes impossible to answer them? Everybody's running around everywhere thinking they actually exist! It's the silliest damn thing that's ever been seen! And anything that I can say all comes out gibberish ranting, sounds like reading the label on the bottle of Dr. Bronner's soap that you can find in health food stores. "All One, Eternally One, All One or none! Exceptions Eternally? Absolute none!" And so on, *ad infinitum*; it's great stuff, but does anyone take it seriously? The man's raving!

There is a very beautiful phrase in the Islamic *Call to*

## 12. The Dr. Bronner's Bottle

*Prayer* that sums up and expresses this as best as can be done. *"La 'illaha il' Allahu."* Since the root of the name for God, *'Allah,'* is the same as the word for 'What Is,' the phrase can be translated any number of ways, all of them correct. "There is no God but God." "There is no reality but God." "There is nothing which is not God." "What Is, is God." "All there is, is What Is." Great stuff, but does anyone really understand?

As there is no 'purpose,' so also it is obvious that 'you,' 'me,' all of 'us,' are not 'doing' anything. Nevertheless the sense is that it is somehow 'right' that 'we' appear to be here... after all, Consciousness is dreaming this, with all the beauty and pain and wonder, so how can it be other than right and beautiful? It's so funny, and nobody gets it. When I say, "it doesn't matter," and, "there is no purpose," some people get angry: "Well then, what's the point of being here? Why get up in the morning?" While in fact the experience is that it is all more beautiful, and more clear, and more simple and enjoyable, even the hard parts, than it ever was before this seeing. Yes, even the chaos and violence and insanity in life. Feeling love and compassion and sadness or anger or revulsion are all so much more clearly felt and deeply experienced without the involvement as to what this might mean or what might result. And yet they also pass more quickly, without a sense of importance or apparent attachment. This awakening

> "...doesn't mean that you can't feel desire, hurt, pain, joy, happiness, suffering or sorrow. You can still feel all of those; they just don't convince you." (Ken Wilber)

There seems to be an idea among seekers that after awakening, life presents you with a different set of experiences, and in particular that the experience of emotions flattens out or goes away. But that's not true. A visual aid that comes to mind to describe this is a graph with a scale going from zero on the bottom to ten on the top. During life your emotional state fluctuates and may be anywhere on this graph, from the pits of despair at zero to the heights of pure joy at ten. What happens when the Understanding occurs is not that the range of experience flattens out, but rather something very different. The range of emotion from zero to ten is still experienced; it's just that there is now an awareness that this range is not all there is. The graph of zero to ten, it is seen, sits on top of an immense range extending down to a hundred, a thousand, a hundred thousand, an infinite expanse which supports and carries that zero to ten range of human emotion and experience. That range is still felt in its totality, but it is seen and felt that that totality is of insignificant amplitude, barely a squiggle on the surface of the infinity of All That Is.

With the understanding that it is all a dream, that there exists nothing other than All That Is, you then re-enter the dream. Like Neo at the end of the movie *The Matrix:* re-enter and continue in the game, with full knowledge that the individual is not 'real.' I used to think that we 'forget' in order to experience separation from the One. We forget all right, but we simply forget that there is no separation to experience; that not only everything that the individual apparently experiences, but also the individual itself, is a fiction, a thought bubble, *lila*, God's play.

Many seekers, when they begin to understand on an intellectual level that all of this is as a dream, quickly come up with the question, "Well then, how do I get out of the dream?" As if that is the next logical step. As if the mind

## 12. The Dr. Bronner's Bottle

thinking this, the one realizing that this is a dream, is not itself illusory, part of the dream. Anything that can arise here in the dream, including thoughts like these and characters like the one you call your'self,' are necessarily themselves dream thoughts and dream characters. Nisargadatta Maharaj:

> "The very idea of going beyond the dream is illusory. Why go anywhere? Just realize that you are dreaming a dream you call the world, and stop looking for ways out. The dream is not your problem. Your problem is that you like one part of the dream and not another. When you have seen the dream as a dream, you have done all that needs to be done."

But just because these 'minds,' here in the dream, are conditioned to think in terms of dualism does not mean they are not capable of thinking otherwise. Just that it is a very unusual and sometimes awkward transition requiring much stretching of boundaries.

It is interesting that most Advaitic teachers do not talk of 'the One.' The word *a-dvaita* means 'not two,' and that is the phrase that is used. To say God and creation, or Unmanifest Source and the manifestation, or What-Is and the dream, are 'not two' seems at first a little awkward, but it is used this way to address a certain maddening confusion that can arise, in which 'oneness' can be taken to represent the dualistic opposite of separation. In phenomenon, the manifestation, one half of a dualistic pair cannot exist without the other; so in that sense one can think there has to be separation in order for there to be oneness. But beyond dualism, in unitive consciousness, unity and separation are 'not two;' Consciousness and the manifestation are 'not two;' there is only unity; separation has never existed.

Our minds have also been trained to think in terms of causation: "The watch implies a watchmaker." However, there is that consistent thread of the perennial teaching in which this is seen as an unnecessary and unjustified leap. The dream does not necessarily imply a dreamer. A Buddhist text says, "No doer is there who does the deed." And there is a phrase in Taoism in which the Tao is described as "the web that has no weaver." This is actually the key. The idea that there is witnessing but no entity of any kind to be a witnesser is incomprehensible to our minds as they have been trained. However that does not mean that this understanding is impossible. If that shift happens, and it is understood at the deepest possible level that there is no individual doing, thinking, experiencing anything, then nothing else need be understood, nothing else need be done.

Realizing always that these are all concepts only and not the Truth. Concepts don't matter. Experiences, even experiences of awakening, don't matter. Because all concepts and all experiences are dreamstuff. All that matters is the Understanding: as Nisargadatta said, the Understanding is all. Because the Understanding is the single point at which What Is (what is not the dream) intersects what is not (what is the dream.)

The funny thing is, you can't get there from here. Or at least, don't ask me. I was blindsided, hijacked, shanghaied in the jungle. And even then, I didn't get 'there.' I was taken 'here,' where 'I' have always been. There is no 'there.' There is only here. Wei Wu Wei writes that there is no 'path' to follow, because all paths lead from here to there, and thus lead away from All That Is, from the only place there is to be, from home. There is no path that leads from here to here. Which is why no practice or study or devotion or

## 12. The Dr. Bronner's Bottle

learning or work or anything 'you' can 'do' on a 'path' will ever get 'you' 'there.' You are already Here.

In traditional Advaita, *jnana yoga* follows the questions, Who am I? (Or perhaps, Who am I not?), Who is experiencing? Who's the dreamer?... And rather than asking them rhetorically, follows them as a mantra, insistently, persistently, to where they lead. Many teachers say that these are precisely the questions which, if followed persistently, *can* get you there. Maybe. But don't ask me.

In my case there is a pure, clear, deep simplicity to it all. In *satsang*, on the 'path' of *jnana yoga*, the idea is to incessantly ask questions, to back your mind into some kind of corner where it will finally be forced beyond itself. I've tried it, during the time when I was learning how to think about what happened in the jungle, and I've tried to take it seriously, but from this perspective it's nonsense. There are no questions that are not immediately answered by the realization that that question, all questions, are empty thoughts. There is no individual understanding this or questioning it. Life appears to happen: thoughts, feelings, actions, experiences. There is no individual doing anything, thinking anything, experiencing anything. Once this is seen, questions just don't hold up.

All there Is, is Presence. And I Am That. You had a question?

The Dr. Bronner's bottle again. It really is pretty funny.

You can get caught up in this and make a lifetime out of it: path, no path; questions, no questions; enlightenment, no enlightenment; and it will still all be nothing, nonsense.

All there is now is for life, the dream, the illusion, to continue to happen while it continues to happen. For enjoyment and appreciation and gratitude to happen. To be in openness in *Sat Chit Ananda* to the Love Compassion Gratitude Outpouring. To rave with Dr. Bronner and Rumi. To know, deeply, that everything simply is; and that the 'I' which knows this is not 'me,' which is not: It is All That Is.

# 13.

## *Deliverance*

*"Whoever discovers the true meaning
of these sayings will never die:
Let the seeker not stop seeking until he finds.
And when he finds, he will be greatly troubled.
And after he has been troubled,
he will be astonished,
and he will reign over the All."*
– Jesus of Nazareth (The Gospel of Thomas)

IT'S APPALLINGLY HARD TO DESCRIBE or explain this no-thing, which after all is why it's called ineffable. Basically either there is seeing or there isn't, either the veil is dropped or it isn't. Just being a mystic or a *yogi* or a shaman of course means little: more dream roles for more dream characters. As long as there is anyone here to understand, there is not understanding. As long as there is anyone here to awaken, there is not awakening. The message of the *sutras* and the shamans is the same: the person of understanding is the one who dies before she dies, who leaves no footprints, who travels no path, because she knows that as a person, as an entity, she is not. But who can do this, what self can cease to be? None, as Wei Wu Wei would say, because none is: it can only happen. Then there is no one to know but only the knowing, and all this world is as in a dream or a vision; only Brilliance beyond light, Love beyond love, clear knowing pure beauty streaming through these transparent forms and no one here at all.

After the jungle, there is an intensely odd and very beautiful quality to the experience of life. In one sense I can only describe everything, all experience, as having a certain emptiness. This is the sense in which everything used to matter, to be vital and important, and is now seen as unreal, empty, not important, an illusion. Once it is seen that the beyond-brilliance of *Sat Chit Ananda* is all that is, the dream continues as a kind of shadow. Yet, at the same moment that all of what appears in the dream is experienced as empty, it is also seen as more deeply beautiful and perfect than ever imagined, precisely because it is not other than *Sat Chit Ananda*, than all that is. Everything that does not matter, that is empty illusion, is at the same time *itself* the beyond-brilliance, the perfect beauty. Somehow there is a balance; these two apparently opposite aspects do not cancel each other out but complement each other. This makes no 'sense,' yet it is how it is.

There is one tradition within Advaita which says that *maya,* the manifestation of the physical universe, is overlaid or superimposed on *Sat Chit Ananda.* I'm no scholar of these things, and can only attempt to describe what is seen here; and the Understanding here is that there is no question of one thing superimposed on another. *Maya*, the manifestation, the physical universe, *is* precisely *Sat Chit Ananda*, is not other than it, does not exist on its own as something separate to be overlaid on top of something else. This is the whole *point!* There *is* no *maya!* The only reason it appears to have its own reality and is commonly taken to be real in itself is because of a misperceiving, a mistaken perception which sees the appearance and not What Is. This is the meaning of Huang Po's comment that "no distinction should be made between the Absolute and the sentient world." No distinction! There is only One. There is not ever in any sense two. All perception of distinction and separation, all perception of duality, and all perception of what is known as physical reality, is mind-created illusion. When a teacher points at the physical world and says, "All this is *maya*," what is being said is that *what you are seeing* is illusion; what all this *is* is All That Is, pure Being Consciousness Bliss Outpouring; it is your perception of it as a physical world that is *maya*, illusion.

Of course in truth there is no gate that opens into All That Is, and no path leads there. There can only be the shift in perception to see *maya*, the unreal, as unreal. Still, for this dream character the Understanding occurred in the context of indigenous spirituality, and so what is known in the dream as 'shamanism' in this case turns out to have been the pathless path to the gateless gate that swung open to reveal what was never hidden, never on the other side. Like any other form of religion or spiritual practice on the planet, shamanism is mostly nonsense, something for the dream characters to do to try to make sense out of it all and comfort themselves while the dream lasts. All that trying and all the trappings of shamanic practice exploded, dissolved in the light of Presence, of All That Is.

Yet there are a very few even in shamanism who also know and have seen: that it is only a dream, and that nothing matters, and that all there is is Awareness, and that they are not. And they go through the motions for others, or perhaps with the passage of time in the dream they do so less and less until no more, and are seen as crazy fools. Who cares? For, while it is known beyond doubt that as a person, an individual, an entity, as 'david,' even as 'spirit,' I am not, do not exist, nor does any other: nevertheless it is equally obvious that as All That Is, I Am.

The seeing that occurred in the jungle was and is self-validating in the sense that it is absolute and needs no confirmation. Everything is seen in its light; it relativizes everything and is itself relativized by nothing. Nevertheless, in the dream, the dream character continues to function as such. And that dream character, that body/mind instrument, will be impacted by the occurrence of the Understanding.

It seems that in most cases the Understanding comes after some period of seeking and of coming to an intellectual understanding of the teachings of the perennial wisdom, and in such cases there would likely be at least something of a recognition when it happened. In this case however there was very little if any preparation in terms of being exposed to the basic concepts. In one way this was a deep and beautiful grace and blessing; I have seen the intellectual comprehension of the concepts involved become itself a tremendous block to many spiritual seekers, and in this case I was spared that, the Understanding happening naturally, spontaneously and innocently.

But in another sense it made the impact greater, and without preparation the body/mind was thrown into a kind of chaos. For this reason I find Suzanne Segal's account

## 13. Deliverance

quite poignant; there is a deep appreciation of what she went through. Although in a sense she had more preparation than in my case, having trained in Transcendental Meditation with Maharishi Mahesh Yogi, still it did not seem to have provided her with the necessary parameters to comprehend the awakening when it happened. Perhaps even more significantly, she was not provided with any meaningful support after it occurred, and spent the next twelve years with psychotherapists engaged in "an all-out effort to pathologize the emptiness of personal self in an effort to get rid of it."

In my case, the shamanic context could not itself provide an adequate system of ideas and experience in which to ground and comprehend and express what had happened. I knew that there was "nobody home," that there was not and never had been a 'david,' that what I had always thought of as 'myself' was a fiction. I also knew that Brilliant Presence was All, outpouring. This was beautiful and perfect, but at the same time it produced what at the time I called a severe 'disconnect;' a sense of discontinuity not only from any sense of personal past or history or beliefs or purpose, but also a total disconnect from what was apparently the experience of every other being on the planet, as far as I knew. Within our social and cultural context, the possibility that there had been some kind of psychotic dissociative break and that the david thing had gone quite insane seemed a very plausible explanation.

And so what followed was once again miraculous, unearned Grace. As a result of the unconventional way in which the Understanding occurred in this case there was not the discovering of the relationship with a guru in the traditional way. Yet there is something, perhaps similar, as this unfolds: simply being, resting, in this Brilliance, letting this tremendous Grace take hold: clearing, opening into this Peace that passes understanding.

Almost everyone I've heard of for whom this nameless thing appears to have been genuine seems to have gone into a long gestation period. Robert Adams, Tony Parsons, Suzanne Segal, Douglas Harding, and others; even Ramana Maharshi: ten, twelve, twenty years before any 'coming out.' In the Zen tradition, when a student monk comes to awakening he stays on in the role of student for another ten years of 'stabilizing.' Even Hui-Neng, the Sixth Zen Patriarch went and hid in the mountains for fifteen years after it happened.

Makes sense here. Jed McKenna calls it a "damn peculiar ten years" and I'd have to agree. It simply takes a while for the body/mind organism to adjust. Everything that people think is important and makes sense, is seen to be completely absurd, meaningless. And what people don't even see, is Perfect, beautiful, complete, needs no words. There is an inclination, even greater than previously, toward silence and solitude even though there is obviously no such thing.

Hui-Neng says that while the Understanding is sudden, what he calls 'deliverance' is gradual indeed. Near as I can figure, the mind/body thing is impacted by the happening of the Understanding, and that can take some adjustment. How can it be otherwise? In some cases perhaps the transition can be smooth: if for example you live in a culture and a time in which you are saturated in the the basic elements of the Teaching all your life, the period of adjustment in the body/mind organism may be very mild.

## 13. Deliverance

Clearly in my case it was different, almost the complete opposite. After a lifetime of experiencing life as almost unbearably confusing and painful, of fighting against life and everything it brought, very different patterns and habits and ways of thinking were laid down in the conditioning. There was no background of the Teaching to fall back on or refer to. And, there was no community or other resources for support immediately after the happening.

There is a tradition in Buddhism of something called *Pratyeka-bodhi,* 'solitary realization.' It refers to Awakening when it occurs outside of the usual transmission of teaching from master to disciple, and without the usual background or preparation or support. In such a case, the road to deliverance might well be even more "damn peculiar" than otherwise. Perhaps Ramesh was thinking of something like this when he said to me,

> "So, the Awakening can be of different kinds, yes. The experience you had was, as you said, 'no one home;' there is, truly, no david. And that is truly when there is no identification. And because that happened in your case, you had a problem living your life... therefore yours is a unique case."

When I came across Jesus' comment at the beginning of *The Gospel of Thomas,* it was the first time I'd found a teacher saying that *after* the 'finding' of awakening, one can be greatly disturbed, greatly troubled. Depending on the conditioning of the body/mind in question, this may not always be the case, but it was the case here. This period of disturbance is itself 'deliverance,' the rearranging of the patterning and conditioning of the life of the body/mind in the light of the new conditioning provided in the Understanding. And underlying it all is the constant, total amazement of awareness as the All, which never dies.

But this all has to do with how the body/mind organism responds and adjusts to the varying ways in which the Understanding occurs. It has always been quite clear that the Understanding itself is ultimately complete and simple and total. Those who argue that there is gradual awakening, or awakening in stages or degrees, or a even some process of deepening into it, seem to me to be missing something very essential and integral to the Understanding itself. It is not something of time and space, and it cannot take up time or space. It is not an experience, is not a process. It is a piercing of time and space by the pivotal intuitive insight that all time and all space and all things and all entities including the one in whom the insight is occurring, all are not. How can this be other than instantaneous, immediate? It can't be partial; it's either/or.

And all this is apparent only; it is seen that there is nothing here: words, ideas, thoughts, all meaningless; "a tale told by an idiot, full of sound a fury, signifying nothing." What Is, is great beauty, great love, great silence, and that really is all. Once again it doesn't translate, doesn't seem to be communicable, expressible.

# 14.

## Spinning Out

*"There was a door to which I found no key;
there was a veil past which I could not see:
some little talk awhile
of me and Thee there seemed;
and then no more of Thee and me."*
- Omar Khayyam

—

*"It's all the same fuckin' thing, man."*
- Janis Joplin

Who am I? The age-old question. Certainly not this body; temporary, changing, physical molecules and atoms and particles that even the physicists tell us ultimately don't exist as such. Certainly not this mind, thoughts that come from I know not where and which I cannot control. Ultimately it comes to this: the only thing of which we can be sure is the Consciousness deep inside, deep behind and beyond personality, prior to all the variations of who or what I have thought I was; the sense, the knowing, "I Am." The irreducible intuited Self, the Life Force that exists and knows it exists. That is all, the only constant. All the rest is a construct, a fabrication.

Under all the layers, each of us has this same experience of "I Am" existence. The same experience of Self. Inexplicably, this common experience is attributed to various selves, each having the exact same experience of Self. This impersonal Self is deemed personal, an 'individual' self inhabiting each individual body/mind. After all, that is what seems apparent. But you don't have to dig very far before this makes no sense. The idea that there are separate, individual selves is only possible because in each apparent self there is experience of Self. This experience has been misconstrued to be a personal experience that belongs to a personal body/mind. The Life Force, the Self animating one body and mind is deemed different from that animating another because the expression of that Self is different in each. We concentrate on the inconstant, variable expression and miss the constant that lies beneath.

The constant: there is only One. There is only one Self, one Awareness, Consciousness finding expression in the many apparent bodies and minds. My knowing "I Am" is the same Self knowing as you knowing "I Am." Reality is that which underlies appearances: the Self, the "I Am," Awareness, Absolute. What we call individuals are only apparent, relative constructs. In fact, all of what is called physical and mental 'reality' is only appearance, relativity. Which is why truly there is nothing happening here, despite what it seems. Despite appearances, nothing in manifest physical 'reality' is real, nothing is happening, and 'david,' along with everything else, is a concept, an idea, a thought bubble which ultimately does not exist.

## 14. Spinning Out

And so, living happens with much more neutrality. There is no need to strive or to struggle or to become: all of 'us' already *are* the One, Self, Awareness. What seems to be happening here in apparent 'reality' is not real and has no effect on who I Am, on Self, on Awareness. The wave arises for a time in the ocean, goes the analogy, but it is never other than the ocean, and it returns into the ocean, and the nature of the ocean is unchanged. Nothing has happened. Experiences are not important: in fact nothing is more important than anything else, because nothing is happening here. If there is no importance, then attachment to outcome gradually falls away.

And when I look at 'others' there is a shocking, naked intimacy: I see the same Self that I Am, expressing in a different appearance.

Nisargadatta Maharaj used to tell his listeners repeatedly, "Back up. Go back." Whatever level you are at, whatever place you are thinking or experiencing from, go back from there, find the place or the level which is before that, prior to that. A similar direction is contained in Jed McKenna's injunction, "Further." No matter where you are or where you are coming from, as long as 'you' exist there is a level beneath, prior to that, beyond that, which is where you want to be. Everything else is just dream stuff, layers of mask. Back up, go back, to the I Am which is prior to all. Rumi:

>"Sometimes you hear a voice through the door
>		calling you,
>	as a fish out of water
>		hears the surf's 'come back!'
>This turn toward what you deeply love
>		saves you."

For a while after it happened, after the jungle, there was an acute awareness of transition, of an Understanding having occurred as a leap, and a sense that this mind and body had yet to catch up. There seemed to be the weight and momentum not only of the life and history of this body/mind, but also that of a culture and a race having a belief that things are otherwise than what was seen now in the light of the Understanding. In daily living the mind or body would respond with a thought or action with which it was accustomed to responding. It was actually pretty amusing, kept me entertained during that time, because there was no 'content,' no supporting emotion or belief which had previously been there and which originally gave rise to these thoughts and actions. They were 'empty.'

Somewhere I came across that analogy of the electric fan which continues to spin for a while after the plug has been pulled. Without the original support, it would seem that these habitual thoughts and actions would fall away, and to some extent this has proved true. Much of that momentum has wound down. On the other hand, to an amusing extent, the david thing continues to behave more or less like david. The organism will respond as it responds, according to the programming and conditioning. It is not a matter of any importance.

After the Realization occurs it can appear from the outside as if nothing has changed and it appears from the inside like nothing is the same. That too is an approximation, and not true, but it's the gist. This is the meaning of the Zen saying, "Before awakening, chop wood, carry water. After awakening, chop wood, carry water." Chopping wood and carrying water are the normal, basic, necessary, everyday occupations in the simple agrarian society where this

## 14. Spinning Out

saying originated. The point is simply that things seem to carry on pretty much as before. Life goes on. Within, there is Understanding of What Is, where before there was the dream state. But from without, the organism continues its appointed rounds. Why not?

There may be some changes in the organism's routine that those close to it might notice. A little more drawn to silence and solitude perhaps; a little less interest in activities or conversations. Depending on the prevailing culture, the general impression may be that the one so affected is just a little weirder. But the natural functioning of the organism continues in much the same way as it did.

I know that this body is inanimate, not an individual; an appearance only, animated by Self, the One, Awareness. It does not even have a life of its own. Rather, it is being lived. There is an acute awareness of this body/mind organism being lived, rather than autonomously living. What I once called 'my mind' is a stream of thoughts; thoughts that do not originate from any 'me' but from the One Awareness. There is no individual, no david. Everything that appears to happen here, including the thoughts and actions that arise in this mind and body, arise spontaneously from Awareness. In spite of 'my' apparent deliberations.

Since it is obvious that there is no one here to have control over 'my' thoughts or over the course of events in this apparent 'reality,' concepts of guilt and pride and responsibility and obligation all become meaningless. Sure, our societies would find it difficult to exist and function without fostering the belief in these concepts to control individuals and populations; but none of these concepts exist in the What Is of Awareness. Everything arises spontaneously in Awareness. Nothing needs to happen or needs not to happen. There is no point, no purpose, no 'why?'

'Why?' questions are fundamentally unanswerable. Most go through life constantly asking 'why?' and, without realizing it, accepting responses which are not answers to the question. If we ask why the sky is blue, the answer, whether it is scientific or mythic or poetic, does not tell why the sky is blue, but rather *how it is that* the sky is blue. If we ask why we feel depressed or happy, the answer can be an explanation as to *how it is that* we feel these ways, but which still begs the question. We talk around the 'why?' giving reasons how it is that something is so, not realizing that the 'why?' goes unanswered. There is no answer, there is no 'why?' Everything arises spontaneously in Awareness. The constant asking of 'why?' is simply the mind's attempt to grasp for control.

It is interesting that in a young child, the incessant asking of 'why?' arises at about the same time, the same age, as the emerging sense of separation as an individual self. The mind thinks, if only I could latch on to a reason 'why?' all this is happening, I would be in control and be able to sort this all out. So the mind settles for non-answers and maintains its illusion of control, rather than recognize that there is no answer and admit it has no control. There is no point, no purpose, no meaning. Therefore no importance. Therefore no involvement. Nothing needs to be any different.

For one raised with religious beliefs, a fundamental shift is encountered here. Even when those religious beliefs were long ago understood to be blind, misconceived constructs, still there remained the kernel, the sense of the Other.

## 14. Spinning Out

Martin Buber's *I and Thou*; Rudolph Otto's numinous sense of *The Idea of the Holy*. Even when a belief in God as a personal being had fallen away, still this idea of the Other had been maintained. An Other toward whom to direct the human sense of awe. Some One toward whom to feel the gratitude. Source. Spirit.

The tendency, without being aware of it, when one hears about this on an intellectual level, is to make 'Presence' or 'Consciousness' that Other, that Spirit; just change the name. You can hear a lot of people talking about Consciousness exactly the way they used to talk about God, or Spirit. Ultimately there is no Other because there is no individual; there is no Thou because there is no I; there is no Spirit because there is nothing which is not Spirit. The split of dualism is not; there is only One. I Am not other than this One.

Trapped in the world of concepts and duality, the mind looses traction, slips, spins out.
The thought comes, "there is nothing to think about."
Then there is Stillness,
there is Awareness.

# Three

*More intimate
than any imagining:
I am not
present;
what Presence
Is,
I am.*

## 15.

# No Guru, No Method, No Teacher

*"No masters, only you
the master is you -
wonderful, no?"*
- Ikkyu

—

*"If you do not follow somebody, you feel very lonely.
Be lonely then."*
- J. Krishnamurti

It has become obvious that none of this is what it once seemed.
We are all dream characters in a dream.

Source, Spirit, God, Goddess, gods...
or: 'my true self,' 'my higher self...'
or: *devas*, angels, spirit guides, forces good or evil...
or: guru, *sat-guru*, master, teacher...
these are all concepts, human ideas, constructs;

and, as such, dream characters here with us
in the dream.

There is no separate 'God,' just as there is
no separate 'us.'
All these are projections. What there is, is
This.
All That Is.
This is not just another name for God.
Not a being named 'God' or 'Source' or anything else,
outside of, other than, What Is.
In all of reality, there are not two. There is only
All That Is. This.

You, who you really are when you say "I am"
and I, who I really am when I say "I am"
are the same "I am"
All That Is.
'you,' 'me,' 'we,' apparent individuals,
are dream characters in the dream which
'I,' All That Is,
dreams.

There is no we, no me, no you.
Even the dream is within
All That Is.
That is who You really are,
not the you you think you are.

In what I began to read after the jungle, and among the people I came across, much importance is made of this thing called awakening or enlightenment. Although I have used the word 'awaken' to express the moment of the shift in perception that occurred in the jungle, at times it seems

## 15. No Guru, No Method, No Teacher

that this is a misnomer; that the word in this context makes very little sense.

There is a sense in which there is no 'awakening,' no enlightenment, because there is no 'one' to awaken. Who would this be? Who is awakened?

'Me,' david? Of course not: david is a dream character, an idea, a fiction; not the dreamer, and therefore obviously cannot awaken. There is no 'david' to *do* anything, including awaken.

Or is it 'Who I Really Am' that has 'awakened;' Presence, Awareness, All That Is?

But of course Awareness has never been asleep, has no need to awaken to anything; Awareness is always already All There Is.

Clearly then, there is no one to awaken. 'Awakening' is only an analogy, a concept, a pointer. The seeker community tends to take it literally, but like most analogies it only takes you so far.

What has happened is more like this: in the dream, in the case of the dream character 'david,' All That Is stops pretending that 'It' is asleep. What has always been awake lets the misunderstanding that there is some one to be asleep and some one to awaken, fall away.

That is all. And the dream continues, as before. The misunderstanding has fallen away, but the misunderstanding was not real anyway, so what has happened? Nothing. The dream character 'david' now knows he is only a dream, not 'real;' knows it is all a dream. But even this dream character's 'knowing' is part of the dream, part of the unfolding of the script of the dream for that dream character, and nothing has happened. The dream character goes on being the dream character.

'Nothing happens' precisely because what appears to be happening is not, and what is happening is what appears as 'no thing.'

Meanwhile, some of the dream characters I was brought into contact with in those months after returning from the jungle are evidently making careers out of this awakening, enlightenment gig. I gradually came to realize that I had stumbled upon an extremely bizarre phenomenon of which I had been unaware: an entire enlightenment-seeker subculture populated with all manner of teachers and teachings ranging from the profound to the utterly ludicrous. This is okay of course, in fact it's wonderful; it's part of the dream. And, on the ludicrous end of the spectrum, it makes for a lot of silliness. Dream characters who publicly profess that they have "awakened to God consciousness" and can now, for a fee, show other dream characters how they too can awaken. At best, highly dubious; at worst, blatant hucksterism. Much ranting about what 'level' of awakening they have 'attained;' about the second level of the first stage or the third stage past the fourth level where no one on the planet is, at present, but they will be soon.

Convoluted, artificial complexity and foolish arrogance. The Truth has a radiant, radical simplicity which negates the possibility of any claim to it. Experiences can be claimed. Knowledge can be claimed. Authority, lineage, transmission, can be claimed. However: once your heart and brain

## 15. No Guru, No Method, No Teacher

are ripped open and what is left of you is found standing in Truth as Truth, any idea of claiming it will reduce you to tears or laughter.

There is nothing to claim or achieve. As the eighth century Zen master Hui Hai put it somewhat bluntly,

> "If you understand the meaning of all this, it implies that you know there is nothing to be achieved. Anyone who supposes they can achieve it by getting hold of, or grasping at something is full of self-conceit – an arrogant person with perverted views."

But of course if you're a dream character whose role in the dream is to make a career out of awakening, simplicity won't do. You have to have an organization, and develop a distinctive teaching; you have to gather a gaggle of followers, and very publicly (and with much drama) work on getting yourself and selected disciples through all those many levels of advanced enlightenment. Which, if there really was the understanding that there is no 'you' and 'you' aren't 'doing' anything, there wouldn't be any bothering about because there would be the knowing that these things don't exist, they're just constructs in the dream. But then of course you also wouldn't be able to gain prestige or importance and make lots of money giving seminars, convincing people they need their primary personality matrixes modified.

Money is necessary for living in the modern world, and there's an honorable tradition of gifting money or its equivalent to support teachers, monks, ashrams, monasteries. But there's a clear line here because on a basic level money and spiritual teaching don't mix. There is an attempt to justify charging a fee for hearing the teaching by appealing to the 'energetic exchange' theory, which says that any time you get something of value you should pay for it. It doesn't take much reflection to see that's bullshit: anything you have of true value, you didn't pay for.

The theory of fair exchange makes sense for things within the dream. But once there is talking about What Is, about seeing no individuals and no separation, about the realization of what you always already are, then the whole concept of one person charging another person money for this is quite blatantly meaningless. Truth is gift, and it is only passing through 'us;' it cannot be bought and sold.

This game of money for spirituality is a whitewash job. It's widely practiced and widely accepted, but it's the spiritual community's dirty little secret; nobody's really comfortable with it, because everybody knows in their hearts that charging money for access to spiritual teaching, even indirectly, is inauthentic and basically inconsistent with the Teaching itself.

Even when it is said that the money is to run the ashram, to finance the organization, to fund the travel schedule, to spread this 'vitally important message' to as many people as possible; even then this kind of sales pitch is still an appeal to ego, to every ego's desire to be part of something big and important.

Euphemistically calling it a 'donation' when it is set up in such a way that guilt and social pressure make it difficult to refuse, is dishonest. Once you have an ashram, once you have a church, you have to pass the basket and give sermons soliciting contributions. But any time you bring money into the temple, you run the risk of some firebrand carpenter from the countryside coming along and turning over the tables.

## 15. No Guru, No Method, No Teacher

The morning the old Zen or Advaita masters realized the Self, they went back to chopping wood, carrying water. If someone wanted to talk with them, they talked, then went back to work. Where is it written that teachers can't work to support themselves, that they have to live off their followers? Who says there has to be an organization? Who says teachers have to rack up huge expenses traveling all over the world giving lectures and seminars and *satsang*? What ego, what sense of individual self is behind this idea that the message of one teacher is so vital, so precious, that it needs to be heard, full time, by the whole world? The old Chinese Ch'an masters were named after whichever mountain they lived on, and if you wanted to hear the Teaching you went and found one of them. This tended to weed out the weekend warriors and limit the field to those who were ready to give up their lives to hear this.

Be still. Who's engaging in all this activity, taking on this importance, believing the hype that what is happening has some special significance? Who thinks it's important that great numbers of dream characters wake up, and that it's your job to do it? What's with this Advaita televangelism crusade crap?

Behind the New Age pleasantries, this messianic idea of being the anointed one, saving the world, is insidious. Stop. The Teaching is universal, and there are many teachers, and they are always already where they need to be. In the Understanding it is known that the world doesn't need any special message from any special teacher. That's all being taken care of. The dream in Consciousness is unfolding perfectly, and personality cults around popular and well-funded spiritual teachers are part of that unfolding; but not in the way they, or their devotees, might think.

There's an amazing amount of this going on, here in the dream. The blind leading the blind. Watching this nonsense, realizing they take it seriously, I can't help laughing because of course the question arises: Who? *Who Cares?* Who thinks it's important, who is organizing? It's all concepts and doesn't exist! The only one who cares, who is keeping track, who gives importance to a role, is the thinking mind, the ego, the apparent individual who still thinks he or she is *there* to be awakened or to carry a message; and the incongruity between this and the subject matter is so huge that it just makes for terrific entertainment.

It is yet another amazing grace that the first teachers of Advaita that I encountered turned out to be false teachers; characters who believe they are awakened but who have been misled, and remain trapped in ego. And trapped also in the money and spiritual prestige game. An odd experience, and rather confusing at the time, because on the one hand they obviously knew a lot more than I did, having studied the teaching deeply for a long time; but on the other hand they didn't know anything at all about what they claimed. They use Ramesh's name, claiming him as their teacher and claiming 'lineage' through him, but it is instructive to hear what the Ramesh has to say about that. "No wonder you were a little confused for awhile," he laughs. "They still think *they* are the ones *doing* it all!"

But I am very grateful for the experience coming when it did because it has led to a clear insight as to what the Understanding is not. One of the most striking aspects of the experience was to witness the extent to which people, ardent seekers, want to believe that these teachers are the real thing; and follow them, and obey what they say, and submit to their demands even when it is harmful and

## 15. No Guru, No Method, No Teacher

exploitative and has nothing to do with the teaching. I began to realize that most people, most seekers, have no way of knowing whether a teacher is the real thing or not.

Again, everything arises in the perfect unfolding of the dream in Consciousness, and there is nothing 'wrong' needing to be corrected. When a desperate seeker, just coming off a harrowing experience with some bogus, ego-driven, phony guru, asks why there are these false teachers, the only possible answer is: so that exactly this can be experienced. This too is part of the overall functioning of totality.

Even so, compassion is stirred, and I've got news for the enlightenment-seekers out there. To an extent much greater than you would like to believe, these emperors and empresses have no clothes.

If a teacher wants anything from you, demands anything from you, solicits anything from you, even if it is couched in the most spiritual terms of advancing your own awakening, then it is exceedingly likely that they have not awakened, that the Understanding is not there. If they ask for money in any form, if they demand your loyalty, if they thrive on your adulation, if they suggest that having sex with them is part of the 'transmission' or 'initiation,' if they want your time or services or possessions in exchange for what you are 'getting,' if they insist that you live in a certain way or perform certain actions, if they want anything at all from you; I assure you that it is supremely unlikely that they are what they say they are, that they have what you are seeking, or that awakening has occurred.

How can this be said so categorically? Simple. When

there is Understanding, none of these things matter. When the Understanding is there, there is the knowing that this is not how things work. This is not how things work at all! When the Understanding is there, there will not be concern about any of these things, because the Understanding renders all these things forever irrelevant.

Despite traditions that suggest the contrary, there will not even be caring whether anyone wakes up or not, whether anyone wants to listen or not. There is no one to care, no one for whom any of these things could be important.

Money, sex, loyalty, services, possessions; these are elements in the dream. When they are necessary they will be provided. If they are provided, they can be enjoyed. When they are not provided that is okay too.

A big fund-raising to run a dramatic crusade to bring the message of personal enlightenment to the whole planet is all very exciting, but it has nothing to do with *im*personal awakening to the true nature of What Is. If you need to create drama and excitement, stay asleep; in Wayne Liquorman's words, once realization happens things get very ordinary.

There is a stunningly beautiful simplicity to it all. You can say, "Awakening is the understanding that there is no one to awaken. There is no individual here doing anything. Consciousness is all there is." And you will have expressed the totality of the teaching. That's really all there is to this. All of this simply Is. There is no individual, no seeker, no teacher, no purpose, no outcome. It all simply Is. All That Is is Presence. That's it: that's the whole shebang. Done, completed. *Parasamgaté*. And, the dream goes on.

## 15. No Guru, No Method, No Teacher

So, with this understanding, enjoy it. Get up, have breakfast, go to work. 'Do' what seems right to do, knowing there is no 'you' and 'you' aren't 'doing' anything.

As the Zen saying has it,
"If you understand, things are just as they are.
If you do not understand, things are just as they are."

Again, this time from Rumi:
"We rarely hear the inward music,
but we're all dancing to it nevertheless."

Like 'you' have a choice. Can you see? It all is as it is. The mechanism, the method of functioning if you will, by which the dream operates, by which functioning occurs here in Consciousness, is the same whether it is realized or not. This is why it is said that when the Understanding occurs, nothing happens. Nothing changes. Consciousness streams, functions, operates in a body/mind organism in which the Understanding has occurred in the same manner that it operates in the body/mind organisms in which there is not Understanding. Awakening or Enlightenment does not automatically suspend the normal means and method by which the dream unfolds; there is no transfiguration into a super human being of light or some such with paranormal powers, like in some of the fanciful storytelling. Who is there to be transfigured? Who is there to do anything?

Humans seem possessed of the idea that there is something we can do to get what we want, and we have been convinced that there is something we have to do, or that we should be doing.

Listen. There is nothing you need to do. Nothing you need to make better or improve. Nothing to purify or sanctify or consecrate. Nothing to accomplish, nothing to prove. Nothing to construct. Nothing to deconstruct. Nothing to work at or to learn, nothing and no one to teach. Not even anything to understand or to 'get.' Nothing to balance or adjust or heal. Nothing to become.

Of course if it is in the dream of All That Is for a mind/body object to appear to 'do' any of these things, then that will happen: something for the dream characters to do while the dream lasts. Students of the Teaching often struggle to reconcile the idea of free will with that of determination; the idea that 'you are always already All That Is and there is nothing you can do to attain it,' with admonitions to earnestness in self-inquiry, questioning, and investigation. But there is no conflict: the teaching of 'always already' does not mean you must stop all efforts. That stopping itself would be an effort!

If you are to understand the teaching, then 'you,' as an ego, as an identified 'self,' will be motivated to perform what is necessary for that understanding to occur. If studying or meditating or working are to happen, they will happen. That itself is part of 'always already.' They are not important in themselves, but they will happen if they are to happen.

The complete Understanding is not likely to happen while sitting on your butt, avoiding the elements of the Teaching, refusing to face your misconceptions, and thinking only of everything else. But what appears as motivation and deliberation, earnestness and determination, choice and action is simply the operating of the mechanism by which the whole manifestation unfolds. The misperception is to take

## 15. No Guru, No Method, No Teacher

it personally, as *your* motivation, *your* deliberation, *your* choice and action; it is completely *im*personal, simply the totality unfolding as it is. It is what you always already are.

It is a matter of the underlying understanding: practices and tasks and all of living are not undertaken with a personal intent, or for the attainment of a goal, or to become a better person, or to save the world, or because 'I should.' There is only watching the body/mind, which you are not, have thoughts occur to it, be motivated, perform actions… or not. There is only complete simplicity: an openness, a consent, to letting happen what will happen, and to letting the misconceptions fall away.

## 16.

## *Free Fall*

*"There is no such thing as an entity.
Now you know you are awake
because you are here and you have
that knowledge.
There is nothing else other than this knowledge,
no entity."*
– *Nisargadatta Maharaj*

ONE ARRIVES FOR THE FIRST TIME in India and is assaulted, overwhelmed, swept away by sensory input. Smells, textures, sights, sounds, tastes: the mind/body organism responds in amazement. There has been the nothing that happened in the jungle; the Brilliance, the seeing, the no one home. There has been the learning and absorption of some Advaita ideas as a way to parse and express this nothing. Then, incomprehensibly, the mind/body thing finds itself hurtling across the planet to meet a teacher in Bombay. This is entirely puzzling: there is no reason for this. The mind is all but blank. There is no expectation; there can be none; there is no possible purpose, no possible outcome. In fact, the david thing has no idea what the fuck is going on, and is astonished to find itself, exhausted and jet-lagged, in the tropical heat of a Bombay night, zigzagging through the crowded streets in a tiny ancient taxi piloted by a nearly naked Hindu driver who speaks no English, a pink plastic figure of Ganesha, the elephant-headed god, swinging wildly from the mirror; and headed, hopefully, toward downtown Bombay and a hotel room.

That first night in India, there is a dream.

I am very high up, in an airplane perhaps, looking down at the ground below. The ground is covered with large flat squares, down there on the ground. Reminiscent somewhat of flying over England or Ireland with the patchwork of square fields, but much simpler; just flat squares of very muted colors, most of them simply gray. Someone next to me says, "Those squares look flat, two dimensional, but actually they are big three-dimensional cubes; they have a height that we can't perceive from here."

I look at her; she seems sincere enough, but there is something strange about the way she is insisting on this, like she is repeating something she has heard but doesn't really know it for herself. And I say, "I know what you mean; because of perspective, from a distance things can seem flat. But that isn't the case here. In this case, those squares actually are just flat. If they had height, they would look different: you'd be able to tell."

Somehow I know this to be true, that the person next to me is subtly misperceiving, or adding embellishment that isn't there; but as I say it, I realize that this will just be a discussion, an argument. Even though I know it with

## 16. Free Fall

certainty, there is no way to prove it one way or the other unless someone were to go down there, get closer, and see for sure. One would have to jump, and fall all the way down there, and of course that would be impossible, foolish, out of the question, because falling from this height would mean certain death. As I think this, I realize that I am already falling through the sky.

No sense of intent or decision or will to jump, or act of jumping. Just that it had happened.

There's not a lot of complication here. Dreams arise as part of the natural functioning of the mind/body just as anything else arises. In the sleeping dream, feelings and sensations arise just as they do in the waking dream. The mind/body does not know the difference between a sleeping dream and the waking dream and it does not like the idea of jumping out of an airplane.

First, there is a moment of horror. There is thinking, my god, what has happened, I'm falling toward the earth, in a few moments I'm going to hit and go splat and this whole life will be over. Panic. Dread. Then, a moment of denial and frantic activity: wait, maybe there's something I've missed: maybe there's a parachute strapped to my back; maybe there's a body of water I can land in and somehow, miraculously, survive this.

Then, still falling, the acceptance. So. This is how it is going to be. The moment has come. This body will in fact go splat and die. Since there's no way out, that's okay. Not such a bad way to go: I probably won't even feel it, the lights will just go out. And meanwhile, there is this last amazing experience: falling this great distance, with no impedance, no protection:

total free fall. Astonishingly beautiful. Complete letting go.

All of this in little more than an instant: the mind/body thing reacts to an unplanned jump out of an airplane in its predictable way according to its programming; it has its moment of fear, its moment of denial, its moment of acceptance. Then, unsupported, it goes quiet. In this dream too, as in the waking dream, the mind/body is a dream character. The dreamer is dreaming, and the dream continues.

The air rushing around me as I drop; and, detached and quite neutral, I see the squares on the ground, speeding toward me and quite close now. It's perfectly amusing because it doesn't matter in the least, but I can't help noticing that what was intuited, sitting back there in the plane, was true; even from this close, they are just flat squares, not cubes, with no height or depth.

Then, in the very instant of hitting the ground, there is a change. At the moment I reach the level of the ground where the squares are, they transform. They had indeed been flat and mostly gray; only now, as if suddenly given life, instantly they morph into wondrous, unearthly, three dimensional objects with subtle, gentle shapes and shading. And they are not just big cubes, as my companion in the plane had insisted so confidently; they are quite simple, nothing elaborate or grandiose, but nevertheless they are unimaginably, indescribably beautiful.

And with this, right at what would be the moment of impact, when I would have lost consciousness, the dream simply ends. There is no shock, no jolt. There is deep dreamless sleep. Later, the next morning when I wake up, the dream and its natural, abrupt ending is clear in memory.

## 16. Free Fall

And there is a realization: well yes, of course:
The only way to know is to jump.
Jumping means certain death.
Jumping has already happened.

And this 'happening' has no more significance or value than brushing one's teeth. There is no meaningful way to talk about it, there is no way to construct a sentence because there is no object and no doer and nothing done and no time frame. It just Is. It would be nonsense and impossible to talk about this as if there were anything personal or significant or special about it.

In the dream, everything *is* flat and gray, and an observer from that distance can only say things are flat, or try to pretend that they are not. Or, perhaps, like my companion in the plane, to repeat what has been heard, that some have said that things are not as they seem; but even then there can only be an approximation. It is only with jumping, and being annihilated, that the true depth and beauty and wonder of What Is can be seen and experienced and known.

For a moment there is a sense, an awareness that the jumper has indeed died, and in the instant of that death has understood what otherwise cannot be; but that too is a joke because there never was a jumper. No one jumped. In the waking dream as in the sleeping dream, jumping happened. The dancing happens. The dreaming happens. And the astonishing, breathtaking beauty is that All of This; dancing, dreaming, jumping, simply Is.

# 17.

## LOVE

*"Love is an endless mystery
for it has nothing else to explain it."*
*- Tagore*

—

*"Whisper words of wisdom:
let it be."*
*- Lennon/McCartney*

IN THE BEGINNING OF HIS BOOK, *The Final Truth*, Ramesh writes,

> "The final truth cannot be accepted unless the mind is empty of the 'me' and the heart is full of love."

And a few days ago, in our conversation, he told me,

> "david – do you want to know how to live life? Let it be! Let it happen. Everything that everyone is 'doing' – let it happen!
>
> "Be still, 'do' whatever 'you' want, and don't bother about the world!
>
> "Be still. Be still means, don't think! You see? It's so simple!"

The past few days, I have been sitting listening during the morning talks; and much of the time there is not even putting meaning to the words. Listening intently, but not with the intellect.

Just being here, in what I call Presence, the one Presence that I am. Reflecting itself in itself without a mirror.

Ramesh talks about 'the Understanding,' but This has nothing to do with the mind comprehending anything. I am learning different words, names for Presence; but the knowing, the felt truth, is that it is much, much more intimate, more familiar, than the words 'Consciousness' or 'Truth' or 'Source' can convey. It is the most intimate thing, not in any way separate or distant.

The realization is that even in the many years when I thought I was david, and this intimate Presence was covered, layered over with thinking and with the sense of being an individual self, still even then it has always been here.

Not other. Under the conditioning, around the edges, barely perceived, but nonetheless here. Like a sort of haunting; if I would in any way look at it I would not see it, yet it was here.

Now it is clear and present, always here, always has been, always will be, is not other, is at no distance whatever. This Presence I feel always here, reflecting. It is the thing with which I am most intimate, most familiar. It is my own heart, the Heart of God, overwhelmingly beautiful, overwhelmingly compassionate, overwhelmingly loving.

## 17. Love

> "You stand inside me
> naked infinite Love...
>
> we're lost where the mind can't find us,
> utterly lost" (Ikkyu)

The human race has no idea what love is.

The other day one of the seekers here was talking about prayer; about the feeling of emptiness or even a feeling of being lost, that comes with a certain intellectual understanding of "Consciousness is all there is," when it is realized that there is no one to pray to.

There cannot help but be a smile and the feeling, "So what?" Can you see? This realization, and the feeling of emptiness, are perfect love, gift. The sense is that there is always immense gratitude overflowing, outpouring, there is no longer any need of anyone or anything to be grateful *to*. Presence is *here*. Where else? In Presence, there is the upwelling of love and gratitude outpouring in Presence. Reflecting itself in itself without a mirror.

Nothing is wanted. Everything is absolutely perfect. *This* does not know 'end.' Tomorrow david leaves to return to Vermont, but this does not end, because there is nothing separate. Even when david dies, it does not end, because this Presence is more intimate to what I am than 'david' is.

It is my own heart, the Heart of Presence, outpouring infinite beauty love compassion bliss. The Heart of Infinite All, radiant Brilliance, more intimate than any imagining, is the only reality, the only truth.

I am not present;
>what Presence is, I am.

I am not aware;
>what Awareness is, I am.

I do not love;
>what Love is, I am.

There is no 'other'
>which can be liked or disliked.

There can be no 'Other'
>to either thank or implore.

And so I cannot say 'I love'
>but rather 'I am in Love,'
>>inside Love.

Where else could I be?
Where else is there?

# 18.

## *Morning Talks*

*"Pure knowledge is not imparted by another:
it comes unasked.
It is the one that is listening:
it is your own true nature."*
– *Nisargadatta Maharaj*
—
*"I show the truth to living beings –
and then they are no longer living beings."*
– *Tung-shan*

PEOPLE FROM ALL OVER THE WORLD come to the morning talks in this living room in Bombay, some of whom have been searching for years and have been with Zen masters, gurus, teachers of all kinds. They have heard of this teacher of 'pure Advaita,' and have come with perhaps some expectation, or at least a hope, of finally hearing what they need to hear, the real thing, the teaching which will unveil the Ultimate Understanding, the Final Truth, Self Realization, Total Awakening.

What they get is a little guy sitting in the corner going on *ad nauseam* about this idea of whether or not you are the 'doer' of what you think are your actions. Most of the people who show up don't stay long. After a few sessions they leave, to go home or go on to another teacher who will talk about 'more important' things. This idea of 'doership' is too mundane, too simple; seems so secondary, so irrelevant.

Of course, make no mistake, from the point of view of the total Understanding this teaching about whether you are the doer is in fact redundant; the question does not even arise. With the Understanding comes the natural and spontaneous apperception that there is no one here, no individual to either be the doer or not be the doer. So the question is moot. What you think of as yourself; the whole package of body, mind, personality, ego, sense of individuality, personal history; none of that even exists as such, as anything other than an idea, a story, a concept in Consciousness. The discussion of whether or not 'you' can be a doer or not is, as Wei Wu Wei writes, like discussing whether the bird in the empty cage is captive. The cage is empty! There is nobody home!

At the morning talks recently there has been a musician who plays traditional Indian flute for the group after the talks. The flute does not know music: it does not know 'G' from 'B flat;' it does not know tempo or emphasis, and cannot make music come out of itself: it's just a hollow bamboo stick with holes in it! It is the musician who has the knowledge and the skill and the intention and the dexterity, and whose breath blows through the instrument and whose fingers manipulate the openings so that beautiful music flows out. When the music is ended, no one congratulates the wooden stick on the music it made:

it is the musician who is applauded and thanked for this beautiful gift of music.

It is precisely so with what we think of as our 'selves.' We are instruments, hollow sticks, through which the Breath, the Spirit, the Energy which is Presence, All That Is, Consciousness, flows. Just as it is not the flute making the note, but the Musician making the note through the instrument, so it is the breath which is Presence which animates this mind and body and comes out through this mouth to make it seem that this mouth is speaking words.

The basic misunderstanding, the basic ignorance, is this unwitting usurpation of the role of Musician by the instrument. This inversion of the truth is spontaneously realized when the Understanding occurs. It becomes obvious that there is no individual, that there is 'nobody home,' no entity here to be the doer or not. Because awakening is simply the Understanding that there is no one here to awaken.

But: this Realization happens spontaneously when the Understanding occurs. From the point of view of the seeker, you can't get there from here. Because there is no 'you,' there is no question of 'getting,' and there is no 'there' to get. The intellectual comprehension that there can be no individual entities will not in any way help the average seeker because in his or her own daily life a deep belief in a personal self and personal 'doership' will remain. And with it the accompanying misery of pride and arrogance, shame and guilt, fear, hatred and malice, all of which arise from the belief that there is someone there to be doing anything.

All attempts to extricate oneself from the dilemma only strengthen the sense of individual self of the one apparently making the attempts. There is no way out of the predicament, the paradox, because the one who thinks he or she is in the paradoxical predicament is itself an hallucination, a mind-generated fantasy, the bird in the empty cage. For the rest of your life you can continue as you have done; you can go to talks and seminars and retreats given by the most enlightened masters, and hear wonderful things about Enlightenment and Total Realization and *Sat Chit Ananda*, and have immense spiritual experiences of great beauty, but when you open your eyes you will be back at the same questions, with the same longings, because there will still be 'you.'

And so: Consciousness is stirring the pot with this insidious little teaching about 'doership' coming through this unassuming little Indian man sitting in a flat in Bombay. Yes, on the surface it perhaps seems insignificant compared to other things you may have heard. It may even seem hard to concentrate on it, when surely there must be more to "It" than this, surely there must be more to look for. And there is: this is not itself the center. But it is a way in to the center. And if you can let it in, performing the investigation that is suggested, and staying with it, and if there is an openness that allows this to take hold, then a truly amazing thing may indeed happen.

Because this teaching that appears to be relatively insignificant can be, small as it is, the little key which if allowed into the lock and allowed to turn, will swing open the vast gates. 'I am not the doer of any action:' the significance of this is not that it is any great or total realization in itself. The significance lies in where it will lead. If you really get this, really get that there is no one to get it, it will be like a line of computer code, which when introduced into the computer will re-write the whole operating system. Will cause a cascade failure of all the systems that you think of as 'yourself.' Will set in motion the surrender and apprehension which otherwise can in no way be achieved by a 'you,' and which is the Complete Understanding of awakening: the knowing that there is no one here to understand or awaken or know. There is only the Peace that passes understanding, the breath of Presence blowing through this hollow stick.

And the music thus made, which appears as the everyday thoughts and words and actions of 'you' and 'others' is nothing other than Presence playing through these instruments, and truly is the ultimate gift, beyond beauty.

# 19.

## TEACHING TRUTH

*"There are trivial truths and there are great truths.
The opposite of a trivial truth is plainly false.
The opposite of a great truth is also true."*
— Neils Bohr

*"Profound things are simple.
If it is not simple, it cannot be true.
But simple things are difficult."*
— Douglas Harding

### I

"THOSE WHO WERE QUALIFIED to teach, those few like the Maharshi, said that silence was more efficacious, but in early stages teaching can only be given via a series of untruths diminishing in inveracity in ratio to the pupil's apprehension of the falsity of what he is being taught. Truth cannot be communicated. It can only be laid bare." (Wei Wu Wei)

The ordinary person's acceptance of the illusions of the

individual self, physical 'reality', birth, death, creation, destruction, free will, personal achievement, (in short, *maya*) as truth has so inverted the perception of truth and falsehood, that what is true is generally perceived as false and what is false is given credence as truth. In this environment, a teacher who speaks the naked truth will be perceived by the ordinary person as speaking falsehood or, perhaps, as lunatic. Through no fault of his own, the listener, because of his conditioning, will not give himself the chance to hear or understand what is being said.

Thus out of compassion for the listener, in order to initiate the process of coming to understanding, the teacher will sometimes begin by couching a small amount of truth in images, illustrations or thought categories which are known *to the teacher* to be essentially erroneous. The *listener* on the other hand will perceive this teaching as mostly 'true' (i.e. familiar) with a small and perhaps puzzling element of what seems to be 'untruth.' If this is explored and his own presuppositions challenged, the listener may with help understand the truth of what he had perceived as the small untruth. It may then be possible for the teacher to gradually, in his teachings, introduce more elements of truth and just as gradually to reduce the falsehood used to make the truth comprehensible.

At some point the listener begins to recognize the inconsistency and incompatibility of the conventional imagery that is being used as a vehicle with the truth that is being conveyed. When the listener thus "apprehends the falsehood of what he is being taught," the teacher is free to dispense with the vehicle and "lay the truth bare" in a way which the listener would previously have found unacceptable.

## 19. Teaching Truth

Since truth is beyond concepts and language, this exposing of the truth will necessarily include less and less in the way of statements of What Is, and more pointers by way of what is not (i.e. the *via negativa*) until perhaps at length the listener may actually reach a point where she is able to hear and understand the truth in silence, about which Ramana Maharshi said that it is the only accurate expression of Truth but unfortunately very few are capable of hearing it. Only in silence is there freedom from the dualism inherent in the subject-object structure of language and thought.

## II

TRUTH, REALIZATION, THE SELF, the Understanding, is One, a-dvaita, not–two. But how the teaching, consisting of pointers toward the Understanding, is expressed in or through any 'teacher' or 'sage' will vary greatly; and that expression will be to a significant degree determined by the programming and conditioning of the body/mind organism in which it is expressed. In particular, the heart of the teaching, the 'basis' or irreducible core, will find a unique expression in the case of each in which the apperception has occurred. And this will be shaped to a great extent by the way, the manner, the context, the circumstances, in which the event of the Awakening occurred in each case.

This can perhaps be better illustrated than explained.

For Ramana Maharshi, the Awakening occurred as a young boy. Having the overwhelming feeling that he was about to die, he lay down and let a vivid experience of death occur, experiencing what it would be like for the bodily and mental functions to cease in death. When this had occurred, there was the realization that the 'I' that one thinks one is dies with the body and mind; yet while this false 'I' and everything else disappears, still there remains a sense of pure existence, the awareness 'I am.' This, he realized, is what the 'I' truly is; not the body or mind or personality or sense of being a separate self, all of which die, but rather the 'I-I' which is eternal. In the case of Ramana Maharshi, this is the central understanding; and so his teaching reflected this, telling listeners to "simply be," to "follow the I am," and to "abide in the I."

Nisargadatta Maharaj's account of how Realization happened is quite different. He states that his guru told him that he was not who he thought he was, not the body, but rather that he was in truth nothing other than the Absolute. He says he believed his guru, took his words to heart, and after three years of meditation and concentration on this, the Understanding was complete. And so this is the point on which all of Maharaj's teaching centers, and he addressed his listeners uncompromisingly by speaking in the first person as the Absolute, "I am That," not as a separate individual; and he insisted that no question be asked which was based on identification with the body.

From one who studied with a teacher or a guru before awakening occurred, there will likely come a teaching that a teacher or a guru is the way. From one in whom awakening happened spontaneously, without a teacher, may come the idea that a guru is not necessary. One whose awakening follows an intense period of meditation and is inextricably linked with a powerful mystical experience, may well teach meditation and mysticism.

## 19. Teaching Truth

You can read the ancient masters; Huang Po, Hui-Neng, and others; or modern teachers such as Tony Parsons or Adyashanti, and find further examples. These expressions of the core teaching, what is continually returned to as the basis, may seem to vary greatly or at least be very different in emphasis. And that difference is due for the most part to the different backgrounds, cultures, tendencies, circumstances, and events in each of the body/mind instruments, and particularly the event of the awakening itself.

In the case of what I have come to call, with some affection, 'the david thing,' the irreducible core of the Understanding was expressed in the first thought which formed when there was that sudden shift of perception and it was clearly seen that "there's nobody home!" There is Presence, Being, Consciousness. There is this apparent mind/body in which and as which Presence streams, functions, experiences. And that is all; there is no separate individual self or entity or person except as a mere thought construct.

And so the expression here necessarily revolves around this basis and returns always to this: that it is the sense of individual self that is the illusion, the 'bondage,' the essential 'endarkenment.' When this illusory sense of individual self is seen through, falls away, then there is simply What Is, there is awakening from the dream of separate, individual selfhood.

What is awakened to, what is Understood, is only One. Yet each occurrence in a body/mind instrument is different, according to the infinite variables in the programming and conditioning of each instrument and in the script or part or 'destiny' each plays in the infinite unfolding in Consciousness. Each has a different flavor, a different emphasis.

If the Understanding is a house, some come in through the front door, some the back. Some enter through windows, perhaps slipping in unnoticed or perhaps smashing the window and setting off all the alarms. One may come down the chimney, another tear through the roof shingles one by one. One may fall from a great height and crash through the roof and land on the floor in a pile of dust and debris while yet another may hand his hat to the butler as he steps from the porch into the parlor.

And these different manners in which it occurs will lend a different feel, different color, different flavor, to the expression, the description, of the One Taste. The way Ramesh talks about the Understanding and the way Tony Parsons talks about Presence are quite different, have a very different tone. Wayne Liquorman says you have no choice; Gangaji says all you have is choice. They are all pointing to exactly the same thing. All part of the infinite unfolding of totality. In form and expression, the teaching is never the same twice. Yet always the Understanding itself is not-two. All the pointers are toward What-Is.

# 20.

# *Not Taxi*

*"There is a Presence that is unnameable
which thought cannot touch.
It is not your possession; it is what you are."*
*- Adyashanti*

*"What we call 'I' is just a swinging door
which moves when we inhale and when we exhale.
It just moves; that is all...
there is nothing:
no 'I,' no world, no mind or body;
just a swinging door."*
*- Shunryu Suzuki Roshi*

Wherever you go in Bombay, there are the desperately poor and dirty, the beggars who reach up from the places on the street or in the gutter where they live and sleep, pulling on your pant leg, or the more able-bodied following you, asking, pleading for help, for a few rupees. Many hang out at the street intersections, and when traffic stops at a red light they approach your taxi, bare feet, torn clothing, dirty hands extended in through the windows, pleading eyes.

One day, returning from the morning talk at Ramesh's apartment, one such beggar more pathetic than most approached the open back window as the taxi came to a stop in traffic. I looked out to see an Indian man hardly four and a half feet tall; his eyes were on a level with mine where I sat in the tiny ancient Padmini. He had no arms, but from one shoulder grew a hand, which rested on the door of the car, palm upward, as his face pressed inward toward mine. His head and shoulders and face were deformed as well, hunched and misshapen. He showed the scars and filth and abuse of a life on the streets, and his mouth moved with a barely audible litany of pleading and supplication, well practiced from a lifetime, until his eyes caught mine and then he stopped, everything stopped, and there we stayed, our faces hardly two feet apart, eyes staring into each other's.

There are such moments in which "nothing happens," in which it is suddenly clear that what appears to be happening is not; and what is happening can only appear as no thing. The roles stopped; his begging routine stopped completely, and there was no move to give him a coin. Both forms went completely empty and still, and the boundaries evaporated.

It is difficult to describe the sense that is experienced in these moments. Whatever feeling might have been starting to arise stopped, and there was no pity, no anguish, no aversion, no awkwardness or discomfort, hardly even compassion. As I looked at him it was clear I was staring at myself, and clear that I was staring at God. The twisted physical form of this beggar seemed so transparent, stretched so shimmeringly thin in the heat of the tropical city, and the Brilliance streaming through him and around him so visible, that it was impossible not to see him and the street scene behind him as dream forms and the light of the Brilliance as the obvious underlying reality unable to be hidden. In that moment there was a sense of intense neutral quietness: as our eyes stared into each other there was nothing to do, nothing to say, nothing to feel, nothing to think.

As the taxi pulled away, I turned to my friend sitting next to me, perhaps to express something of what happened or to ask what she had seen, but there were still no coherent thoughts and no words, and when we turned back to look there was no sign of the small misshapen human form anywhere.

A couple of days later at the morning talks I was asked, essentially, "What would happen to the Understanding if david were not so well off?" My thoughts immediately went to the armless beggar and the many others I have encountered living, sleeping, wandering in the streets of Bombay, and to the sense of intense stillness that occurs in those moments. I had not put it into thought or words; I had fumbled with it once or twice, as in the taxi that time when I had turned to my friend, but it had not articulated. Now came the realization that that question, that problem, only arises if there is identification as one of the body/mind organisms.

If there is identification as a body/mind, then the whole thought process arises: "Oh my god, 'I' am so lucky, 'I' am so well off, 'I' am so comfortable, and this poor guy is in a bad way. 'I' feel bad, 'I' feel terrible, 'I' have to do something about this." Or conversely, if the situation is reversed: "'I' have it hard, 'I' don't have what 'I' want or need, these other people have more than 'I' do, 'I' need to do something... or better yet, one or all of 'them' need to do something to help 'me.'" It's all driven by the 'I' sense of individual self and comparison with other apparent individual selves.

But when there is not identification as one of those apparent individuals, then simply all this is happening. In one body/mind is arising happiness. In another body/mind is happening poverty. In this one, anger; in this one, wealth and hatred; in another, disease and peace; in another, perfect health and complete boredom! Infinite combinations of attributes and experiencing in these billions of body/minds. One of these body/minds is this one. But it really doesn't matter.

Intellectually or emotionally, this can seem a difficult, tricky subject. "It really doesn't matter," sounds about as politically incorrect as anything can. It seems an easy thing to say, sitting here in comfort. Would the same thought be occurring in this body/mind if it was one living on the streets of Bombay? And the only answer is that whatever thought occurs is the thought that arises in Consciousness in each body/mind in each moment. It simply cannot be approached either intellectually or emotionally; both of these are responses of the individual, and these boundaries do not exist except as illusory and temporary props. In the Understanding, the boundaries simply dissolve. Awakening has occurred in beggars and in kings. Many beggars and many kings remain unenlightened in the dream. It really doesn't matter.

## 20. Not Taxi

This time on the way back to the hotel, the taxi driver wanted to practice his English. I wasn't paying much attention, reading something I had been given, until at one point he had been quiet awhile and I looked up to see him watching me in the rear view mirror. Looking at me intently, he said distinctly, "I not taxi. I driv-*ing*," with the emphasis on the participle "...*ing*." An enunciation of pure non-duality worthy of a master, like something right out of Wei Wu Wei. Not the apparent entity that you think you see, but the functioning, the happening. Yes my friend, you are indeed.

> "When your individuality is dissolved, you will not see individuals anywhere, it is just a functioning in Consciousness.
>
> "If it clicks with you, it is very easy to understand. If it does not, it is most difficult. It is very profound and very simple, if understood right.
>
> "What I am saying is not the general run of common spiritual knowledge." (Nisargadatta Maharaj)

## 21.

## Don't Know

*"Authentic consciousness sees only
a radiant infinity in the heart of all souls,
and breathes into its lungs only the
atmosphere of an eternity
too simple to believe."*
— Ken Wilber

*"The wise know nothing at all –
well, maybe one song."*
— Ikkyu

THIS PERIOD OF DIRECT CONTACT with Ramesh lasts a little over two years; visits, letters, conversations. During that time there is increasing clarity about what is known, and the Brilliance outpouring widens and deepens. When there is a shared seeing and shared understanding of That which no one else sees or understands... this is quite hard to put into words.

The experience of visiting Ramesh repeatedly during these years is profoundly reassuring. In the early days especially, his thinking is quite precise, and this is immeasurably helpful in distinguishing, conceptually, the elements that are inherent in the Understanding from those that remain as part of the body/mind conditioning, and both of these from the Babel of extraneous ideas and opinions on the subject.

'The body/mind organism,' 'conditioning and programming,' 'Consciousness' (as the basic concept for All-That-Is) and 'the Understanding' (as a defining term for the knowing, the inseeing): while not originally or exclusively Ramesh's, these concepts are received from him and become part of the underlying framework that emerges during this time to facilitate comprehending, and therefore a kind of easing into, the no-thing no-one no-where no-when that is here since the jungle.

Yet it is also true that from the time I first arrive at 10 Sindhula House, there is some dissonance. Although the recognition is there from him almost immediately, Ramesh by this time is no longer using the uncompromising nondual language of his earlier books, with which there had been such resonance that I had traveled across the globe to see him. He spends our first conversations going on about how 'you are not the doer' of any action. He talks about how what everyone wants is simply to be comfortable with oneself and others.

Oneself? Others? I am nonplussed, and it is some while before I can articulate to him that what he is talking about makes no sense in the context here. There is clearly no 'one' here, no one to either be a doer or not: the question does not even arise. How can it? This has nothing to do with being comfortable, as he himself wrote in his earlier books.

## 21. Don't Know

"...The total annihilation of the phenomenal object with which there is identification as a separate entity..." Phrases like this are about as quintessentially vintage Ramesh as you can get. Yet he no longer uses this language: instead, he asks visitors 'what it is they want most out of life,' and spends the time giving advice on relationships with 'others.'

What life, what relationship, what others? All is streaming Presence: any perceived 'other' is I! Only knowing this can remove suffering: all else is bondage. If this is known, how can there be a teaching of anything else?

You see, when the shift in perspective occurred that night in the jungle, without any training or background or terminology or concepts, when that Understanding first expressed itself in the thought, the concept, 'my god, there's nobody home;' in that instant, the center of experiencing and functioning and identity was displaced, and it was known, without labels, that the 'I' who is and who experiences and functions is not 'david', but experiences and functions through the instrument of 'david', as likewise through all others. This is the center, the irreducible essence, as far as it can be expressed, of the Understanding here, and it is utterly simple.

All there is, is Presence, Awareness, Consciousness; and within Consciousness this apparent body/mind instrument which in itself does not exist separately as a person or an entity or a thing but only as a thought, a dream, in Consciousness; through which and as which there is experiencing, but there is no 'one' here experiencing! There is mental and physical and psychological and emotional functioning here, to be sure. And this functioning is unique in this body/mind organism, as it is in all such. But this is impersonal functioning in, as, by, impersonal Presence; it does not add up to a separate personal entity, of which there are none!

Ramesh, on the other hand, draws on an immense tradition of thought and discussion on this subject, and has spent a lifetime and many books developing and expounding on such ideas as noumenon and phenomenon; reality, doership, entity and ego; working mind and thinking mind, intellectual understanding and the complete Understanding. He also operates within the Indian tradition of the guru being responsible for the guidance, spiritual and otherwise, of those who come to him.

And what do I know? Gurus, after all, are known for their strange ways. Who is there to say? I have come here to hear 'the teaching coming through Ramesh,' and much of that teaching is extremely helpful. And so at first there is working with him during this time, to find the correspondences between the knowing that is here, and his sense of what this is all about, including his structure of concepts. There is immense gratitude here for the great benefit and clarity which he contributes. And there is the growth of what can only be called a tremendous love for Ramesh. And therefore also, there is giving him the benefit of the considerable doubt in all this when at times there seems to be significant divergence.

Nevertheless, as each of his new books comes out there is some discouragement as they trend further from the pure awareness of What Is and more toward simple stories and guides for everyday living. And the conversations with him become more frustrating as he insists more rigorously that awakening or the Understanding consists only of the awareness that the individual is not the doer of any action, and that the individual self always remains. This is not what is known here.

This idea that 'you are not the doer of any action' is central to Ramesh's thought. It was there from the beginning, in the experience of awakening with Maharaj. Somewhere early on, he came across a quote attributed to the Buddha: "Events happen, deeds are done, but there is no individual doer thereof." This became the basis of his teaching, and anyone who has heard him speak has heard this aphorism a thousand times. (Although it remains somewhat odd that when asked, he could never say where the quote was from; and in all my research, and that of others I know, a source for this has never been found, nor have I ever seen it quoted outside Ramesh's own works or the works of those who heard it from him.)

At first, when pressed, Ramesh concedes that the idea of non-doership, along with the investigation he recommends to seekers so that they could discover this for themselves, is a teaching device. Its usefulness lies in the fact that once one is convinced that they are not the agent who does anything, the sense of self will itself begin to crumble. In his early books, he is quite clear that enlightenment consists of "a total disidentification with a body/mind organism as a separate entity;" and the "sense of doership" is, if not equated, at least closely linked with the "sense of a separate entity," so that when one disappears the other does as well.

But during the time I know him, this idea that 'you are not the doer' seems to progress from a concept used as a teaching device to itself being the centerpoint. At first, Ramesh's teaching is that when 'you are not the doer' is understood, the flash of awakening may then occur, and what remains is a shadowy ego which only occasionally interrupts the unattached 'working mind' and the impersonal witnessing. But later, 'you are not the doer' becomes itself the awakening, and the ego remains; you always exist as a separate entity, albeit with the understanding that it is not you who are doing anything.

But in fact, the understanding that 'you are not the doer' is not the center. It's useful as a step, as a way into: 'you are not,' and indeed it can be a valuable and helpful step. But it is nothing in itself. If it is the center, then the individual self is maintained. And that is what is not.

> "Realization is of the fact that you are not a person... Personal entity and enlightenment cannot go together." (Nisargadatta Maharaj)

After each visit to Bombay, there is the sense that it is finished; there is no reason or need to return. I dislike travel and dislike India and dislike Bombay; it is all unnecessary and difficult, and this body's health fails each time I make the trip. And for what? Yet each time, a few months pass and there is traveling again. What do I know? Unfinished business, apparently.

It is no secret that Ramesh and I have a somewhat public falling-out at my last visit. He is by now teaching without qualification that each person always exists as a separate individual entity: pure dualism. And he dismisses accounts of the loss of any identification as a separate entity as inaccurate and confusing. When objections are raised that this contradicts all the teachers and masters of the perennial wisdom, including and especially his own teacher, he shouts it down: everyone else was wrong, they were not qualified to speak, what they said was just confusing.

## 21. Don't Know

There are many ways these things could be interpreted, and each evening in the hotel room they are all weighed. I am acutely alert to the archetype of the student who loves his teacher until the student reaches a certain level of understanding; then if the teacher disagrees or tries to rein him in, the student says the teacher has lost it, and leaves. Also aware of the archetype in which the teacher creates this situation intentionally to kick the student out of the nest. Neither applies here; there simply has never been that relationship between 'Ramesh' and 'david.'

And the 'crazy wisdom' prototype also does not fit. Ramesh has played that card before. Always there was a little glint in his eye that let you know (if you could read it) that something was afoot; and always when the joke had gone far enough and he had made his point, he would set things straight. There is nothing like that here now. Whatever else is going on, Ramesh is dead serious – which itself is unusual and raises concern.

And yes, all of this is concepts, and all teachings are only pointers and not themselves truth. Which is why the masters use the negative way, saying what the awareness is not. Ramesh's repudiation of these masters and his aggressive insistence on your existence as an individual person as separate entity is hardly *via negativa*.

Finally, I can only repeat to him all that is known here; that there is nothing here, only the Presence which is all, streaming through these apparent forms; and I tell him that whatever purpose this teaching of his may have, I know he is talking nonsense. The presumption is that he knows this as well.

In the end, after investigating to see that there is clarity within, there can be only a smile and a shake of the head at the tricks that are played, at the complexity and the sometimes apparently odd ways that this totality unfolds in Consciousness. And as the days of this last visit wear on, there is growing sadness, and great love for the expression and the form in which Presence is perceived as Ramesh.

There can come a time, with any friend or teacher for whom there is love and respect, when it may become unavoidably clear that a change is occurring. Clear that in a subtle and uncanny sense there is some kind of 'slippage' in the body/mind system. There may be a sense that it is not only the outer speaking or teaching which has changed; that there is also not the single-pointed attention, not the sense of total presence; that arguments become full of an apparent struggle to assert, rather than a resting in what needs no asserting. It can sometimes be subtle, and if one had reason not to see this kind of thing, it could be easily dismissed. Other times it is more blatant and cannot be explained away or disregarded.

From a lesser teacher, off on a tangent, one might expect arguments that are confused and self-contradictory; a manner aggressive, abrupt and belligerent; and defensive and increasingly erratic behavior. Discussions then may easily get caught up in pointless opinions and arguments approving of certain experiences and ideas and ways of expression, vehemently disapproving of others. And always an insistence on the separate self; lacking, even repudiating, the essential basis, the inseeing of pure not-two-ness. All of this dream-bound and very little of it making much sense or having anything to do with the Understanding of What Is.

## 21. Don't Know

In any case, none of it really matters. My time here is finished. Whatever the 'cause,' it is here necessarily that there is a parting of ways on the essence of the teaching. And who knows? Perhaps that in itself is Ramesh's gift, and explanation enough for all of this. Perhaps it is simply this certain coming-about that came about, nothing else; and that too is gift beyond reasoning.

Most who come to see Ramesh do so as seekers and students, and their concepts and comprehension come to reflect his teaching. For them he is the touchstone, the point to check back with for truth and accuracy. As well it should be; such is the guru/disciple relationship. There is a deep enduring wisdom in Ramesh. There will be many who will continue to find him and his teaching of great benefit. As did I.

But here, there is another Touchstone: always and forever that Understanding, that Seeing, that in-perceiving of What Is, which first exploded here in that shift of perspective, in that time out of time in the jungle, and since then has never not been. That is all that is known, and it simply cannot be compromised, diluted or revised for the sake of agreement.

All of this, whatever it may be, however it may unfold, is always part of the infinite expression of Presence. It is as it is. As long as it is seen as a matter of separate individuals, there will be a problem. The only reason, the only truth, the only explanation for mystifying events is that all there is, is Presence. There is no Ramesh, there is no david. What Ramesh is, I am. Which apparent instrument what event happens in, is insignificant. What do we know? The universe operates on a need-to-know basis, and the dream characters don't need to know. They will play out their parts regardless.

More and more there is increasing awareness that, other than the complete certainty of what is known since the jungle, I know nothing. As david I am not; all this world is not; all there is is Presence streaming here in perfect Outpouring; and this Presence is what 'I' is. Yet even this is not something I know: It is what I Am. And other than this, everything is simply, "don't know."

And always, everywhere, this perfect Brilliance, this deep Stillness; it is no thing, it has no name. Outpouring constantly, in perfect beauty lacking nothing. And seen always; never not seen. But seen not as from this mind/body; there is no one here to see.

Nothing can contain this, nothing can hold this. Not the Catholicism of my youth, not the forays into Zen and Tao in later years. Not native shamanism, not the dogmatic and institutionalized Advaita of the first teachers I encountered, not even beloved Ramesh and his vicissitudes. No guru, no method, no teacher.

And once again I leave Bombay and return to Vermont: as if there is any place to be left, or any to return to; as if there is any one leaving or returning. And nothing comes to an end, because there is nothing separate. Only the Heart of Presence, outpouring; the only reality, the only truth.

"*What did he mean?*

At that time, I nearly misunderstood my former master's intent.

*I wonder if the former master was actually enlightened.*

If he was not enlightened, how could he have known to answer in such a way? If he was enlightened, why did he go to the trouble of answering in such a way?

*What teaching did you receive when you were with him?*

Although I was there, I didn't receive any teaching.

*Since you didn't receive any teaching from him, why are you remembering him in this way?*

Why should I turn my back on him?

*Do you agree with him or not?*

I agree with half and don't agree with half.

*Why don't you agree completely?*

If I agreed completely, then I would be ungrateful to my former master."

– from *The Record of Tung-shan*

# *Four*

*In this
annihilation,
every longing,
hunger, and
thirst
is dissolved,
perfected,
healed
and made
forever
irrelevant.*

# 22.

---

## *Question/Answer*

*"A voice comes to your soul, saying:
Lift your foot, cross over;
move into the emptiness
of question and answer and question."*
        *- Rumi*

---

*"Keep asking those deep questions, sleep on -
when you wake even you'll be gone!"*
        *- Ikkyu*

### I

**Y**OU MUST CONTINUE TO ASK QUESTIONS, *pursuing each question as it arises, with great earnestness.*

Any question which may arise here is answered immediately, and they all have the same answer.

And that is?

That that question, that thought, like all thoughts, is empty. When there is the misconception, the idea that there is a separate entity here out of whose individual mind the thought or question arises, then questions are taken as important. When all is seen as it is, all thoughts, feelings, and actions are seen to arise as the infinite expression of Consciousness. Whatever arises can only be the perfect unfolding in Consciousness, however it appears to the apparent individual. These body/mind things are only instruments, objects in Consciousness and therefore cannot possibly know the basis, the purpose, the reason by which Consciousness works. When any question is asked in this context, the question dissolves. All simply is as it is.

*Well, there you are. So, that's good. (pause.) How long has it been since you awakened to this?*

Here we go again. You should know better. Since who awakened?

*What you call this body/mind thing, the apparent individual.*

You miss my point. There is no one here. The body/mind is an object only; the individual is only apparent, a character in the dream. It cannot be the character in a dream who awakens.

*So, it is the dreamer who awakens.*

The idea of 'awakening' is only an analogy; be careful not to begin taking it literally. Any analogy breaks down eventually, and this one does here. The Dreamer is Consciousness, which is All That Is: it has never been asleep, has no need to awaken.

*So, who awakens?*

The analogy of awakening, like any analogy, can have a certain limited usefulness. It is one of the straws grasped at in an attempt to describe the indescribable, to communicate what cannot be communicated. It also has its drawbacks. In particular, it can be used to make a demarcation, a distinction. A false separation between those perceived individuals who have awakened and those perceived individuals who have not. This is artificial, a construct of the mind. There is only Consciousness, streaming through and expressing as all these body/mind things. What happens in one body/mind thing as distinct from another is insignificant unless you believe they exist as individual persons and you identify as one of them. As the Third Zen Patriarch wrote, "Distinctions arise from the clinging needs of the ignorant... What benefit can be derived from attachment to distinctions and separations?"

*Surely there is a difference between one who is awakened and one who is not.*

Not at all. As Huang Po said, "There is just a mysterious, tacit understanding, and no more."

*The difference then is that some of us have this understanding while most do not.*

You are taking it personally, setting up "us and them," which makes nonsense of it. These are the distinctions that the Zen Patriarch was talking about. Please understand, what you are referring to as 'us' or as 'them' are personal reference points which are seen here to be illusory, purely mythical in spite of being taken quite seriously by you and just about everyone else. There is Understanding. There is no one here to *have* understanding, or to have anything for that matter.

*But you yourself use words like 'you' and 'everyone.'*

If you went to a foreign country, you'd find it hard to communicate unless you learned and used the language that the locals used. Our language is structured in a way that makes it all but impossible to speak without using personal pronouns and other words which seem to refer to individuals. This makes things difficult, but language must still be used. Trying to avoid these words altogether just results in stilted and awkward speech which calls attention to itself and fails to communicate. So one must continue to use the conventions of language which include personal pronouns to refer to an experience and an understanding which is completely *im*personal.

It's a little like continuing to talk about 'sunrise' and 'sunset' even when you know quite well that the sun doesn't revolve around the earth, and so it doesn't rise or set but only appears to because of the earth's own rotation. When I use the terms 'I' or 'me' they refer to nothing personal at all, since it's completely obvious from this perspective that there is no person here. There is only All That Is, streaming through all these apparent forms. On the other hand, when you say something like, "some of us have the understanding but most do not," it's evident that you are taking the distinction between yourself as an individual and others as individuals quite seriously, and are busy comparing and judging between them.

## 22. Question/Answer

To return to your earlier comment, earnestly asking questions should not be seen as an end in itself. Asking questions does not actually lead anywhere. In the tradition of *jnana yoga*, asking questions operates a bit like the Zen *koan*, gradually backing the mind into a corner or exhausting it to the point that it realizes that while questions can go on forever, Truth will never be found there. The Third Zen Patriarch again: "To seek Mind with the discriminating mind is the greatest of mistakes."

The problem, you see, is that all questions arise out of their answers. You can't ask a question about Self, or Truth, or the Understanding, that you don't already, on some level, know the answer to: if you didn't know the answer, the question never could have occurred to you.

That's why the great Zen and Advaita masters rarely answered a question; they redirected it. The point of asking a question is not to get the answer, which you already have; despite what you may believe, there's really no benefit in getting answers. All the answers in the world will not lead to Understanding. All answers are within the dream, as are all questions. What you want is no-answer, which can only be arrived at by no-question. For each body/mind, there is only one no-question, what I sometimes call the dangerous question, the asking of which contains the end to all questions, the asking of which stops you, annihilates 'you.'

If a question arises, then by all means ask it. Sometimes it is all that can happen. But there is nothing sacred about asking questions. It is when the questions cease and the mind is empty that there is an opening.

## II

*W*HEN YOU SAY, 'THERE'S NOBODY HOME,' *what do you mean? Who isn't home?*

It is the sense of being a separate self, an individual, a separate autonomous independent entity.

*So the separate self is no longer home.*

Yes, although I tend to say the *sense* of being a separate self is what is no longer there, because the separate self as such has never existed, was *never* there, was only an idea – and a mistaken one.

*The ego?*

I tend to equate the ego with the sense of a separate self, yes. Others may mean different things by the ego.

*But some teachers say the ego is still there, but transformed or made 'harmless.'*

You're referring to Ramana Maharshi's analogy of the burnt rope. He said the ego of the sage is like a burnt rope; it is harmless in that it cannot any longer be used to hold anyone in the 'bondage' of *samsara*. Some teachers take this and say that although the rope is burnt, it is still there. But in fact, it is *not* still there, *as* a rope. The ego is not still there, as an ego, as a sense of separate self. What is still there is the appearance: various forms of functioning in the body/mind instrument. But this functioning does not add up to a separate entity. It never did.

## 22. Question/Answer

Have you ever actually experienced a burnt rope? This is another one of those agricultural parables that might be a little hard to understand in the modern world. The burnt rope phenomenon is quite an extraordinary thing. When I was twelve, the tool shed on the farm burned; and as I was picking through the charred remains with my father, to salvage tools and hardware, I came across what appeared to be the big coil of manila rope that we used on the farm for jobs like felling trees.

I was surprised that it had survived the fire, but when my hand tried to close on it, the fingers passed through the fine powdery ash with no resistance. There's something about natural manila or sisal rope that causes it to burn thoroughly, but for the ashes to remain in place and retain the appearance of the whole rope. This is the meaning of the Maharshi's image; what remains is not a rope (the 'ego') at all, but only looks like one! There is only the appearance of a rope, not a rope itself!

But like all analogies this one too only goes so far. Unlike the rope that burns and is then only an appearance of a rope made of ash, the ego never really existed in the first place: it was only a mistaken idea. So then, this is where that other traditional analogy takes over, the image of the coil of rope that was mistaken for a snake. At first the response is fear; then when it is realized that it is only a coil of rope and not a snake at all, the experience is quite different. But what has changed? Nothing, because there never was a snake there, it was only a mistaken idea. The separate self, the ego, was never there; only the idea, the *sense* of being an individual, which turns out to be misled.

And yet even that's not the point. Finally, even that falls

away. Even the appearance never was: always everywhere there is only the changeless Self. This, at least, is what is understood here.

This is what is meant when the Understanding or awakening is called a shift in perception. Wei Wu Wei said it well;

> "...merely a readjustment is needed, such readjustment being the abandonment of identification with an inexistent individual self..."

*But I heard Wei Wu Wei wasn't enlightened.*

And?

*He had Alzheimer's at the end, so he wasn't enlightened.*

Whoa! One thing at a time here. First, whether or not Terrence Gray was awakened is a moot question. As I read his books, it seems there are at least a couple of places where he says himself that he is not. This need to label someone enlightened or unenlightened is misplaced: it is based on a belief in the separate self. If there are no separate individual selves, who's awakened? All there is, is Presence. Separating and making distinctions and comparing is the illusion.

Whether the one we know as Wei Wu Wei was enlightened or not, his works are among the clearest and most uncompromisingly accurate renditions of the teaching you can find. The complete Understanding and the ability to express it accurately don't necessarily go hand in hand. Some of the truly, deeply awakened can't express it at all, while some of the best expressions come from those who have an excellent intuitive grasp of the meaning of the teaching on an

## 22. Question/Answer

intellectual level, even though it may not have gone deep enough that they no longer experience any separate self.

Now: this Alzheimer's thing needs to be laid to rest. This is part of the misconception that with awakening the sage becomes an elevated or perfect human being. Alzheimer's is a physical disease, affecting the organism. It results from genetic and environmental factors, and so in our terminology it is a matter of the programming and conditioning of that body/mind organism. As such it is no different than any other disease; no different from Ramana Maharshi's or Nisargadatta Maharaj's cancer. Since it affects the physical cells of the brain the results are not very pretty, but it's still a disease of the organism, and arises as part of the organic functioning of that body/mind.

The so-called sage knows that whatever arises is the perfect unfolding of totality in Consciousness; and in which dream character what event happens is irrelevant. The body/mind organism of the sage has no special immunity conferred upon it at awakening. The Understanding is not a vaccine, against Alzheimer's or anything else.

*But someone who has Alzheimer's isn't going to be making much sense a lot of the time.*

It sure isn't going to look very pretty. It'll be quite disturbing to those who need perfect enlightened beings to look up to, or have fantasies of disease-free enlightened living; or have absorbed some New Age ideas about causing your own sickness.

But if the awakening has truly occurred, and there was no longer any sense of a separate self, and then the body/

mind organism succumbs to an organic disease, you can't go back and retroactively say that the awakening didn't happen after all. It did. Then, the disease happened. Life is like that. It's messy. It includes everything.

*Seems like that introduces a lot of confusion, or potential confusion.*

Confusion is already there. What's 'wrong' with confusion? Again, it's part of the overall functioning. In duality, you can't have light without dark, up without down, beauty without ugliness, clarity without confusion. Declaring war on confusion and trying to eliminate it completely is misguided. Remember what Maharaj said to someone who wanted out of the dream?

> "The dream is not your problem. Your problem is that you like one part of the dream and not another."

Trying to eliminate the parts of the dream you don't like will keep you occupied, but it will also keep you frustrated: it can never succeed because the manifestation is inherently dualistic. Awakening is seeing What Is, and acceptance of the whole – the whole messy lot. You don't necessarily have to like it, but it's What Is.

*I don't understand. Just because there's confusion doesn't mean I still shouldn't try to be as clear as I can.*

Then be as clear as you can! If you have been given that kind of motivation, you may be instrumental in contributing to the overall balance. But be aware that despite your best efforts, it's always possible that the things you say or do may have unintended consequences. In spite of trying to be clear, it may be that what you say will still be confusing

## 22. Question/Answer

to some people, and may actually add to the overall confusion, even though that wasn't your intent.

The point is that it's not up to you. All of this, the overall balance, is being taken care of, in ways that are not up to the body/mind mechanisms and which they cannot begin to comprehend, with the level of cognition allotted to them. Knowing this, there is no intent here: just a consent to, a cooperation with, whatever arises. And sure, 'whatever arises' may include a motivation to be clear. Just don't be surprised if that is not the outcome, because the outcome is not up to you. And the ultimate outcome in the long term will be to maintain the balance of clarity and confusion in totality.

# 23.

## Perspective

"We dance 'round in a ring and suppose
while the Secret sits in the middle and knows."
- Robert Frost

—

"When we Understand, we are at the center
of the circle, and there we sit
while Yes and No chase each other
around the circumference."
- Chuang Tzu

### I

*I*N A SENSE, IT IS ALL A MATTER of perception, of perspective. The ultimate Understanding spoken of in the perennial wisdom can be seen as a massive and total shift or alteration in perspective. But just how massive or total is hard to imagine until it occurs.

When I was in high school in the late sixties and early seventies, Edwin Abbott's *Flatland* became popular among students. The small book was originally written in 1884, but it found new interest and several reprintings as it resonated with the counterculture and mood of the Nixon years. Flatland is a two dimensional universe inhabited by two dimensional beings who know only width and length, such as the stick figures you might draw on paper. Existing on the flat plane of the paper, they know nothing of height or depth, which do not exist in their world. Consequently they have never thought of these 'unreal' directions or dimensions and have no words for them; our words 'height' or 'depth,' 'above' and 'below,' as well as the ideas or concepts which these words represent to us, do not exist in their world.

The book narrates the experiences of one such two dimensional being, a square, when his comfortable two dimensional life is invaded one day by an incomprehensible creature from another dimension: a sphere. Only gradually was the square able to come to comprehend the initially disorienting experience of a third dimension. Needless to say, the great difficulty arose when the square tried to express his experience to other two dimensional figures like himself. How does one describe 'above' in a context where there exist only forward, back, and two directions of sideways? The square tried using existing words ('forward, but not forward, a different forward,') and tried using new words he had learned from the sphere (but 'above' was only nonsense syllables to the Flatlanders.) So the square, who knew he had had real experiences of this third dimension, found himself being regarded as an idiot talking nonsense.

The experience of the Flatland square will be familiar to anyone who has had a spiritual or mystical experience of 'Otherness,' of another dimension beyond our familiar physical three dimensions, and then tried to express this to

## 23. Perspective

others in comprehensible language. And it can be useful as a metaphor to illustrate or express how the Understanding cannot be described in any terms or concepts available here. But the shift in perspective inherent in the Understanding is even more total than the inclusion of another dimension. Rather than the mere addition of a dimension, it is a shift out of all dimensions in that it is not a question of seeing differently or of seeing new or different things, but of the disappearance of the one who sees.

In a sense, the Understanding is the opposite of the discovery of the third dimension by the two-dimensional Flatlander. In the common shared experience of this world of duality and process, what is experienced is always the triad of the experiencer, what is experienced, and the experience itself. There appears to be the doer of an action, the thing acted upon, and the action. The one who thinks, that which is thought of, and the thought. The seer, that which is seen, and sight. And so on; even the one who is, *what* one is, and the being of that.

But in the unity consciousness of the Understanding, these perceived discreet dimensions of otherness collapse into Oneness and in place of the 'split mind' perception of experiencer, the experienced, and the experience, there is in 'whole mind' only experien*cing*. No doer, no object, no thing done, only function*ing*. Only see*ing*. Only be*ing*, not in the sense of *a* being, but rather *be-ing*. All there is, is not some-one conscious of some-thing, but rather simply impersonal *Conscious-ness*. Consciousness is all there is, and Consciousness is the functioning, the seeing, the being, the experiencing, which is perceived by split mind as some one doing or being some thing.

How does this shift occur? How does one go from perceiving with split mind to the Understanding of whole mind? Well, the point is that one doesn't. No one ever understands, in this sense. There is only understand*ing*, and the Understanding is that there is no one to understand and no thing to be understood. The very essence of the Understanding is that while events seem to be happening, and deeds appear to be done, "no one does it, nor is anything done; it is pure doing." (Wei Wu Wei) There is no individual to do or understand anything. There is no thing to be done or understood. Appearances notwithstanding, there are no discreet individuals or entities of any kind, any where. This seeking, this quest for understanding, ultimately leads to the annihilation of the seeker; to the realization that there never was a seeker to begin with, that the entire world perceived by split mind, including the perceiver, is an elaborate illusion. Wei Wu Wei:

> "It is important to understand that there is nothing to acquire, but only an error to be exposed, because acquiring necessarily involves using, and so strengthening that spurious 'I' whose dissolution we require. For this merely a readjustment is needed, such readjustment being the abandonment of identification with an inexistent individual self, an abandonment which leaves us unblindfolded and awake in our eternal nature.
>
> "To seek to persuade ourselves that we do not exist as individual entities is, however, to ask the eye to believe that what it is looking at is not there. But it is not we alone who have no existence as entities: there are not any anywhere in the reality of the cosmos, never have been, and never could be. Only whole-mind can reveal this knowledge as direct cognition which, once realized, is obvious. This is the total readjustment. And only 'I' remains."

## 23. Perspective

It's not new or even unusual to think of all this world and life as an illusion or a dream: the analogy is all around us, from Shakespeare, ("we are such stuff as dreams are made on,") to nursery rhymes, ("merrily, merrily, merrily, merrily, life is but a dream.") What hardly anyone realizes is that the one who might think he understands this is himself a dream character, part of the illusion. That the mind which thinks, "life is but a dream" does not itself have an existence apart from the dream; that this thought arises only within and as part of the dream.

Naturally, this is enough to put off most of the human race. Does exist. Cannot be expressed.

## II

*T*WO MORE EXAMPLES:

Get in an airplane in Oklahoma. Fly straight south. What do you fly over? If you answer 'Texas,' I have news for you. There is no such thing as 'Texas.' If you look down while flying south, you will not see any such thing as Texas. You will see what is there: arid desert, farm land, mountains, rivers, roads, cities. Texas is only an idea; it exists only as an agreed-upon conceptual construct. There is nothing 'real' about the border between Texas and Oklahoma, and you will not see it if you fly over it. The delineation, the distinction, the decision to call this bit of land Texas and a few feet over here to call it Oklahoma, exists only in the mind, as a thought construct. The separation into discreet separate entities is a layer added in thought only. This distinction, this naming, this separation, these 'things' as separate entities, do not exist except as ideas.

'You' and 'me' are 'Texas.'

Next time you go to a movie, stop when you leave the theater and think about what you have just seen. When you start to describe the movie, I would ask you to stop. The movie may be what you saw, but it is not what was there. You were in the movie theater for some two hours, and for almost the entire time you were staring steadily at the screen in the front of the theater; yet if I asked you to describe that screen to me, you might look at me blankly. Because of the beams of colored light that were projected at the screen the entire time, you did not see the screen, even though it was there and you were looking at it. There were no 'real' people or landscapes or events up there on the screen, although you probably got caught up in the story and the emotion of the movie as if it were real; that's what you go to movies for, and if you spent any time during the movie thinking, 'this isn't real,' it probably wasn't a very good movie. The projection of light onto the screen caused the appearance of people and places and events that looked real and evoked mental and emotional responses in you; but all the time you never saw the screen, which is what you were actually staring at for two hours and without which the projected light would not have fallen on anything and you would not have been able to see the movie either.

'You' and 'me' are the movie.

## III

*I*T'S ALSO ALL A MATTER OF PERSPECTIVE in an even simpler, more subtle way. How we perceive things, and therefore what we call 'real,' or 'true,' or 'right,' has to do with

## 23. Perspective

our perspective from where we sit in the overall continuum. This is basic, but is so often completely overlooked. The tendency is to absolutize one's own perspective, to make everything relative to that, when in fact our perspective is what is relative. The entire 'history of humanity' including the present is filled with every form of exploitation and subjugation and injustice and intolerance, all of it made possible by the fact that from some perspective, from some point of view, it seems justified. Clearly, the basic assumptions about the way things are, are in fact very relative and dependent on perspective, on one's relative position in the overall spectrum.

The Understanding carries with it a massive shift in this perspective. To the dream characters, things in life matter and are important. From the latest war, to the environment, to what your children are being taught in school, to the way that man just looked at you, things and events are thought to have significance and to be important. That's what seems to make life worth living. Thinking of things as important and having value; causes, crusades, principles, values, getting involved in what you believe is right, working against what you believe is wrong, making the world a better place.

But in the Understanding, it is seen that all this only serves to further the illusion and perpetuate suffering. Values, seen as absolute in the dream, upon examination turn out to be arbitrary. The values espoused in one body/mind are dependent on the programming and conditioning from a certain time and nation and culture and race and family, and are the opposite of values held just as dearly in another body/mind.

Right, wrong; good, evil; important, unimportant; according to whom? From whose perspective? It is the way of all the earth for most people to feel that those things that are closest to them are most important. From your perspective, you will most likely feel more distraught over the death of one family member than you will over the death of thousands in a foreign country you have never seen. From one perspective, an act of terror is evidence of evil; from another, it is evidence that God is great. It is neither; it just is. It all simply arises in the wholeness of Consciousness, which is totally impersonal, and entirely neutral. Right or wrong, important or not, are only your projections, from your perspective.

But the 'perspective,' as it were, of impersonal Consciousness is unfathomably immense. Uncountable zillions of life forms in uncountable billions of solar systems, matter and life and energy in forms we cannot imagine and on scales that make all life we know, all this planet itself, all of the universe that we know or can imagine, hardly noticeable. The beauty is that in fact all this we know is *more* than noticed, is in fact nothing other than Consciousness, is Consciousness Itself, as perceived by us as these things. But that anything we may think we are, or think we know, or believe we want, or believe to be 'right,' is of any special importance, is simply a matter of our extremely limited perspective.

Anyone who writes or talks about this subject will at one time or another be inundated with questions around this issue of importance and value, right and wrong, good and evil. How can there be evil in the world; how can there be natural disasters; how can there be wars; how can a God allow poverty, or violence; how can a God, or Presence, or Consciousness, allow children to suffer?

## 23. Perspective

All of us have experienced (or been close to someone who has) some form of tragedy, some form of violence or loss or misfortune or pain. Some more than others. There is no escape from this; it is of the nature of this dream 'reality' that it contains what is experienced as pleasure and pain, good stuff and bad stuff, and no one knows what the next moment will bring, or what the overall mix will be for any body/mind. There is no answer, no reason, from within the dream.

> "Suffering is a call for inquiry. All pain needs investigation." (Nisargadatta Maharaj)

Suffering and pain raise questions like nothing else does. Inquire into it; investigate it. The "Why?" question gets nowhere; that is only the ego/mind seeking for nonexistent control. It will never be satisfied, and leads only to resentment and more suffering. Instead, investigate into the suffering. Who is it that is suffering? From whose perspective is this unacceptable?

Buddha said, *samsara* is *dukha*. Taking the dream to be real is not what *causes* suffering; it *is* the suffering. The only possible solution to the question of evil and suffering is to see through the illusion. Suffering in all its forms is the greatest invitation to awaken, and it is never far away.

Or in the immortal words of Humphrey Bogart's Rick, in *Casablanca,*

> "It doesn't take much to see that the problems of three little people don't amount to a hill of beans in this crazy world. Someday you'll understand that."

## 24.

## *Incredibly Simple*

*"Please understand that there is only one thing
to be understood, and that is that you are
the formless, timeless unborn."*
*- Nisargadatta Maharaj*

*"Here is just emptiness. There is no
getting my ego out of the way, and all that stuff.
There is just the seeing,
shining in great brilliance and clarity."*
*- Douglas Harding*

*L*OOK, IT'S ALL SO INCREDIBLY SIMPLE. There is no one here. This is not a figure of speech. I mean there is truly no one here, no person, no individual speaking to you. You look at me and think there is a person here talking to you, trying to tell you something. I assure you, there is not. Look at me. If there were not Consciousness streaming through this body, what would be here? What would this body be if Consciousness were not here? A corpse, of course! Dead matter. There is nothing else here. There is only the appearance of a body, and Consciousness which animates it. You, along with the rest of the world, have assumed that there is a discreet individual person here: that the Consciousness which is the animating force here is an individual consciousness, unique to this body and separate from the consciousness in other bodies.

This is based on appearances: there appear to be separate bodies, so the assumption is that there are separate consciousness-es. The belief in this assumption blinds you to seeing What Is, and is also the cause of your experience of this life as disquieting, confusing, unhappy, and generally full of fear and suffering. But it is not the case. There is in no way an individual sitting here talking to you. This body is nothing, an appearance in the dream. All there is is Consciousness, and it is Consciousness which is streaming through this appearance.

There is nothing here that exists in and of itself. What we call the human being is not an independent being, not an originating mechanism, not a transmitter. It is a relay station, a pass-through mechanism for Consciousness, the One Consciousness, All That Is. That is what I am, talking to you. And it is the same One Consciousness listening to this, looking back at me out of those eyes you call your own. What I am when I say 'I Am' is exactly the same as what you are when you say 'I Am.'

Once seen, the irony of the situation is staggering. Look: what you think of as your'self,' what you perceive as an individual person, this idea of being a separate entity, a body-mind-personality-soul-intellect: this is a subsequent by-product, an artifact, an almost accidental side effect of this streaming, this flowing of Consciousness. It is the

## 24. Incredibly Simple

streaming of Consciousness in this organism which the organism inaccurately perceives as a 'mind' which it thinks is its own: it is the very Consciousness streaming in this organism which allows this perception at all, which makes it possible for this organism to think it is other than that same Consciousness. A simple, innocent misperception. And a silly one, because the very One who appears to be thinking this, who appears not to see, not to understand that it is not as a separate individual and is only as All That Is, is Itself the very I-ness that is the only Is-ness of all seeing, of all understanding.

Look into what is behind this perception. Investigate what you think of as your'self.' This is the purpose, the meaning of all spirituality, of all seeking, of your very being: to understand this amazing intricate play of Consciousness by seeing what is this illusion, this mistaken perception, and what is its source which makes it possible. What you are, you always already are. It is by seeing what you are *not* that there is a stepping away from it, stepping out of the misconceived role of a separate fearful individual.

When you step out of what you are not, what remains is not something you have to become, but what you always already are. That is why there is nothing you have to do, or become, or learn, or practice, or work at, or purify. It is completely effortless to be in your natural state. What is full of difficult, constant effort is maintaining this false and unnatural idea of being somebody, of being an individual, a separate something. You are a non-entity! Let it go! When it is let go of, you rest in the effortlessness of All That Is, of what could be called your natural state.

Effortlessness is not something that can be attained by effort. No-mind is not a state that can be achieved by the mind. Peace cannot be achieved by striving. Trying to be *aware* of 'just being in the present moment' is a contradiction in terms; being 'self-consciously' aware of it takes you out of it. Trying to be *aware* of "I Am' is a similar contradiction, and for the same reason. You can't try to be happy any more than you can try to go to sleep or try to act naturally. You only act naturally when you're not trying, not thinking, but simply going about life. People would come from all over India and the whole world to see Ramana Maharshi and ask him for advice on the spiritual path. His advice? "Just be yourself."

This is what Nisargadatta Maharaj said of your natural state, of what you are naturally, spontaneously, without effort:

> "This state is before the appearance of beingness.
> It is prior to or beyond beingness
> and non-beingness.
> I Am, in that state which existed before the arrival
> of beingness and non-beingness.
> With the arrival of the waking state, all the world
> becomes manifest;
> because of my beingness, my world is manifest.
> That also is observed by that state which is prior
> to beingness,
> and you are That!"

## 25.

## NEVER INTERFERE

*"To free people from the idea that they suffer is the greatest compassion."*
- *Tony Parsons*

—

*"Greater than the greatest good in life is to know who we are."*
- *Nisargadatta Maharaj*

To QUESTIONS AS TO WHY he was not out helping the world, or working to ease suffering, or at least trying to reach more people with the teaching, Ramana Maharshi would answer; first, how do you know I am not? (Your judgments are based on physical appearances only.) And secondly, why do you assume that there is something that needs to be done, that the world needs helping or that people need to hear a teaching?

From a certain perspective, there seem to be many ironies to this whole awakening thing. One such apparent irony has to do with why social action seems to be engaged in by so few of the truly awakened. These body/mind instruments in whom is known first hand and without doubt the dream-like and illusory nature of what others call the 'real' world, to whom this world truly appears, in the Buddha's words,

> "as a star at dawn, a bubble floating on a stream; a flickering lamp, a flash of lightning in a summer cloud; an echo, a rainbow, a phantom, and a dream;"
> (*The Diamond Sutra*)

– such would seem thereby to be in a unique position to effect change, dispel evil, propagate peace and beauty, heal pain and sickness, and generally improve conditions all around. Yet it is precisely these who most often have the least inclination to do anything of the sort. There are some exceptions of course, rare examples both historic and current of awakened healers, activists and miracle-workers. The spiritual and mental technologies exist to bend and stretch the apparent laws of time and nature. But the way of the *yogi*, the adept specializing in such means, and that of the *jnani*, the sage who surrenders into the self-annihilation of Self Realization are widely divergent if not strictly mutually exclusive paths.

For the most part,
> "The one who has fully investigated himself, the one who has come to Understand, will never try to interfere with the play of Consciousness."
> (Nisargadatta Maharaj)

The profound awareness is that everything is perfect as it is:
> "That is perfect. This is perfect. Perfect comes from Perfect. Take Perfect from Perfect, and the remainder is Perfect." (*Isha Upanishad*)

And by 'perfect' I do not mean any kind of judgment about

## 25. Never Interfere

good or bad, or being better than something else. I mean it in the sense that,

> "The Understanding is perfect as vast space is perfect, where nothing is lacking and nothing is in excess." (Seng-Ts'an)

To use Nisargadatta's terms again,

> "This dream you call the world is not the problem; your problem is that you like certain parts of the dream and dislike others. Once you have seen the dream as a dream, you have done all that needs to be done."

It may be helpful to let go of the idea that God has somehow screwed up and needs your help and involvement, or that of the sage, to set things right. What is, cannot but be the perfect unfolding in Consciousness. And if an adjustment is needed to maintain the cosmic balance, some 'one,' perhaps 'you,' will be irresistibly motivated to perform an action which will serve that purpose. And that too will be the perfect unfolding. Just don't take it personally.

It is hardly surprising that to these body/mind instruments, with their limited perspective and from this small corner of the universe, some events may not seem very attractive. In fact given the programming and conditioning and overall situation, many aspects of what we call life here can seem extremely unpleasant, horrific, and frankly unacceptable.

The perspective of awakening is not that these do not exist, but that somehow in a way not comprehensible to human minds they are part of the overall balance and perfect unfolding, and are accepted as such. This is the 'acceptance of what is' spoken of by the sages. It is not that on awakening the horrible and painful things that happen in life are found to be any less horrible or painful. In fact this awareness is often even more acute. But the whole is seen from a different perspective which renders the issue moot. The idea that there is something wrong, that something needs to be fixed, that "somebody needs to do something about this," is an integral part of the 'divine hypnosis' of *samsara*.

As Adyashanti so succinctly puts it, "The idea that there is a problem... that's the wild hair in the ass of humanity." As with so many issues and problems; on awakening the problems and questions are not solved, they simple dissolve.

> "With the belief in the individual entity/doer, problems never cease. When the illusory nature of the individual is seen, problems never arise." (Ramesh)

# 26.

## Dream Machine

*"He who knows does not speak.
He who speaks does not know."*
*- Lao Tzu*

—

*"Authority of any kind,
especially in the field of understanding,
is the most destructive thing.
Leaders destroy the followers
and followers destroy the leaders."*
*- J. Krishnamurti*

Occasionally, someone will ask, point-blank, "Are you awakened?" or, "Are you enlightened?" On the surface this seems to be a perfectly reasonable and straightforward question, deserving an equally forthright answer. I recently came across an internet web site that was devoted to "finding your spiritual teacher." It was all about sorting through all the teachers and gurus out there and deciding which was authentic and would be the best teacher for you. This web site included a checklist of indicators and tests, one of which being that you should be able to ask a prospective teacher, "Are you yourself enlightened?" and he or she should be able to clearly and unhesitatingly give you a direct yes or no response. If not, you should immediately go elsewhere; any truly enlightened individual should be able to tell you so in a straightforward manner and any hedging or fudging on this question is a sign that the individual in question is a charlatan.

Although this is probably well meant, the difficulty arises in that the unawakened mind of the dream character, with its conditioning and limitations, is attempting to put itself in a position to establish the criteria whereby awakening is to be evaluated, which by definition it does not and cannot understand. It is not that anything is being evaded here; it is simply that from the point of view of awakening the question, "Are you awakened" simply does not make any sense whatsoever. It is like asking, "What color is a kilometer?" Or, as Nisargadatta Maharaj suggested, like asking about "the child of a barren woman." The questioner is sincerely earnest, and there is a wish to answer in a way that will be helpful, but once again the questions which are so pressing before awakening dissolve into meaninglessness and irrelevance when it happens. From the awakened perspective, the question, "Are you awakened?" is a fundamentally mistaken question: any answer is the wrong answer because the premise of the question is mistaken. It is like a Zen *koan* in that it is inherently unanswerable.

Awakening or enlightenment is also called "Self Realization," because it is a matter of realizing who or what the Self actually is. It is the realization of who the 'I' is and who 'I' is not. The very essence of awakening is the realization that there is no one here to awaken; that there is no

## 26. Dream Machine

individual, are no individuals. The Self is All That Is, there is nothing which It is not; "Consciousness is all there is." The appearance of an individual self as a separate entity and as the originator or 'doer' of anything is the primary illusion, the basic 'endarkenment' from which any enlightenment occurs.

> "From the perspective of the infinite it is obvious that the individual self absolutely does not exist. The idea that we have a self that controls, arbitrates, or is the doer behind our actions, is absurd. The individual self is nothing but an idea of who we are. Ideas are ideas – and nothing more." (Suzanne Segal)

Any questions about the nature or the activities of this purely mythical beast called 'me' are therefore revealed to be nonsensical. The simple question, "What are you doing?" for example, can only be met with laughter or a simple shake of the head, unless it is sensed that the questioner may be open to hearing the real answer: "Doing? Me? There is no 'me' to 'do' anything, nor has there ever been. Nor, if you could but see it, is there a 'you' to 'do' any 'thing' either; nor any 'things' for 'us' to be doing." Consciousness is all there is, flowing, streaming through these instruments in a manner which, in accordance with the perfect unfolding of totality, is perceived as discreet individual entities autonomously performing actions, but in truth this is not the case. There is no individual, no entity, no separate self here to do anything or to be anything, awakened or enlightened included.

There may be times, in *satsang* or private conversation, when a true *jnani* may find it necessary to admit that the complete Understanding has occurred. Still, our well-meaning web site author notwithstanding, any'one' who generally proclaims to all listeners that he or she is enlightened is highly unlikely to be, for if they were they would understand that such a statement is inherently self-contradictory. Who? Who is enlightened, you silly goose? If you were what you say you are, you would know better!

It's a little like that ubiquitous New Age slogan, "We are all one." Surely well meant but obviously self-contradictory; doesn't anyone see that if there are 'we' then there is not 'one' (but many), and if truly all there is is 'one,' there cannot possibly in any way be 'we'? Similarly, setting one's 'self' apart as one enlightened, as an individual entity distinct from 'others' who are not, is only to demonstrate the depth of the dream state. When there is Understanding, there cannot possibly in any way be a 'me' to claim it.

There is a great preoccupation among spiritual seekers with this subject of awakening or enlightenment. Much thought and many conversations revolve around questions about which teacher or writer is enlightened and which is not; whether or not a certain advanced student has 'gained' enlightenment yet; or even how close one is oneself to awakening. All of this preoccupation, and indeed the entire subject, becomes irrelevant in the event: all there is is Consciousness, functioning in and as these apparent forms. How can there be question of the apparent forms doing or gaining or becoming anything? All of this is a happening in Consciousness. What happens, happens. In which apparent form what dream event happens is of no significance. Who is it that cares?

All this is part of the timeless secret of enlightenment, but fear not; it is and always has been an open secret, the truth laid open always for everyone to see. As the sage Huang Po repeated over and over, "It is right in front of you!" The point is that true awareness, the true Understanding, cannot

## 26. Dream Machine

possibly be faked. The light of the ultimate Understanding, even when it occurs in and is expressed through a mostly illiterate, uncultured body/mind organism, renders the most erudite and sophisticated intellectual comprehension of the teachings to be still just ignorant bumbling about in the dream. This has been demonstrated by sages throughout the ages, from Hui-Neng in fifth century China to Nisargadatta Maharaj in twentieth century Bombay.

On the other hand there are those who may have had transformative mystical experiences of Oneness and have also a commanding intellectual grasp of the teachings, together with a charismatic personality and an inclination to teach others. They will gather many followers and become quite successful in the guru business. When the blind lead the blind, none of the followers can see that the leader himself carries a white cane. But to the truly awakened, such a teacher gives himself away every time he opens his mouth.

Awakening is not an experience, and it is not knowledge. Knowledge is only a veil over the Known. And a highly misleading one at that. True awakening is a knowing and a seeing that goes beyond any knowledge and any experience; What Is, is, and cannot be contradicted, while those still in the dream can only guess and approximate.

Like so many things that have come before and many fads yet to come, Advaita and the teachings of not-two-ness, having existed all through 'human history,' have recently been hungrily devoured by the American Dream Machine and have come out the other end in a form more palatable to the sensibilities of modern western dream characters but hardly recognizable to those few throughout the ages in whom this unspeakable thing has happened, for whom the 'pop' of shift of focus, shift of perception, is so complete that there is Understanding, there is knowing that there is no one there to shift; that there is no one there to know that there is no one there to shift, to awaken.

In the *Bhagavad Gita,* Krishna tells Arjuna that from among all the people on the earth, "only one in many thousands seeks me: and of those who seek, hardly one in those many thousands realizes my true nature." Taking this scriptural passage literally and attempting to do the math to calculate how many 'enlightened ones' there are in the world at any given time is problematic. Krishna was making a point, and I doubt it had to do with counting numbers of individuals. Nevertheless it does give some insight into the traditional awareness as to the infrequency of the occurrence of true enlightenment.

Ken Wilber takes a shot at something similar in *One Taste*. He relates how he once asked a Chinese Ch'an (Zen) teacher how many truly enlightened masters there had been throughout history, and the immediate answer was, "Maybe one thousand altogether." Assuming for the sake of argument as few as a billion Chinese over the same time period: one thousand out of one billion comes to, yes, 0.0000001 percent of the population. Again, taking the numbers literally misses the point; there is a larger sense to this, regardless of the actual percentages, which has been recognized as part of the perennial wisdom:

> "And that means, unmistakably, that the rest of the population were (and are) involved in, at best, various types of horizontal, translative, merely legitimate religion... magical practices, mythical beliefs, egoic petitionary prayer... ways to give meaning to the separate self...

## 26. Dream Machine

> "Thus, without in any way belittling the truly stunning contributions of the glorious Eastern traditions, the point is fairly straightforward: radical transformative spirituality is extremely rare, anywhere in history, and anywhere in the world. (The numbers for the West are even more depressing. I rest my case.)" (Ken Wilber)

To modern western sensibilities, this is not acceptable: it seems elitist, exclusive, politically totally incorrect. Liberation, enlightenment, should be open to anyone who puts in the effort, not arbitrarily as a prize in some divine lottery system. Besides, it doesn't sell; nobody is going to buy a ticket if the odds are one in several million.

And so, in the American Dream Machine version (which, by the way, is not limited to America), enlightenment is redefined to include anyone who has had an enlightening experience. We now have 'awakening lite,' in which you can call yourself awakened while still enjoying being fast asleep, and it is happening all over the place.

The result is a kind of tent revivalist *satsang* movement. According to many of the teachers on the guru circuit, awakening is happening wherever they go, to people just like you, and it's the next great wave in the evolution of humankind to the next level of cosmic consciousness. Where have we heard this before?

Everywhere, and about everything. It is the way of all the earth, the 'divine hypnosis,' to be deceived and to stay asleep pursuing individual and collective liberation, personal and group enlightenment, when the only truth is completely *im*personal and can be found only in the annihilation of the illusory individual.

"If a guru says 'I am enlightened,' it means the ego is enlightened so stay away. Western teachers who say this are preachers and only write books to load more garbage on seekers and more money in their pockets. They will attract so many students but in this Kali Yuga [the current dark age of ignorance in Hindu mythology] it is the falsehood which will draw the crowds. The Truth and the true gurus will be neglected. The Truth will be held by the honest and the honest will not be followed. Only the dishonest will be followed." (H.W.L. Poonja)

There are many teachers on the tent revival *satsang* circuit talking about enlightenment as the next great step in the evolution of the human race, and it's all very exciting because that step is happening now, with lots more people waking up than was ever the case at any other time in history.

This kind of thing is just confused and dream-bound thinking. Enlightenment has nothing to do with turning points in history, with lots of people waking up. It has nothing to do with evolution. As Jed McKenna notes, "If anything, enlightenment is evolution derailed." Evolution is a completely dualistic concept. Individuals, or the whole race, growing and changing and developing and becoming better over time: this is a description of dualism, of how dualism operates. Evolution is about change in relative objects. Enlightenment is the opposite; it is about realizing the Truth, absolute subjectivity, which is unchanging.

The whole concept of evolution assumes the existence of separate individual entities, a collective species or 'race' of such entities, and their existence in something called time. It also involves a whole set of value judgments as to what condition the human race is in now, and in what direction it should be going.

## 26. Dream Machine

This way of seeing things, and the way of seeing things after true awakening or Understanding has occurred, are mutually exclusive. When awakening occurs, the whole context which contains individuals, the race, time, and value judgments is seen as an illusion, a dream. Awakening, enlightenment, means popping out of the context in which evolution makes any sense.

> "Anything that implies a continuity, a sequence, a passing from stage to stage cannot be the Real. There is no progress in Reality; it is final, perfect, unrelated. Reality is not the result of a process; it is an explosion." (Nisargadatta Maharaj)

Someone, perhaps it was Robert Adams, once suggested that there should be a Great Gathering Of Awakened Beings, and anybody who showed up would be immediately disqualified. (Ironically, there is such a gathering now, annually. Most of the well-known teachers who have published books and tour the world giving *satsang* attend and give presentations. I get fliers for it in the mail.)

Honestly, I just received something else in the mail: a pre-publication notice for a popular spiritual teacher's new book, hawked with the tagline that at this pivotal moment in 'our human history,' the deepest truths that were once available only to 'the most rare beings' are now being made available to you; along with the admonition to order not one, but *several* copies – 'to encourage media interest!'

I find it startling, to put it mildly, that the spiritual seeker community apparently considers this sort of thing acceptable coming from a leading teacher and a publishing house devoted exclusively to spiritual publications. Advertisements for SUV's and Caribbean vacations use the same emotional hooks – but usually come across with a little more integrity! Transparent deluded manipulative exploitative nonsense. And even perhaps on some level the idea behind it was well meant; somebody who really believes they are an awakened being and that they are going to save the world by awakening 'more people than ever before!'

Recall Wilber's assessment that true awakening is "extremely rare, anywhere in history, and anywhere in the world." There is nothing amiss about trying to help people of course, but pay attention: telling individuals that they are so special that they have won the big prize and can now be an 'enlightened being' – *when there is still a 'being,' a 'me' there to get involved in it* – is ultimately not helping them or anyone else. Yes, there is suffering; but this is taking advantage of that suffering and in the end multiplying it, not ending it. This kind of stuff will always be said, will always happen. But leading spiritual teachers at least should know better.

But they don't. Blind leading blind, so nobody knows the difference. Please, dear hearts, so much suffering is perpetuated by believing this crap. Listen. There are no awakened beings. Never have been. Awakening doesn't happen to people like you or to people like me because awakening doesn't happen *to* anyone. There is nobody home. There is no one here to awaken. Thinking that you are an awakened one, or that it is possible that you might become an awakened one, or that your teacher is an awakened one, or that there is at least one awakened one in a cave in the Himalaya somewhere, is called being asleep. Awakening means popping out of the context in which awakening makes any sense.

# 27.

# CONFUSED THINKING

> *"Your vision will become clear*
> *when you look into your heart.*
> *Who looks outside, dreams.*
> *Who looks within, awakens."*
> – Carl Jung

THIS 'BLIND LEADING THE BLIND' THING would be funny if it weren't so tragic: it would be tragic were it not so damn funny. Somebody comes along saying they have 'achieved full enlightenment.' (Comically redundant expression, that; what other kind is there? Half full?) Now, how the hell can 99.9999999 percent (so to speak) of the population of characters wandering around here in the dream evaluate such a claim? How can they tell? But that question doesn't seem to occur to anybody. A remarkable number seem eager to believe the claim anyway.

If, as the masters have asserted, only a *jnani* can recognize a *jnani;* if only when realization has occurred can there be recognition of when realization has occurred; then just about anyone can make the claim and get away with it — as long as they manage to avoid the .0000001 percent who know better. Which shouldn't be difficult. And once there are enough of them, all those who make the claim can authorize and certify each other; and the radical one millionth of a percent in whom there is actually the seeing of What Is are marginalized as weirdos. Then you've got a self-contained self-perpetuating mainstream system going which is utterly phony and no different than any other activity in the dream, and which hardly anybody can tell is phony. The one millionth of a percent don't care: it's all a ridiculous dream! Why interfere with something that is working perfectly? But for the identified characters slogging along in the dream and caught in the suffering of trying to make some sense out of it, it's really quite tragic.

Here's the funny part. Imagine a conference where the world's top experts on human sexuality are convened. One after another these doctors, and specialists in human behavior, and research psychologists, go to the podium to deliver scholarly lectures on the subject of orgasm. As the conference goes on, it might become obvious that none of these experts have actually experienced orgasm themselves: it's all intellectual. 'After long years of arduous research and many austerities I can now tell you that I have finally achieved full orgasm. And I can confirm what all the ancient texts have said: that the very essence of orgasm consists of getting red in the face and screaming, after which you become a perfect person and everybody thinks you're wonderful.'

Huh? But wait: nobody in the audience has experienced orgasm either, so how would they know that the speakers are all hot air? After all, these specialists are presented as

## 27. Confused Thinking

the 'experts,' and another 'expert' has certified their expertness, and they certainly sound impressive, so... they must be right! So everybody asks questions and takes notes. And later they all sign up for the advanced seminar, in which it is promised that they too (for a few hundred dollars) can learn the disciplines necessary to get red in the face and scream; at which time they will enter the ranks of those who have been certified as having attained full orgasm and become perfect wonderful people.

Of the thousands in attendance at the conference, there are just two people in the back of the hall, with absolutely no scholarly qualifications at all, but with a different kind of knowing; who look at each other, laugh, and walk out.

There is a lot of confused thinking in this awakening business, and it would be helpful to make a distinction. Many spiritual seekers, and many spiritual teachers, talk about having had "an awakening experience." They have had a profound experience of Oneness, of meaning (or perhaps several such experiences); and as a result everything, including themselves, looks different and new. On the one hand, there perhaps is no better way to express this than to say that it's like waking up. There are no exclusive rights to the analogy anyway; it means what everybody does every morning when they wake up from sleep, so why not use the analogy to refer to a renewing experience?

On the other hand, this kind of waking up has nothing whatever to do with what is being talked about here as awakening. The very fact that it is referred to as "*an* awakening," or "a *series* of awakening experiences..." is a tip-off. One experience among many. The effects of such experiences may be brief or may last for a long time, sometimes for years, before they fade. Then if you're lucky there will be another one. Such experiences are profound, and beautiful, and bring about change, and nothing is ever the same. They are very wonderful; indeed this is the most profound and most meaningful thing that a human being can experience. It is what is called mystical experience, and it brings with it mystical knowledge.

But it is still a dream experience by a dream character. What this kind of waking up is referring to is a dream character having an experience, in the dream, of waking up relative to their prior level of awareness in the dream. But anything that can happen to a dream character is still in the dream, is still a dream event. It is still part of 'everything,' the everything that is not. It is not what is being talked about here, is not what has been talked about by the sages, as awakening. This awakening talked about by the sages is not part of 'everything.' It is the end of everything. It is not an experience, and it is not knowledge. It is not *an* awakening, it is *It*. It is not relative, it is Absolute. It is All That Is. It is that the dream, including the dream character in which this occurs, is seen through, and as such ceases to exist; is seen to have never existed.

True awakening is the total annihilation of the sense of a separate self. How can it be total annihilation if it keeps happening every other weekend – or every third year? Sounds like there's something left to annihilate. Once the total annihilation of any sense of being a separate self has happened, who is there to totally annihilate, *again*? It does become obvious that what these teachers are talking about cannot be the same as what is being talked about here, as what is talked about by the masters as 'ultimate,' as 'final,' as 'complete.' 'Gone, completed, beyond.'

## 27. Confused Thinking

You could say that this 'end of everything' is the end of the everything that is not; that's why when awakening occurs, it is said that nothing happens. There is no great experience in the dream, there is no great knowledge gained in the dream, there is no event at all, because all events are in the dream.

Those who are selling 'awakening lite' will tell you that something wonderful happens. A true teacher will tell you that nothing at all happens. There is the stepping out of what happens, the stepping out of the idea of one to whom things happen. This is the meaning of Wayne Liquorman's comment to the effect that if you want dramatic, beautiful, profound experiences, stay in the dream; once awakening happens, things get very ordinary.

Some teachers, such as Ramesh, get away from this confusion by using the language of awakening very little, if at all; by referring to the end of everything as 'the Understanding.' Of course that introduces its own set of potential confusions, as people think it has something to do with comprehending something, which it does not.

And of course all of this confusion is itself simply part of the perfect unfolding of totality in Consciousness.

Much of the misunderstanding seems to spring from an innocent underestimation. Reading the original accounts of total annihilation of self, most readers would, naturally enough, think that these accounts don't make much sense: after all, there's the 'enlightened master' continuing to live and teach and certainly look like a separate self. The modern critical sense is to distrust these accounts as fanciful hagiography or devotional embellishments, or as somehow allegorical. After all, nobody knows anybody around *now* who appears to meet these descriptions. Hence the underestimation: awakening can't possibly be *that* rare, *that* strange.

In short, the accounts of awakening related by the masters just don't correspond with anything that is *believed* to be real and true, or valuable and helpful toward making the world a better and more enlightened place. And so, the accounts of what it is to realize the dream as dream are reinterpreted, in the light of what 'we know' – in the dream! This kind of thinking of course misses the whole point of what is trying to be conveyed, and is in itself just more dream.

In spiritual circles there is great value placed on personal growth, personal improvement, becoming a better person, becoming more aware, teaching others how to become better, making the world a better and more enlightened place. The hope for a better future, the belief in an upward spiritual evolution that carries the whole race with it, is like the belief that there is something wrong and something that needs to be done. It seems hard-wired into the human mechanism but is in fact the device by which the 'divine hypnosis' operates, keeping the dream characters motivated and occupied in the dream. This belief is an illusion, and it is what creates suffering.

In Truth, in the Absolute, in All That Is, there is no evolution, no progress, no becoming better, no becoming. All is as it is. The idea that the world is in bad shape and that the present point in history is pivotal and that something has to be done, is as old as the human mind; it has always seemed thus, at every point in 'human history.' In truth

## 27. Confused Thinking

everything is in perfect balance; the world never gets better and never gets worse, although to the apparent individual instruments it may seem that it does.

Teachers who draw on these recurring themes in the dream to appeal to the ego's hopes and dreams and to popularize their message are deluding themselves and others and have not seen beyond the dream.

This belief in ongoing evolution, the dream of becoming a better person, the goal of improving oneself and others and society and making the world a better place: all these and more certainly seem to be noble beliefs and goals by any standards. Our cultures value them as ideals and it is believed that these high goals are what keep individuals and the human race from descending or regressing into chaos. And of course it is the 'divine hypnosis' itself that allows these beliefs, because without them the dream would not go on.

But as Buddhist teacher Chogyam Trungpa Rinpoche has noted,

> "Enlightenment is the great and final disappointment, the dissolution of all our egoic fantasies and grand hopes."

This is true seeing, and it will never sell in the revival tents. What is being said here is not a politically correct message, or even a spiritually correct message. It is not a comforting message, and it will never in any culture be popular. It is only the truth, as near as can be told. All is as it is.

The ego seeks fulfillment, and if awakening is marketed as satisfying that need, then what is being offered is bogus. True awakening is awakening to the annihilation, the dissolution *of that which seeks fulfillment.*

> "Transformative spirituality, authentic spirituality, is revolutionary. It does not legitimate the world, it breaks the world; it does not console the world, it shatters it. And it does not render the self content, it renders it undone." (Ken Wilber)

And of course, as you may perhaps intuit at this point, the wonderful aching beauty is that in this annihilation every longing, hunger and thirst that any mind/body apparatus ever felt is resolved and dissolved, perfected, healed and made forever irrelevant. The ego seeks fulfillment, but what is Understood in this annihilation is so huge that no mind, no ego, no heart could ever possibly hold it. The human race has no idea what fulfillment truly is.

# Five

*Acceptance
is infinite;
and it starts
here,
in your own
heart.
Whatever arises
is accepted.*

# 28.

## SURRENDER REVISITED

*"Whatever happens. Whatever
what is is is what
I want. Only that. But that."*
— *Galway Kinnell*

*"Earthly things must be known to be loved.
Divine things must be loved to be known."*
— *Blaise Pascal*

*L*ET THIS BE CLEAR FROM THE START. It is a question that arises often: at a certain point the implications of this annihilation, this total surrender of the sense of individual self, will begin to sink in and you will begin to suspect that what is being talked about here is not compatible with the continuation of the familiar, of life as you know it. The question will arise: is it really necessary to die completely, to surrender everything? Isn't there some more moderate, less radical way of going about this, some middle way to be found while not rejecting this life and myself as an individual?

And there will be many teachers, in fact most, who will comfort you by saying; 'Yes, of course there is. All that talk of utter annihilation is metaphorical. Enlightenment is to be found even as you continue your everyday life. It is important to honor who you are; negating that is being… well, negative.' Other teachers will take it a little deeper and tell you; 'It is not the dying, not the surrender which is important, but only your attachment. Dying is good, not dying is good. Are dying and not dying equally good to you?' And if you can say; 'Sure: surrender, not surrender, who cares;' then you don't have to surrender.

All of this sounds quite reasonable from the point of view of the dream. But from the Understanding, it's just silliness. It is all predicated on the idea of there being someone there to die or not die, to surrender or not surrender, to continue a life or be attached or be free. When there is the Understanding it is obvious that there is no such entity as 'you' to either be free or not, to surrender or die or not. It is the very idea that there is such an entity which is incompatible with the Understanding. This movement to protect that sense of individual, this aversion to complete annihilation, runs very deep in the illusory self. It is the ego's sense of self preservation. When faced with his own surrender and death, Jesus sweat blood and prayed that he be allowed to pass this cup by without drinking from it. But he recognized that this is not possible. "Yet not my will, but Thine be done."

The basic Understanding is that you do not exist as an independent entity or agent, but only as an object in the dream of Consciousness. All this bargaining about surrender and death is just an attempt by that illusory agent, that non-existent doer, that fictitious individual to continue on in its

## 28. Surrender Revisited

mythical life. Nisargadatta Maharaj called the individual self the "child of a barren woman." It's hard for any such individual to take this seriously, to accept that it has no existence other than as a myth, a construct in mind. But without this total acceptance, this complete surrender, the Understanding, enlightenment, awakening, is – by definition! – not possible.

It is the ego-rebellion of the mere object in Consciousness, the usurpation of subjectivity, the setting itself up as a separate entity unto itself, which is the basic error, encoded in such myths as the Judeo-Christian story of the 'fall from grace,' the 'original sin,' of the first humans. It is this mistaken concept of a separate, self-determining individual, taken to extreme, which results in arrogant and destructive behavior toward others, toward environment, and so on; but even in its most basic, benign form is the cause of separation, anxiety, and suffering.

What is being asked is whether it is possible to awaken while remaining comfortably asleep. This is what the sense of individual self, the ego, wants. And, there are a multitude of teachers who will cater to this, who will bring you a wonderful experience in the dream and call it awakening. 'Awakening lite.' But listen to or read the true masters; the Buddha, Ramana Maharshi, Nisargadatta Maharaj, Huang Po, Hui-Neng, Wei Wu Wei, even Rumi or Teresa of Avila, among others. When they talk about the Understanding, awakening, acceptance, surrender, they use words like complete, final, total, utter, absolute. The very basis of the Understanding is that you are not. This cannot be accepted without at the same time surrendering every vestige of the idea that one is. Totally.

Only the one who loses his or her life will find It.

From here, it's obvious. There is no reason or motivation to water down this truth or make it more acceptable or politically or spiritually correct so that more dream characters can believe in it while staying in the dream. Why would there be any such inclination? What Is, is. If you hear this and it is not acceptable to you, that's perfect and wonderful: it is the perfect unfolding of the role for that dream character. Why would there be any interest in changing that? That this complete surrender of self should occur in the case of any dream characters at all, that any should wake up in the dream, is a great mystery in any case. Why should there be any motivation to make the Teaching more moderate, more palatable, more widely acceptable? Acceptable to whom? Comforting to whom? Thinking that there should be such an accommodation is foolishness, is continuing to take the dream and the dream characters seriously; is confused thinking, taking illusion for truth and what is true for mere illusion.

Essentially, the Teaching contained in the perennial wisdom is what Ken Wilber calls an 'instrumental injunction.' Such an injunction is an invitation. It lays out a way of thinking, perhaps even a set of practices, a kind of recipe that says, "If you want to know this, try this." Try thinking this way, try doing this investigation, try letting go of these cherished ideas, and see what happens.

Of course perhaps even then nothing may happen; there are no guarantees. Many have tried these ideas and fallen flat and gone back to their old ways. That is as it should be. But if it is to be approached at all, it must start somehow.

## 28. Surrender Revisited

Absolutely no one can directly convey what It is, or what It is like. But if you attend to and follow the Teaching, and by unspeakable Grace it sinks in and takes hold, it becomes possible that direct experience and understanding of what is pointed to, what is presented indirectly by the Teaching, may occur.

Then you will be in a position to discuss, verify, question or reject various ways in which the Teaching is expressed, should 'you' still have any interest in doing so. But until then, the idea of diluting the Teaching to be more acceptable to dream characters, more compatible with what dream characters already believe and hold dear, is a silly waste of time.

Within the dream, the common wisdom is that you must understand something before you can accept it. But this will lead at best only to intellectual understanding and intellectual acceptance. Characters in the dream cannot understand, evaluate, or judge waking up from that dream in any meaningful way. By its nature, awakening turns the whole dream on its head. Nothing applies. Rather, the Understanding must be accepted before it can be understood. There must be awakening before there can be any evaluation or real understanding of awakening.

That's why it's called surrender.

And the complete, total surrender and the complete, final Understanding, are the same.

# 29.

## Too Many Words

*"I Am
Light within Light.
If you see this
be careful.
Tell no one what you've seen."*
*- Rumi*

—

*"Only one koan matters - you."*
*- Ikkyu*

*I*T SEEMS A SHAME there have to be so many words. Volumes and volumes, from time immemorial. So much verbosity, talking in circles around What Is. Of course, it has to be. "The Tao that can be spoken is not the Tao," Lao Tzu famously started, but that didn't prevent him from going on to write the whole *Tao Te Ching*. Seng-Ts'an did it more succinctly, somewhere in the seventh century, with his *Hsin-Hsin Ming*. It's all there, in just eight small pages, the whole thing. The *Heart Sutra* got it down to two pages, but then has had uncountable treatises written about it since. Ramana Maharshi and Nisargadatta Maharaj didn't write much, so others wrote down what they said, volumes of it. Wei Wu Wei, the eccentric Irishman, made pretty good sense of it, worked it out in what, six, eight books? Ramesh, what is it, some twenty books now and still going?

But you see, it's necessary. It cannot be spoken, so it must be spoken around. Does exist, cannot be expressed. As Wei Wu Wei lamented, even the best writing is like taking pot shots at the moon. No way will you be able to hit it. What is not of the dream is not of the dream, and cannot be expressed in dream terms, but dream terms are all we have. In the language of two-dimensional Flatland, where there exist only length and width, there are no words for height or depth. And with no words, no corresponding thoughts. No thought, no experience, because no such thing 'exists.' It is always right here in front of everyone, but no one sees it. How then can you show it to them? If they could see it by looking at it, they would have seen it already.

One usually starts like that. One points to what is seen and says; here, see? And everyone stares at you blankly. So then, the words start. Parables. Funny little stories. Sideways slants. Sentences, ideas, started and not finished, left for the listener to follow. If you finish the sentence, the listener hears it finished, and it's finished. So if you leave it unfinished, at least there's a sense of something unfinished there, which may lead beyond. May. May not. Doesn't matter.

Eventually, U.G. Krishnamurti's apparently monstrous nihilism is the only thing that survives: there is nothing here for you. I have nothing for you. You have no true self, and the false self you think you are is of no significance.

## 29. Too Many Words

Go away. Sleep your happy dream life. Why would you want this anyway? Self-annihilation is never chosen. The only ones who come to this are dragged kicking and screaming. Or are tricked, lured into the jungle and then ripped open, hollowed out, gutted. Or accosted at a bus stop; blasted, moorings cut, left to drift. If you are going to be so dragged, so tricked, fine. Has nothing to do with me or with you.

Meanwhile, all these words, all these books, come out anyway. They also have nothing to do with me or with you. There cannot not be writing, there cannot not be talking, there cannot not be reading and listening. In the immense overall pattern of galaxies swirling and planets being born and civilizations dying and words spewing forth, not a thing is misplaced or wasted. And so this writing, this talking, happens, and there follow the so-called results for which it was brought into being. But in the unfolding of the infinite expression of What Is, who knows or is to judge the result? Can the speck of dust in the arm of a swirling galaxy know why it swirls?

Yes, perhaps there is someone somewhere who may benefit at just the right moment from these words; at some time, near or far, perhaps this is what someone needs, and they read or hear and if not awakening, at least a deepening, a going back, happens. Maybe. Perhaps the only result is that this happens, *this* is experienced, whatever this is, here now. This conversation, this reading, this feeling, this nuance in Consciousness, never before experienced in quite this way or in quite this combination. This would be reason enough.

# 30.

## *STOP*

*"Everybody understands the single drop
merging into the ocean.
One in a million understands the ocean
merging into a single drop."*
— *Kabir*

---

*"Sitting quiet is most essential.
Don't waste your time by not doing this."*
— *H.W.L. Poonja*

### I

Stop. Please, just stop.

Stop talking, stop objecting. Just for a moment let quietness happen.

Notice how you cannot do that, you cannot bring that about. Notice how objections and judgements and resistance continue to arise as long as they continue to arise.

Let it be. Let quietness, stillness, be.

Notice how nearly every thought you have is a 'me' thought, an 'I' thought. Almost every thought you have starts with 'I' or is about 'me' or 'mine.' '*I* feel..., *I* think..., but it's not that way for *me*..., and *my* experience..., where *I* am coming from...,' and so on. Even when those words are not used, the thought is important to *you* because *you* think of it as *your* thought. *Your* opinion. Something *you* feel about *your*self or *your* 'reality.' Drop it.

> "Do not seek the truth: only cease to cherish opinions... If you wish to know the truth, then hold no opinion for or against anything. To set up what you like against what you dislike is a disease of the mind." (Seng-Ts'an)

When you are given the unspeakable grace, the unbelievable, undeserved, unearned gift, of being able to see, to notice, that what you are thinking is an opinion, or is something by which you identify yourself; the gift of being able to listen to yourself; then stop. Honor the gift by stopping. And let it drop. The opinion. Let it drop. The bit of identity contained in every statement about yourself, every comment involving yourself, every question coming from yourself; let it drop. Let the grace of this moment of catching yourself having an opinion, talking as an 'I;' let that grace stop you.

> "Do you want to know how to live life? Be still. Be still means, don't think. You see? It's so simple!" (Ramesh)

"Be still" does not mean to stop moving the body. "Be still" does not mean to try to stop all thoughts and feelings from

## 30. Stop

arising. Thoughts and feelings will always arise. "Be still" means letting go of that secondary level of thought; opinion, judgement, commentary. This is what it means to stop.

No thought you have ever had is true. No opinion you have ever held is right. Let them go. No idea you have of yourself, or of who or what you are, has ever corresponded to reality. Or ever will. Let them go.

Comparing, sifting, learning, struggling, imagining, feeling, thinking, all chasing after wind. Instead there is the awesome, overwhelming gift of stopping, of letting it drop.

> "You must have a clear understanding that all things are only a manifestation of the mind itself. Everything, *everything* in this world is nothing but a complex manifestation of one's mental activities." (*Lankavatara Sutra*)

Let it stop. Let it drop away. Stop taking it seriously. Stop taking it at all. Let it be. Be still. Simply stop. Let grace stop you.

## II

FOR EVERY ACTION THERE IS AN EQUAL and opposite reaction. For every force applied, there is an equal force applied back. The 'world,' the universe, *maya* only exists because of resistance to it: you push against it, it pushes back.

The only way to freedom is surrender. You stop pushing, asserting yourself, and illusion stops pushing back, asserting itself. Stop pushing, putting energy into the system, and there is no energy in the system to push back.

Stop telling the story, and without that constant input of energy the story collapses. This, I suppose, is the law of *karma*. The only way beyond is to stop; stop creating it.

This is the purpose of self-inquiry. Who is it that is doing all this acting, all this pushing? The ego, the sense of a separate self, has convinced you that the only way to survive is to push, to act, to make things happen. Because then the illusion will push back, and seem real, and that is the only way that the sense of self, which relies on separation, can survive.

Self inquiry brings this to awareness. Who is it that is doing all this? Who is it who thinks, 'I' have to do something? Who is the one who is thinking this? When this inquiry begins, some of the pushing stops, and so some of the pushing back stops, and things quiet down a little. As long as you are involved in pushing, in making things happen, you appear to be the one doing things. The individual self is convinced that if it doesn't do something, nothing will get done, and it won't be able to survive. Which is true. It won't. But You will.

If you stop, something amazing happens. The individual stops being involved, stops acting; and amazingly, everything continues to happen. Without 'you' doing it. Because, surprise, 'you' were never doing it.

Try this as an experiment, if you can. The sense of separate self will panic as you come to the point where you stop doing anything; it may actually prevent you from stopping. But if the grace of stopping happens, and there is the experience of watching everything continue to happen, you will never again be able to believe there was ever anyone there doing anything.

# 31.

# *Explode Your Brain*

*"You take your imagining for facts
and my facts for imagination..."*
*- Nisargadatta Maharaj*

*"Oh, God help me! What a difference there is
between hearing and believing these words,
and being led in this way
to realize how true they are!"*
*- St. Teresa of Avila*

ULTIMATELY, ANYONE WHO HAS EVER attempted to write about this, or talk about it, with the idea or intent of communicating some of it, is engaged in a futile, pointless task. There is a basic problem here. And now I don't mean that what is outside human knowledge or experience or categories is inexpressible, which is also true. There is another basic problem, on the other end, the receiving end.

Human beings learn by association. The way the human mind is constructed, the way it is wired, is that it always has to have something to relate to. If something new is encountered, the mind will look in its data banks for something similar, however approximately, in order to make a comparison. If it finds something it has encountered before which is somewhat or in some way similar, it will say, okay, this new thing is like this old thing, but different in the following ways. The new thing can then be seen, assimilated, categorized, learned. Education professionals call this 'schematic development.'

But if there can be found nothing in the memory banks that in any way corresponds to any aspect of the new thing, then to the mind it will have no meaning and the new thing will not be learned or assimilated. The mind does not know what to do with it. In fact, scientists who study these things tell us that our eyes, for example, physically see many times more things each day, each moment, than our brains think we see. The nervous system filters out most of what is physically seen, because it is not familiar and therefore judged to be not important.

This is not something we can blame ourselves for, and resolve to correct, and take a seminar to learn to do differently. It's simply the way the organism functions. This filtering mechanism occurs on the level of the autonomic nervous system, before what you think of as your conscious self or your thoughts or your will or your intention even have a crack at it. We have all experienced the phenomenon of learning something new and subsequently seeing it everywhere, whereas before it had never been noticed. It had always been there, everywhere, and surely our physical eyes had 'seen' it, but until the brain recognizes it as something that relates to something it knows, it is not truly seen.

## 31. Explode Your Brain

Given this mechanism, it is a wonder that anything is ever learned at all. As it is, learning happens only incrementally, by way of what is familiar, what is already known. And we tend to learn more in the direction in which we were started. Wei Wu Wei puts this well at the beginning of his *Ask The Awakened:*

> "Perhaps the most serious handicap is that we start on the wrong foot. In the end this is likely to be fatal, and, I fear, generally is. We have a basic conditioning, probably in some form of Christian religion, of which very little remains today but its ethical content, or in one of the modern psychologies, that of Freud, Adler, or Jung, or in some scientific discipline, all of which are fundamentally and implacably dualist. Then the urge manifests, and we start reading.

> "Every time we happen on a statement or sentiment that fits in with our conditioned notions we adopt it, perhaps with enthusiasm, at the same time ignoring, as though they did not exist, the statements and sentiments which either we did not like or did not understand. And every time we re-read the Masters or the sutras we seize upon further chosen morsels, as our own jigsaw puzzle builds up within us, until we have a personal patchwork that corresponds with nothing on earth that could matter in the least. Not in a thousand million *kalpas* could such a process produce the essential understanding that the urge is obliging us to seek.

> "We are required to do exactly the opposite of all that."

The "opposite of all that" which is required for the Understanding of What Is, is what is known in Zen as 'beginner mind,' a state of open awareness, a state of what Stephen Levine calls "don't know." Spiritual teachers often make use of the image of the innocence of a young child in trying to express the empty openness necessary if one is to be able to truly hear the Truth.

But who can approach the teaching like this? One hears the sage's words, and immediately the mind associates the words with what it knows as their familiar definitions, and thinks it knows what has been said. This is why the masters use so many tricks, *koans*, meaningless phrases, stories that lead nowhere, statements that contradict themselves. Carlos Casteneda called the whole process of teaching by these techniques an attempt by the teacher to 'stop the world' of the student. Gangaji calls on seekers to simply "Stop!" But who can stop in this way? "Ooo, that's good," thinks the seeker, "that really resonates. We should all just 'Stop!'" The idea or the expression that one should 'Stop!' is simply added to the personal patchwork and the crazy jigsaw puzzle that corresponds to nothing keeps being built up. The seeker calls it a lifetime of hard earned knowledge or even wisdom, but the masters and sages unequivocally call it ignorance.

I've seen this in action. When I first went to see Ramesh, he was continually telling the people who came to him that the way to the Understanding lies in realizing that there is nothing you can do. You are not the doer of anything; events only happen through you. This was the basis of his teaching, and he repeated it *ad nauseam*. I would see people take notes, writing this down. Then the hand would go up. "So, given this, and I understand it perfectly, how do I go about my life? When I leave here, what should I *do*?"

Ramesh showed infinite patience. I wanted to shake them: haven't you heard anything the man has said? You have just been given the secret of life, the universe, and everything! Stop! Wake up! Let these words explode your brain!

## 31. Explode Your Brain

> "The trouble with students these days is that they seize on words and form their understanding on that basis. In a big notebook they copy down the sayings of some worthless old fellow, wrapping it up in three layers, five layers of carrying cloth, not letting anyone else see it, calling it the 'Dark Meaning' and guarding it as something precious. What a mistake! Blind fools, what sort of juice do they expect to get out of old dried bones?"

These words were spoken by Ch'an master Lin-chi in the seventh century! What has changed?

Sometimes, someone will listen carefully to expressions of the Understanding, that there is no doer of anything, that there are no individuals, that all there is is Consciousness, and that you are That; and they will say, "This all sounds a little theoretical, how do I integrate this into my daily life?" That's usually a good conversation stopper, because the answer is, you don't. Actually, it's one of those questions like, "Are you awakened?" which from the point of view of the seeker is sincere and begs for a decent answer but from the perspective of the Understanding makes no sense, because the premise is back-asswards. It's a little like the tourist who stood next to me as we took in our first view of Cliff Palace, the ancient Anasazi ruins at Mesa Verde, a complete adobe village thousands of years old built into a cliffside in the Colorado desert.

"Humph," he pronounced, "looks like a movie set."

"But you see," I couldn't help but reply, "actually, it's the movie set, if it's a good one, that may look a little like this."

You come across this all the time. Sitting on the porch on a summer evening listening to the insects, someone will say, "That cricket sounds just like a cell phone." Sure, it's all dream, all illusion, but even within the dream the cricket is just itself: it was there before there were cell phones, and it is the cell phone that came later and was programmed to (poorly) imitate the chirp of a cricket. This is a perspective, a mind-set, which obfuscates clear understanding. As a first step, at least get clear on what it is that is real, and what it is that is the illusion, the construct, the derivative.

Asking how you integrate the Understanding into your daily life is like asking how you incorporate total freedom into captivity. You don't. Maybe it's the other way around, what remains of your 'life' might be incorporated into the freedom of the Truth. But in fact there isn't anything there to incorporate. As Jed McKenna puts it,

> "You're talking about reconciling the dreamstate with reality, like it has to add up. Everyone seems to get hooked on that, but you can't do it. Truth and non-truth are irreconcilable. Truth is, non-truth isn't… We can't insist on a truth that makes sense in light of what we know because we don't know anything."

Adyashanti has simply said,

> "There is no such thing as integrating truth into an illusion."

If you insist on trying to fit the teaching into your growing patchwork jigsaw puzzle, your lifetime of learning and knowledge, you will reduce it to just one more meaningless bit of ignorance. Please don't. Don't try to integrate this. Don't take notes and go back and re-read them and compare them to something you read somewhere else. This doesn't work like that. The only way this works is if you stop taking notes and start taking this personally, as it were. Take it very intimately. Let it stop you.

## 31. Explode Your Brain

Don't fit it into a lifetime of hunting and gathering for nuggets. Don't try to compare and sort to see how it fits in with other stuff you've learned, other things that you have heard from other people. Especially if you are a seeker and have been at this awhile, your head is probably full of other people's ideas, half-assimilated into your patchwork, of what Truth or awakening or understanding is. Don't ask, how does this fit in to what I already have accumulated? It doesn't. That isn't what this is about. If you are going to ask questions, ask instead the hard questions, the questions that take you out of anything you have ever known, the questions that could end your life. That's what this is about.

Most of the folk I come across who are 'into' Advaita are intelligent people. They are quick studies, and after they have read a few books and been to a few *satsangs* they figure out what words and ideas are acceptable Advaita concepts. Ask them a question and they don't answer right away; you can almost see the wheels turning in there, weighing and rejecting one answer after another as inappropriate or likely to get them branded as one who doesn't know. They've been to enough teachers that they've learned to try to find that 'right' answer that won't get them shot down. And it's hardly their fault: there are a lot of teachers out there whose sole functioning seems to be shooting down anyone whose answers are not phrased correctly.

What good does this do anyone? Is it necessary to point out that this isn't about 'right' answers? Speak your truth. There is nothing acceptable, there is nothing appropriate. There is only what is. Talking in circles, painfully and awkwardly trying to avoid using personal pronouns, when it is clear that your simple everyday experience is that you live your life as an individual, is pointless. Obviously so. This isn't an area where you can 'fake it until you make it.'

One person says, "I'm glad you came." And the other answers, "Who? Who is glad?" And I think, the Advaita thought police never sleep. An old Ch'an master would give you a whap upside the head with his stick. What are you saying, 'who is glad?' She is glad, you dope, and she's being honest enough to tell you so.

Descriptive, not prescriptive. When there is no sense of a separate self, words referring to such a mythological thing will be superfluous, will naturally be used much less; not because they are avoided, but because they do not express what is, and are used simply because that is the way language is structured, and it is often the most convenient way to speak and be understood. There will not be searching for words or actions or responses which are imagined to be most appropriate, but rather there will be the simple spontaneous expression of what is here.

Speak your truth. That's what this is about. How can it be about saying the right thing, fitting in, using acceptable language? Stop. Go back. Self inquiry is about going deep within to see what is your truth. Never mind what you have heard or what anyone else has said. This is not about learning the right thing from some teacher. A true teacher will deflect any such attempts back to you: what is your truth? Inquire within, find out for yourself. Who are you? Who is the Self from which all these things arise? No one can show you this. No amount of trying to guess right will reveal this. Discover it yourself by being relentlessly and ruthlessly honest, authentic, true.

# 32.

## EXEMPLARY BEHAVIOR

*"The projections of others do not belong to me.
I am never a teacher,
just a lover who has been given a glimpse
of the Beloved."*
*- Llewellyn Vaughan-Lee*

THE BRITISH GENERAL WELLINGTON is said to have commented that a man can be a hero to everyone but his valet. The observation is similar to Jesus' saying that no prophet is without honor except in his home town. Awakening, or the Understanding, does not in any case make a perfect human being or a saint out of the body/mind organism in which it has occurred; and those who feel they know the person most intimately may be the ones most likely to see the everyday imperfections and be the least able to see beyond them.

That awakening should produce a perfect being is a deep misconception, and a popular one. People seem to think they need awakened spiritual masters to begin with, and further that they need their awakened spiritual masters to be the embodiment of a certain set of (usually traditional) virtues. And since most traditional ideas of spirituality are pretty far divorced from physicality, emotions, urges, and feelings, people need their spiritual masters to be divorced from these things as well, especially from what is judged the 'negative' or 'dark' sides of these.

All this is nonsense of course. There is no such entity as an awakened spiritual master to begin with. In the manifestation of Consciousness there are, among other things, these body/mind organisms commonly called human beings. According to the nature of these body/mind organisms, there arise from time to time emotions, urges, needs, thoughts, feelings, physical and emotional impulses. In the Understanding, there is no judgment of any of these as negative or positive, light or dark, desirable or undesirable, appropriate or not. They simply are, and simply arise as part of the purely impersonal functioning of the organisms in Consciousness. From the perspective of the Understanding, when there is no longer identification as this particular body/mind organism, which particular feeling or need or thought or emotion arises in which particular body/mind organism is of no significance. Including the body/mind organism in which the Understanding has occurred. These things arise as part of the functioning of the organisms. So what?

While one in whom awakening has not happened may well be concerned with whether they are or are not acting or emoting or thinking or appearing in an 'appropriate' or 'enlightened' manner, to the body/mind organism in which the Understanding has occurred this is of no particular concern. The whole issue only arises

## 32. Exemplary Behavior

when there is identification as a particular body/mind. Why should there be any special concern or interest here whether the david thing gets sad or angry or occasionally feels confused or acts inconsiderately? These things may not seem desirable, but desirable to whom, and from what perspective? They arise as part of the functioning of all body/mind organisms in Consciousness, according to the programming and conditioning of the organisms.

> "When enlightenment happens, the organism does not become perfect. It is whole and the whole includes both opposites. Seeking perfection is the basic, primary folly and the *jnani* understands that. That is the basis of the understanding. Whatever happens is part of the functioning of Totality." (Ramesh)

In this case, there is much in the conditioning and programming of the david body/mind organism to judge or dislike, for those who are so inclined. Irritable, impatient, a tendency to be easily overwhelmed, and generally poor social skills which can appear as arrogance or dismissiveness; any behavior the origins of which are not understood can be easily labeled.

And to the dismay of some who have been close or intimate, the Understanding itself does not instantly produce a perfect human being, a saint! The dream character to a large extent continues to be the dream character it was, with essentially the same conditioning and programming. It seems certain that this organism was not designed to ever be playing the role of saint or beloved teacher; there is little here to inspire devotion. More like the voice crying out in the wilderness; the iconoclast, the contrarian.

Of course, from the point of view of the body/mind organism in which it occurs, the Understanding itself, whatever else it is, is a massive dose of new conditioning. And so there are apparent shifts. The extreme sensitivity that is here in this body/mind is simply observed, along with its other characteristics, and not judged one way or the other. A certain startling compassion appears where before there was little. And I would have to say that there is a continual occurrence of what can only be called small miracles, considering the rough character in which they are occurring: layers of old patterns of behavior and thinking that, without attention or effort, simply cease or fall away.

The perspective, the perception from 'within' is entirely transformed; I know I am not david, that david never existed except as a hollow and only apparent instrument through which Presence flows. There is no longer any sense of being an individual self; only the deep, constant Brilliance beyond light, the steady, profound Peace beyond peace, and constant upwelling gratitude for and in All. From 'within,' any 'undesirable' characteristics are seen with indifference, perhaps some amusement: undesirable according to whom?!

> *Questioner*: "It is said that a realized person will show exemplary behavior in every way."
> *Maharaj*: "Why? Exemplary according to whose standards?"

Thus there is no particular motive to 'try' to 'change' 'my' 'self' (as none of these concepts have any reality) other than the ongoing acknowledgement (prayer) in All that is... 'Thy will be done'... and the knowledge that this too shall pass. What will be, will be; and then that too shall pass.

## 32. Exemplary Behavior

In the course of this dream there will be apparent change and molding of this body/mind organism as there is of all such, but into what there is no knowing. "My skin is not my own."

This flies in the face of traditional ideas, and the ego-ideals of all the spiritual seekers who want noble, beloved and definitely well behaved spiritual teachers and masters to put on a pedestal and who will show them by example the way to escape from all the messy negative dark stuff of life.

It's fantasy. Listen. There is no escape. What you want to be free from, what you reject, what you want not to be, want your teachers not to be, is It. Is Presence, is Consciousness. This, here. No one needs a spiritual teacher, certainly not one on a pedestal, to show them something else. There is nothing else. Judging it 'dark side' or 'light side' is the illusion. If you're not disillusioned with your spiritual teacher, he isn't doing his job. A spiritual teacher worth his or her salt is in the dis-illusion-ment business.

# 33.

## NATRAJ

*"The Heart is the only Reality.
The mind is only a transient phase.
To remain as one's Self
is to enter the Heart."*
*- Ramana Maharshi*

*"Compassion is but another word for
the refusal to suffer
for imaginary reasons."*
*- Nisargadatta Maharaj*

### I

IN FRONT OF ME ON THE DESK, a rather unwieldy chunk of bronze, the theme of which you may or may not be familiar with. Known as a *Natraj*, or Dancing Shiva. What perhaps some of us knew during our folk/hippie days as the 'Lord of the Dance.' From the primordial Stillness, Shiva dances the world into existence, and all the world exists as long as there is the dancing. The world is the dancing, nothing more.

Of course all the details of the *Natraj* have intricate meaning in the Hindu myth: the number of flames, the number of cobras in Shiva's headdress, the image he's standing on, what he's holding in his hands, and so forth. This is an antique one, found in the depths of *Chor Bazaar* in Bombay; evidently broken and repaired several times, most recently my own brazing a flame back on.

Such is this life – intricate meanings, broken and repaired several times – the living of which is as rich and deep as a Kashmiri carpet, that other artifact I drag back from visits to India. This is what Tony Parsons means when he calls emotions the colors of life. Even the anguish, or the coming apart under stress, or the fear of the unknown, or the courage of moving into it anyway (or the thrill and wonder of being moved into it anyway.) When it is seen that this too shall pass, that this is part of the dance, that whether or why *this* happens in *this* body/mind organism rather than another or none at all is of no significance, then there is just running your fingers through it and actually enjoying, or at least appreciating, the texture, the depth, the indescribable beauty.

None of it taken delivery of, none of it owned, none of it judged. Just constant, total amazement. Day to day. Nothing need be any different from what it is. You do not need to change anything. No one need be any different than they are.

The difficulty with most systems of 'working on yourself,' therapy, self-help and analysis is that they become tools with which to judge ourselves and at the same time tools with which to prop ourselves up by justifying the judging of others. Forget all that. Just be yourSelf. It All just Is.

## 33. Natraj

"Listen:
out beyond ideas of right-doing and wrong-doing there is a field.
I will meet you there." (Rumi)

The ultimate unified field, beyond all concepts of dualism. Where 'I' and 'you' flow together. 'I' is not david. 'You' is not you. Neither is. And, I meet you there. Completely, with nothing lacking. Because the I Am that you are, is the I Am that I am.

The rest is just day to day, and there is no way to do anything wrong. The only thing we can know for sure is that it is right and wonderful and essential for exactly this to be happening, now. Beautiful and Perfect.

The human conditioning, emotions, feelings, thought patterns: all part of this world that has been pulled over our eyes to hide us from the truth. The effect is that we can never see clearly; only "as in a glass, darkly." Always fuzzy thinking, always missing the obvious.

All these forms come and go; all will soon pass. The frustration, the sadness, the wanting things to be different, they too arise in the Quiet Expanse of Accepting Awareness between the thoughts. They will never stop arising; there is no stopping them, and indeed no need to try. There is just watching. Accepting what is. It is the judging that makes us miserable:

> "When the mind is in bondage, the truth is hidden, and everything is murky and unclear, and the burdensome practice of judging brings annoyance and weariness." (Seng-Ts'an)

## II

*I*N THE JUNGLE, THE GREAT QUEST to find 'my' purpose, my path, and above all the way I can help, falls to the ground and disintegrates, laughing. It is taking the dream to be real which creates the emphasis on finding a purpose or meaning; with the constant asking, "why?" or "how?" everything takes on importance. This seeming importance keeps us involved.

A preliminary, intellectual understanding of the Teaching would lead one to conclude that the best way to help is to be empty, to stop trying to be helpful; and the best way to be 'caring' is to stop caring and get out of the way. But it goes deeper than that: What is, is unfolding perfectly. There is no way to not be helpful; there is no way anyone can get in the way.

Attachments and expectations around love, as caring and romantic and fulfilling and satisfying of deep needs, are often more deeply held even than attachments to physical things. And so many spiritual traditions and teachers emphasize non-attachment to others as a spiritual practice, to the point of actively disrupting and negating loving relationships. But truly, the whole emphasis on getting rid of attachments turns out to be misplaced. It's the prescriptive/descriptive fallacy again. Once there is seeing the true nature of things as they are, all things are seen to be elements in the dream and therefore untrue, not necessary, unimportant; and they simply loose their 'hook.' Any attachment to them spontaneously evaporates.

But trying to eliminate attachments in order to bring about the seeing is of course back-asswards once again

## 33. Natraj

and doesn't work. How many people do you know have 'attained' enlightenment, or even happiness for that matter, by doing violence to themselves in this manner, trying to cut out what is naturally there? Like everything, it simply is: and when it is natural for it not to be there, it isn't. You can't make this come about, even by making yourself lonely and miserable.

Emotional attachments and relationships in general, like all behavior, remain inscrutable as long as you're still seeing it all as independently directed individual behavior. Whole sciences have been constructed around this. During and after two divorces and numerous relationships I spent many years working on the commonality in the situations, talking to friends and soul-searching, agonizing, trying to find where I was screwing up.

With the Understanding that all so-called 'human behavior' is Consciousness acting through these instruments and there is no independent doer of any action, the subject becomes moot; and the judgment that there is something not okay and needing to be changed subsides. Shiva, the Lord of the Dance, dances the dance of the Heart; and All of This simply Is.

There are no mistakes. It is not possible to make a mistake. You are not the doer of any action, the experiencer of any experience. How can you be the maker of any mistake?

What happens through these mind/body things, happens. If there is learning to happen, it will happen. Sometimes there is not. Sometimes change happens, sometimes it does not. Sometimes such change follows insight, sometimes it precedes it. The perceived chain of cause and effect and the mandate to better ourselves are seen through as parts of the dream/game.

The source of suffering and unhappiness really is all this attachment, this hanging on to our cherished ideas even though they obviously don't work and have never given anyone lasting happiness. But you see, why would anyone do that? Because you have no choice, obviously. But of course none of it is obvious until the seeing happens.

There is no thing to attain, no where to go. There is only acceptance of what is, on the deepest possible level, and even that only happens if it happens. If one is not ready to hear this, it will not be heard no matter how well articulated. When one is ready to hear it, it can be said in passing by someone on the street and it will strike home. When there is a body/mind organism in which this is ready to happen, a certain word or phrase in a certain context can be, like in the Zen story, the "sound of the pebble against the earthenware pot" which causes the cascade failure of the mind and the occurrence of Realization... which is the only possible end to suffering.

## III

*T*HE SURRENDER INTO COMPLETE ACCEPTANCE of what is, as the perfect unfolding in Consciousness, is a primary characteristic of waking up; it can be found over and over in the writings, and all of the Teaching points to it. Acceptance is very deep, is infinite: and it starts here, in your own heart. Whatever arises is accepted. If resentment arises, there is acceptance that resentment is happening in this body/mind. If there then comes a layer of judgement,

## 33. Natraj

that the resentment should not be happening, then the acceptance can go deeper, to accept that the judgement is happening.

If there is another layer, of feeling bad about yourself perhaps, or an unhappiness that you are the 'kind of person' in whom resentment arises, or feeling bitter or hopeless, or whatever; then that too can be included in the infinite acceptance. If there is an urge to be more mindful or attentive to the root causes of resentment, then there is acceptance that such a motivation is arising. There is no end to the acceptance. And then it extends outward, to events and situations and other people. Deep acceptance, at all levels, of whatever arises; even if it is not liked; even the not-liking itself.

Despite appearances, there is nothing happening here. Nothing that appears to happen matters at all, is of any importance. It is all perfect as it is. How do I know? Because it is what is; how then can it be other than perfect? This becomes obvious when it is seen, is probably incomprehensible and difficult to accept until it is seen.

Meanwhile, of course, there is simply being. Things happen in your life; good things, not so good things. There is watching this happen. Again, if emotions arise, then they too are arising in Consciousness, and there is watching them arise. If thoughts or judgements arise, then there is watching these also. Always knowing, this too shall pass. No assumptions need be made, nothing needs to be labeled or held on to.

Perhaps odd and inexplicable things happen in your life because they are a step toward where 'you' will be needed to be. This is what I call a 'reverse engineering' of cause and effect. From the point of view of Consciousness, as it were, the idea of cause and effect working 'backwards,' the effect causing the happening of the cause, is just as valid as the conventional model of cause followed by its effect.

Or, perhaps the mind/body unit you think of as 'yourself' is being used as a teacher for someone else, and what is happening has nothing to do with 'your' story at all. Or perhaps not, perhaps simply the letting go, the realization that any sense of control is illusory, is itself the 'point.' What do we know? The dream characters do not need to know; they will play out their parts in any case. Even this dream character whose part in the dream is to wake up in the dream and realize it is a dream character. So what? Who cares? Ask yourself, who is it that feels like it cares, feels like it wants to know?

## IV

THIS SENSE OF CARING AND IMPORTANCE runs very deep in the conditioning and is not easily seen through or set aside. Even seekers who are familiar with the concept that 'none of this matters' will be brought up short by this idea that even 'awakening' is part of the script for the dream character in which it occurs, and is of no significance. "Do you really mean to say that the total Understanding is only part of the dream?" Indeed yes, even the occurrence of this realization is an event in the dream, part of the unfolding of the dream, and nothing has happened.

How can anything that happens in the case of any dream character be of any significance? Stop! There's

## 33. Natraj

nothing going on here; it's a dream! To the extent that the Understanding is happening in a dream character (a body/mind organism), it is an event in the dream, and so what? The idea that awakening or enlightenment matters is a seeker fiction. Matters to whom? Who is it that cares?

It has been said that if you want to know when you're getting close to the Understanding being total, to awakening, it's when the importance of awakening happening, in the body/mind you call yourself, fades. Of this awakening consists: the awareness that anything happening to this body/mind, whether it be awakening or death, or misery or luxury, is all happening in the dream to a "child of a barren woman," to use Maharaj's phrase; to a mythological creature, an idea, a fiction, some'one' who can't exist. None of it matters in the slightest. It looks important from the dream, but I confidently assure you it is not.

Now, sometimes, the phrase "The Understanding" is used obliquely to mean "That Which Is Understood". Now in that case, That Which Is Understood is precisely what is *not* of the dream, and pierces the dream at the no-time no-place instant of awakening. But the occurrence of the total Understanding in the case of any specific body/mind organism is, by definition, an occurrence which appears to happen, in the dream, to a dream character; and is as such a part of the unfolding of the dream.

Caring and a sense of importance attached to the whole issue of awakening finds its highest traditional expression in the bodhisattva vow. The bodhisattva concept is just so quintessentially and beautifully Buddhist; sacrificing your own enlightenment until all have 'attained.' The height of altruism, self sacrifice, and high mindedness, taking the "greater love than this, no man hath" theme to the next level. Beautiful; can there be anything greater in human aspiration? Just absolutely sweet and gorgeous, and I hate to be one to break this, but it's malarkey. Completely dream-bound thinking. Wonderful, tear-jerking, romantic drama, and completely irrelevant once the awakening occurs. The whole idea only arises in the dream, when there is taking 'individuals' seriously. If indeed the individual is the child of a barren woman (doesn't exist and never did) then who is there to sacrifice, and who is there to sacrifice for? And of course it's the same with the Christian concept of Jesus 'dying for our sins.' It's all dramatic nonsense, what I tend to call 'silliness' or in Maharaj's term, 'great entertainment.'

This is a difficult point for many. The apparent indifference of the Understanding to these high-drama 'important' and 'spiritual' things in human life can be seen by normal and well-meaning folk as cold-hearted. It's not; it's so the opposite, so completely compassionate, but I don't know of any sage who has been able to explain this adequately and bridge this gap. And it is a gap: from the human perspective, the bodhisattva represents the very highest virtue: from the Understanding, it's irrelevant though somewhat endearing silliness.

Of course it's all venerable ancient tradition, along with karma (whose karma?) and rebirth (no 'one' is born, let alone reborn). But tradition often doesn't hold up in the simplicity of the Brilliance. East or West, thousands of years of tradition have a tendency to corrupt and fabricate. There is a well-meant tendency to teach comforting but dream-bound concepts to give folk some immediate relief. The distinction between these and the Understanding is sometimes subtle and oft lost.

## 33. Natraj

In seminary, I studied enough Catholic theology and New Testament redaction to know that centuries of well-intended parsing of what the original visionary might have meant rarely comes close to the actual Understanding. It certainly seems, for example, that Jesus of Nazareth may very well have lived and taught and died without any of his *sannyasins* (at least not the ones who left the official written record) really getting what he was trying to express. What they passed on as Christianity has just about nothing at all to do with the Understanding which appears to have almost certainly occurred in Jesus' case.

> "Disciples as numerous as grains of sand in the River Ganga, yet not one has come to enlightenment; they err in seeking it as a path taught by others." (Tung-shan)

East or West, generations of well-meaning monks can pretty well garble the message. I am no scholar of these things, of Advaita, Vedanta, Buddhism, or Sanskrit; and there is neither the ability nor the interest to argue the fine points which are so significant to scholars. It would appear that the job description here (at least at the moment) is to describe, within the context of the conditioning of this body/mind character, what the Understanding is, here. This may or may not necessarily correspond to what the scholars have worked out over the centuries.

In a way that is hard to enunciate, the Understanding, the Seeing, when it occurs, is extraordinarily simple, and in a very subtle way many things are immediately transparently clear. Which from the human, intellectual, or moral perspective can easily sound like unacceptable presumption; but to that objection there can only be a shrugging of shoulders here. It is what it is, and if it is not acceptable, that's cool too; after all, there really is no compelling reason for it to be accepted. As soon as there is fiddling around with concepts and modes of expression, the david thing, along with everybody else, is likely to be quite 'wrong.' But what is Understood is very simple. It is What Is. And there can only be pointing toward it from various angles, which pointing in this case, because of the conditioning, will very likely not be in classical form.

And in this completely simple Understanding there is a recognition, not by the mind, of those cases where this same Understanding – in its utter simplicity devoid of complication or embellishment or the interjection of what someone thinks should be right – has occurred. There may seem more affinity with some of these, but the recognition is the same, so that it is quite clear who understands and who does not; who truly saw and who was trying hard; who was faking it and who is clueless. And who is or was pure transparency in the awareness of nonexistence.

Whether alive today or come and gone, it makes little difference. There are those that say the only good Indian guru is a live Indian guru, that citing Maharaj or the Maharshi or the Zen Patriarchs is simply an appeal to characters dead long enough to be no longer controversial. And then there are others, the dead guru societies of seekers and even teachers, huddling forever around the site of a well gone dry and never recognizing the ever-present Perfect Outpouring standing quietly next to them, streaming within them.

Both miss the mark. Within the parameters of the dream, seekers and teachers do the best they can. But in the Understanding there is no birth or death, no coming

## 33. Natraj

or going, and the occasions and forms where there was seeing are all and always I, clearly present, *per omnia saecula saeculorum.*


    look within.
    look within!
    unimaginable, perfect beauty
    in the still, silent heart.
    the one perfect blazing radiant Jewel
    All that is
    what you Are! true Self –
    look and see in the Brilliance.
    nothing to do to know this:
    do not think, and this is known.
    when the mind is still
    when the mind is not other than the heart
    still, silent, radiant heart –
    look within
    don't miss this!
    don't live a life not seeing, not knowing
    this ultimate blinding beauty
    look and be
    do not think – look within – you will know
    who you Are.

# 34.

## METANOESIS

*"Although everyone wants happiness,
most people suffer from tragically mistaken ideas
about what brings it."*
— Roger Walsh

*"If I ever go looking for my heart's desire again,
I won't look any further than my own backyard;
because if it isn't there, I never really lost it
to begin with."*
— 'Dorothy' in The Wizard of Oz

*I*NTERESTING, ISN'T IT, that the American *Declaration of Independence* names as "unalienable rights" life and liberty, but not happiness? The "pursuit of happiness," sure, but not happiness itself. A recognition, it would seem, that no one has an unalienable right to happiness, only to spending one's life and liberty chasing after it. Sounds like a certain frustration factor built in there, doesn't it?

This matter of happiness turns out to be very, very simple.

Happiness is your natural state. The only reason it is not always experienced is because of the layers and barriers that are erected and constantly maintained. It is simply a matter of letting go of these, not of gaining anything new. That is the secret: the "pursuit of happiness" is looking for that something new that will 'make' you happy, and is doomed to eternal frustration because it is looking in the wrong direction.

> "Why are you unhappy? Because 99.9 percent of everything you think, and everything you do, is for your self – and there isn't one!" (Wei Wu Wei)

As always, there is fuzzy thinking around this subject which makes any understanding that much more difficult. Although 'happiness' has a strongly positive connotation among spiritual seekers and 'pleasure' a more negative one, the dictionary definitions of the words suggest that similar sensations underlie both. For our purposes it may be useful to define these concepts with a little more clarity.

Pleasure is part of the cycle of desire. Pleasure is the sensation that occurs when a desire is satisfied. It is the experience of release, the "ahh..." experienced at the moment when there is satisfaction of the desire and the desiring stops. This pleasure is itself very desirable, very addictive. There is the restlessness, irritation, and anxiety that accompany desire, followed by the brief moment of pleasure at the moment of satisfaction. Every body/mind organism is programmed and conditioned differently, and so the particulars will be different in each case; but basically whatever is found to lead to that sensation of release and pleasure will be what is desired, because ultimately it is the pleasure at the release of the desire being satisfied that is desired.

## 34. Metanoesis

The nature of pleasure is that it is a momentary release; the sensation of pleasure is lost almost as soon as it is found, as the cycle of desire, once satisfied, immediately repeats itself. As many have found, there is no way out of the cycle on its own terms. That is why Buddhist teaching has always stressed the cessation of desire itself. But how can the body/mind just stop desiring, and what does that have to do with happiness?

Most "pursuit of happiness" is based on the subliminal idea that happiness is pleasure that doesn't end, at least not so quickly. This leads to the 'if only' method of seeking happiness, which is really only a matter of upping the ante on desire: if only I had this, or if only this happened, then I would be happy. This is a glorified version of the desire/pleasure cycle, and is doomed to the same fate. Lasting happiness can only occur when there is a re-orientation, a stepping out of the desire/pleasure cycle entirely.

> "All you want is to be happy. All your desires, whatever they may be, are of longing for happiness. Basically, you wish yourself well. Desire by itself is not wrong. It is life itself, the urge to grow in knowledge and experience. It is the choices you make that are wrong. To imagine that some little thing – food, sex, power, fame – will make you happy is to deceive yourself. Only something as vast and deep as your real Self can make you truly and lastingly happy."
> (Nisargadatta Maharaj)

At some point in each of our lives we have all had the experience of being happy. It may be hard to describe, but we all somewhere, somehow know the experience, however fleeting, however rare. Otherwise we wouldn't know what it was like, and we wouldn't be striving for it. Remember a time when you were truly happy. It could have been a period of your life, years maybe: or it could have been just a passing moment when you felt the surge, the bliss, the peace, of real happiness. At that moment, whatever else happiness might have felt like, wasn't there a part of it, a component of that experience of being happy, that felt like, "This is perfect. Nothing has to be any different. Everything is just right, just the way it is."

This is an essential component of the experience of happiness, and it is what we only catch a glimpse of in the momentary pleasure of a satisfied desire, before that satisfaction turns to desire again; the experience that nothing has to be changed, nothing has to be different. This, here, now, is perfect. How many times, when someone experiences happiness, do they spontaneously declare, "Oh, this is perfect." Even the popular phrase, "This is as good as it gets," implies that nothing need be added, nothing need be different than this, now.

This is where the subject of happiness becomes very simple, a matter not of acquiring anything new but simply of letting drop the barrier we constantly erect with the pursuit. If there can be a simple turning it around; a coming at it the other way, an opting out of the desire/pleasure cycle, with a simple knowing that this is perfect, now, here, the way things are, and nothing has to be any different: if there can be more than just saying that, more than just believing it, but truly *knowing* it in the heart; then, simply, there is happiness.

When this occurs, there is a transformation of life from an experience of misery or irritation or incompleteness or frustration to an experience of happiness. And it is found that this happiness is unshakable. It is not dependent on

## 34. Metanoesis

anything being attained, or anything changing or being in any way different from how it is; it is also not shakable by the *fear* of something changing; because either way, it is the acceptance of what is.

The literal meaning of the Greek word *metanoesis* (which in the Christian Bible gets translated as 'conversion') is 'changing the mind.' The English language expression, 'I changed my mind' doesn't mean the same thing. It means, the thoughts changed; 'I did think this, but now I think something else.' Same mind, different thoughts. *Metanoesis*, transformation of mind, is different. The Sanskrit word is *paravritti*, and means the same: a turning over or a turning around in the deepest level of the heartmind.

> "There is only a looking in the right direction, an orientation of mind. *Paravritti, metanoesis*, is, doubtless, just that. And no one does it, nor is anything done; it is pure doing." (Wei Wu Wei)

That is where happiness lies: in the re-orientation of mind which allows looking in the right direction; acceptance of what is. Your natural state.

Desires, then, still arise: they are part of the dream, part of the functioning of the body/mind. There is no need for desires themselves to cease as such. But since it is *known* that nothing need be any different from what is, the desires are not pursued. Pleasure, like pain, will happen from time to time. But since nothing need be any different, there is no attempt to either seek out or avoid these experiences. And so the desire is not taken on, not claimed or owned. It is simply there, experienced as part of the dream.

And through it all there is the constant sense of well being, this unshakable happiness, this deep knowing that all is well. This is perfect, this is just right; nothing need be any different from this, now.

# 35.

## THE DIFFERENCE

*"The writing comes in three scripts:*
*one that you and only you can read;*
*one that you and others can read;*
*and one that neither you nor anyone else can read.*
*I am that third script."*
— Shams of Tabriz

—

*"Sometimes naked, sometimes mad,*
*now as scholars, now as fools;*
*thus they appear on the earth – the free ones!"*
— Shankara

---

$S$O OKAY, WHAT IS THE DIFFERENCE between a regular person and a sage?

On the deepest level, distinctions between sage and not-sage are essentially meaningless. Neither exist as such. These distinctions exist only in appearance. In the so-called sage, this is known. Both are body/mind organisms, both with their conditioning, both with emotions arising and actions happening through them. The only 'difference' is that the sage sees that there is no 'one' there; that this is the impersonal functioning of Presence through the instruments of the body/mind organisms, whereas the ordinary person claims the emotion or the action, thinks they are responsible for it, and calls it their own.

*But the emotions or actions arising would be different?*

Not necessarily. Only according to the conditioning of the respective body/mind organisms.

*So if a person got angry a lot before awakening...?*

...Anger might well continue to arise in that body/mind organism after, according to the conditioning. The difference is that the sage would not get involved with the anger once it arose: it would arise and pass in a natural way and be done with it. The sage would not own it or feel guilty about it or try to explain it or justify it or make excuses, or think that he should try to improve himself so it would not happen again. What is there to improve? Anger simply arises as part of the impersonal functioning in Consciousness. That it arises in that particular body/mind organism is of no concern to the sage.

*Okay, could a sage kill someone?*

The sage knows 'he' or 'she' cannot 'do' anything.

*Okay, okay, could the sage be the instrument through which a killing happens?*

Why not? If it is part of the perfect infinite unfolding in

## 35. The Difference

Consciousness for something, anything, or any combination of things to happen, how can they not happen? In traditional terms, if it is the 'destiny' of one body/mind organism according to divine will to be killed and the 'destiny' of another to do the killing, that will happen. And the sage will also understand that society will punish 'him' for that, and that the punishment of that body/mind organism will also be accepted as the 'divine will,' as part of the perfect functioning of totality.

*But why would it be the divine will for a sage...*

Why not? Are you telling me you know the basis or reasons for the divine will?

*Well, I guess it would be unlikely that someone with the conditioning to kill would ever become a sage...*

Now you're trying to get out of it! You've heard many times that there are no preconditions for the Understanding to occur. Quite honestly, the example of killing someone is an extreme one. In a sage there would be no motivation to kill someone; so yes, it might seem to be unlikely. But the dream characters, the body/mind instruments, are hardly in a position to predict this kind of thing. There could be any number of reasons, some comprehensible, some completely incomprehensible from the standpoint of the body/mind instruments, why or how such a thing might be necessary in the perfect unfolding in Consciousness. If it were part of the infinite unfolding for something like this to happen, it would. I don't know if you've noticed, but there does seem to be a tendency for Consciousness to bring about any possible combination, sooner or later.

*Okay, so the sage is really just like an ordinary person? What does he gain, what is the benefit of enlightenment?*

It is the body/mind organisms and their functioning that are alike. The sage knows he is not the body/mind, not a person at all. There is no one to gain anything!

*So the benefit would be for those around him, like the guy's friends maybe, or when he had students...*

Ha! 'The guy's friends,' assuming it's a guy and assuming he has any friends, might find him harder to get along with than before! But yes, sure, there is the potential for great benefit for others. Whether that is realized depends on the conditioning, and also on what unfolds in Consciousness, what the eastern traditions refer to as 'destiny.'

*The conditioning of the students?*

Who says he has any students?

*But wouldn't a sage teach?*

Why? Once again, only if it is in the script in the dream for that 'sage' dream character to teach. Only if it was the 'destiny,' according to the cosmic unfolding, of that 'sage' body/mind organism to talk on the subject, in the functioning of Consciousness.

*Okay, so if he doesn't teach, and he still has these emotions, and he can even do bad stuff....*

What?

## 35. The Difference

*So okay, what is the difference between a regular person and a sage?*

Just the Understanding, my friend. Only the seeing, the knowing; that is all. Just the Peace that passes all understanding. And what good is it? None at all, you could say. Buddha said, "Truly, I obtained nothing from enlightenment." And Huang Po wrote, "There is just a mysterious tacit understanding and no more." The sage is not a superhuman, a regular person with something added. The sage is a regular person with something less; the sense of being a separate self, a separate individual, is gone: there is no one home.

*I've heard that in the sage, everything happens spontaneously.*

Yes. And do you want to know what else? In everyone, everything happens spontaneously. In you, everything happens spontaneously.

*I don't experience it like that.*

Exactly. That's the difference.

*Do you believe that the Understanding can happen to anyone?*

I don't believe anything.

*What?*

There are no beliefs here.

*That's an extraordinary statement.*

Not at all. It's really quite simple. You either know something or you don't. If you know something, you don't have to believe it's true or have faith that it's true; you know it beyond doubt, it simply *is,* and there's no belief involved. On the other hand if you don't know something, the honest thing is to simply say you don't know. But of course there are many psychological and political and social reasons why people can't admit, even to themselves, that they don't know something, so they create a belief; which is essentially saying that you don't really know something is true, but you're going to pretend you do. It's all activity in the dream. There's really only one thing which is not of the dream, only one thing that can be known, and that is the basic consciousness, "I Am." Everything else is just a concept, a construct of mind in the dream, something "I don't know." Everything.

*Okay, but can this Understanding happen to anyone, any body/mind?*

Of course.

*Could it happen to me?*

No, of course not. That's the difference. But it could happen in the case of the body/mind organism which at the moment you *think* is you, and then there would be the understanding that there never was a 'you,' a 'me' for anything to happen to, and that who You are is the Consciousness in which all this appears to happen. The Understanding and the belief in a 'me' are mutually exclusive: if one is there the other will not be.

# Six

*You are
Quiet
Compassionate
Space
in which
the life
that you think of
as 'yourself'
unfolds.*

# 36.

# *Time*

> *"One instant is eternity;*
> *eternity is the now.*
> *When you see through this one instant*
> *you see through the one who sees."*
> – Wu Men

THE BASIC MISUNDERSTANDING, the essential 'endarkenment,' is the belief in discreet individuals existing as separate entities and as the originators, thinkers, or doers of any thoughts, actions, or experiences. Including, of course, the presumed individual thinking this.

> "It is not so very difficult to understand, at least intellectually, that this universe is a dream, but it is almost impossible to accept that the one who is supposed to understand this is himself part of the dream. This belief in oneself is the only real obstruction to the happening of apperception." (Ramesh)

This belief in separate individuals, including the individual which one calls one's self, is part of the larger illusion of space-time. All there is is Consciousness, Presence,

Noumenon. What is perceived as the manifestation, phenomenon, the totality of space-time, is an appearance in Consciousness and not other than it.

It is not terribly difficult or unusual for seekers, after some investigation, to be able to intellectually comprehend the illusory nature of the individual and of separation. Both are functions of the idea of space: it is in space that things, including individuals, appear to be distinct and separate from each other. While it is indeed another matter to include one's own 'self' in this, nevertheless the basic idea can be grasped. After all, the central idea that "all is One" is present in almost all the world religions and spiritual traditions and is one which any spiritual seeker will have been exposed to for some time.

As I have said, the idea that "we are One" is self-contradictory and clouded in fuzzy thinking. But again, nevertheless the basic principle can be understood: the perception of boundaries which creates separation in space into distinct individual entities is illusion; in truth, only Oneness is. When this is spoken of in a group of seekers, there can be seen a general nodding of heads.

Of course this presents its own dilemma: while this principle of 'spatial Oneness,' the illusory nature of the separation of all things in space, is in some circles so familiar as to be a truism, it is clearly not truly and fully understood. True understanding of this would bring the end to all questions, suffering and seeking.

When one moves on to the concept of the illusory nature of time, and begins to talk of 'temporal Oneness' there is not this familiarity, and even intellectual comprehension

## 36. Time

is much harder to come by. Phrases like "there is no such thing as time," or "there is no past or future, only now" can be repeated easily, but any understanding as to what this means is less common. The bookstores are full of books propounding the value of "living in the now." One popular author insists that there is no past or future, but only now, the present moment. At any given time, there exists only the present moment. There is always only "now, and now, and now." Each present moment is followed by the next present moment. More fuzzy thinking. This is merely renaming the 'past, present, and future,' somewhat confusingly as 'now, now, and now.' There is still the concept of sequential time, one present moment following another.

Perhaps it can be helpful to use the model of 'spatial Oneness' (which, once it is understood at least intellectually, exposes the illusion of 'space') to come to an understanding of 'temporal Oneness,' which will in a similar way expose the illusory nature of 'time.' The concepts are parallel:

The idea of discreet separate moments in time is like the belief in discreet separate individuals in space. Just as the separate entities in space are seen not to exist as such, as separate entities, but rather simply as appearances in Consciousness, or as the way Presence manifests: so the separate moments in time can be seen not to exist as such, as sequential moments, but rather simply as appearances in Consciousness, or as the way Present manifests. There are no separate entities: only what can be called This. There are no separate moments: only what can be called Now. There are no individual entities relating to one another: there is only One Presence, and it is All. There are no individual moments following one another: there is only One Present, and it is Eternal.

Put another way: just as there is only one Presence Present, so too there is only one Present Presence.

I'm not sure this can be arrived at intellectually. With the Understanding, the conundrum of time finally simply folds in on itself; the clear understanding that there is no time, of how there is no time, of how time is not, is blindingly simple and obvious, just like the other: just as there is One Presence, so there is One Present.

And yet even this method of explaining 'temporal Oneness' by comparing to 'spatial Oneness' is false. These are not other, not two. Of course. They are a single point. Infinite/Eternal. One Infinite Presence *is* One Eternal Present. There is no thing called Presence which is being present. There is not really 'This' and 'Now.' They are the same; the suchness, the is-ness of This, Now.

In essence, the illusion of time is exactly the same as the illusion of space, which is exactly the same as the illusion of the individual self. They are part of each other, depend on each other, and prop each other up to form *samsara,* the objective manifestation brought about through the agency of perception. This is why the illusion of the individual self, or even simply the illusion of the self as an individual 'doer' of anything, can be used as a focal point toward the Understanding. When this illusion dissolves, the illusions of space and time go with it.

Ramana Maharshi spoke about this connection:
> "What is eternal is not recognized as such, owing to ignorance. Ignorance is the obstruction. Get rid of it and all will be well. This ignorance is identical with the 'I' thought. Seek its source and it will vanish."

## 36. Time

And Wei Wu Wei expresses the same thought in *Posthumous Pieces:*

> "Ignorance of what is eternal is due to the concept of 'time.' The 'I-concept' and the 'time-concept' are inseparable, neither can appear to exist without the other: they are dual aspects of what is erroneously conceived as objective."

Thus we return to the central idea of becoming clear on the issue of subject/object. The belief in the individual self is an identification as that self as subject, which through its perceptions objectifies the rest of the phenomenal universe of space and time. When it is realized that this usurpation of the role of subjectivity is false, that the so-called individual exists not as a subject perceiving but as merely one of the objects appearing in the phenomenon of space and time, then the illusory or dream nature of all such objects and all of space and time can be seen. With the realization that 'there is nobody home,'

> "...the consequent liberation is not only from 'who?' but also from 'where?' and from 'when?' The supposed phenomenal 'subject' has ceased to believe in the impossible, and knows at last what he has always been, and what the phenomenal universe has always been – which knows no who, no where, no when." (Wei Wu Wei)

Then one looks a little differently at the New Age slogan popularized by Ram Das, "Be Here Now." On the level at which it was intended, it works well as a reminder to mindfulness – although even there it begs the basic question, "*who* is to be here now?" But in the Understanding, all three words are seen to be redundant; all there is is being, there is only here, there is nothing other than now. Where else can I possibly be but here, now? Even if there is being lost in a memory of the past, that 'past' exists only as that memory, that thought, happening now, here. Even when there is worrying about the future or daydreaming happening in a body/mind organism, that worrying or daydreaming is what is happening in that organism, here, now. There can never be anything other than being, here, now. There is only here, and it is all, unbounded, undivided. There is only now, and it is eternal, unbounded, undivided. So relax. There is no effort needed to be here now. You cannot not be. Enjoy.

# 37.

# SUBJECT/OBJECT

*"From within or from behind,*
*a light shines through us upon things*
*and makes us aware that we are nothing,*
*but the light is all."*
- R.W. Emerson

—

*"...music heard so deeply*
*That it is not heard at all, but you are the music*
*While the music lasts."*
- T.S. Elliot

**B**E CLEAR WHO IS SUBJECT and who or what is the object. This may sound a little academic, but stay with me here. This is key. Our language betrays us. Every time we speak, even when we speak of the Understanding, of All That Is, we do so by constructing sentences like this one which are pure idiocy. Look at what that sentence does: it sets up 'All That Is' as the *object* about which 'we,' the *subject*, are speaking. 'All That Is,' pure Subjectivity, That in which all objects arise and which as such cannot be an object of anything: and 'we,' body/mind organisms and as such human objects among other objects, usurping the role of subject. Completely inverted, but it is how our whole language and thought structure are constructed. With the Understanding, it is seen so clearly how ironic this is: that it is the streaming of this very Consciousness itself through these limited human objects which is what gives them the ability to erroneously think that they are separate consciousnesses; which is what allows these objects to arrogate for themselves the role of (pseudo)subject.

Sometimes, in the case of some body/mind objects, there is a moment on the way to the Understanding when there is a subtle but vital distinction to be made, and it can easily be missed. At some point in the intellectual understanding of the teaching, it becomes clear that all there is is Consciousness. If so, then there is nothing which is not Consciousness. If so, then even this which is realizing this is Consciousness. If one has been exposed to Advaitic teaching, in particular if one has read Nisargadatta Maharaj, or even if not, the phrase "I am That" will suddenly take on great significance.

Be clear who is Subject and who or what is the object. On the threshold of awakening, on the eve of the annihilation of the false self, the ego will seek to save itself by this subtle misdirection. "Of course, I understand and accept that I am not an individual self. But what I truly am is Consciousness, All That Is; I am That; I am God." One does not have to look far to find teachers who have gone down this road, convinced they have reached awakening, 'God Consciousness.'

There is, unavoidably, a subtleness that is sometimes lost

## 37. Subject/Object

in the translation and transcription of Maharaj's talks. The ancient Sanskrit phrase which parallels Maharaj's "I Am That" is *"Tat tvam asi."* Literally, "That thou art," which preserves "That" as the subject: *"That* (subject) is what you (object) are." Maharaj's native Marathi has a similar language structure, and a truer translation of Maharaj's sense could be, *"That* is what the 'I' *is."*

"I am That:" there is a sense in which this is true, and in one in whom the Understanding has truly happened this can be said with impunity. (Although then there will be no need for it to be said, and little interest in doing so.) Then there is no longer any identification as the separate doer, the separate entity, the small self, the egoic "I." But until then, and especially when one is advanced in the intellectual understanding of the teaching, there is a short circuit that can happen here. Do yourself a favor and don't go there. I assure you, as long as there is an 'I' to say "I am That," that 'I' is the ego. As Ramana Maharshi would say, "Wrong *I!"* Remove the word 'am' and the identification of the 'I' as a separate ego is deflated. *"That* is what the 'I' *is,"* gets the perspective right, keeps it clear who is Subject and who or what is the object.

There is nothing wrong, nothing amiss in all this. It is all the perfect unfolding of totality in Consciousness. All there is is Consciousness, all this happens in Consciousness, so it can be said that it is Consciousness itself which identifies as the body/mind organisms. Even the basic misperception, the usurpation of subjectivity by the object instruments, is not some wrong thing being done that needs to be corrected. The identification as an object is simply what is happening in Consciousness, and it results in what we are calling the dream. When awakening from the dream occurs in the case of a body/mind object, there is the ceasing or the falling away of that identification as a pseudo-subject, and that too is simply what is happening in Consciousness.

When the Understanding occurs and there is that falling away of identification, then there is the end also to the whole subject/object distinction. It is seen that there is no relationship, no 'I and Thou,' for they are the same. 'I' as separate pseudo-subject has never existed: and 'Thou' is not Other, is who 'I' always already is.

The first teacher I heard talking about Advaita made a useful distinction. She is British, so at first I thought it was just a peculiarity since the British frequently use prepositions in a way which is different from the way they are used in America. (Or, "different *to*," as they would say.) But the distinction can be helpful in any case. As concepts, there is a difference between identifying 'as' and identifying 'with'. 'As' in this context is like an equals sign: when there is identification 'as' a body/mind object, you believe you *are* that body and mind. You identify yourself *as being* that body/mind. But identification 'with' is more like what you mean when you say you really identify with a friend who is going through some experience. You don't think you are your friend, but still you "can identify with that," as we say. There is an empathy there, a seeing things through the eyes of your friend.

In the dream, there is identification 'as' a body/mind organism. Almost all the dream characters think they are that particular body and mind, with their own separate consciousness and self. This is the usurping of the role of subject, identifying 'as.' When the Understanding occurs, this falls away and what remains is an identification 'with'

## 37. Subject/Object

a body/mind organism. You know this body/mind is not who you are: it is only an object in the Consciousness which the I is. But the body/mind organism continues to function, and there is an experiencing of life through the eyes of that body/mind organism. This is identifying 'with.'

Teachers of Advaita sometimes use the image of a chauffeur. Because he has access to a nice car and can drive it anywhere, the chauffeur can be deceived into thinking that it is his car (thus arrogating subjectivity.) With the Understanding, there is no chauffeur, only an owner/driver who is very aware of the different functions involved in owning a car and driving one.

# 38.

## AN IMPOSSIBLE WEIGHT

*"A person is not a thing or a process
but an opening through which
the absolute manifests."*
*- Martin Heidegger*

—

*"God only knows; God makes his plan.
The information's unavailable
to the mortal man..."*
*- Paul Simon*

### I

THE ENTIRE DIFFICULTY could be summed up like this: the human object has bitten off more than it can chew, taken on more than it is capable of. Armed with just enough of the Consciousness flowing through it to give it just enough intelligence to facilitate a function it calls thought, the human being believes his or her 'self' to be a separate, independent being, autonomous in itself, having the responsibility of freedom and of choice in its decisions and actions.

But you see, it isn't. The so-called human being is only an object in Consciousness, however much it believes itself to be an independent conscious being, however much it attempts (unwittingly) to usurp the role of Subject.

How can an object in the play of Consciousness, with the entirely limited capacity of an object, a dream character, a character in a movie, not be completely overwhelmed if it attempts to take on the role and responsibilities of Subject, of the dreamer, of the scriptwriter and producer and director of the movie? The human character convinces itself that it has almost complete freedom and therefore responsibility for its actions. It then finds itself nevertheless doing what it is intended to do in the perfect unfolding in the infinite expression of Consciousness, playing its role as it has been scripted. "But I didn't mean to do that!" "I try to be a better person, but I still find myself acting this way." "This didn't happen the way I intended." "I keep doing this. Why can't I learn?"

So much energy is spent berating oneself for not living up to what one has become convinced he or she should be. So much guilt. And an equal amount of energy expended trying to avoid that guilt by faulting someone else for not living up to the same expectations. It's ridiculous. The human organism thinks it is God, and takes on the responsibilities of God, but has only the capacity of a created object. No wonder so many feel so bad about themselves so much of the time.

How can they possibly measure up? It's an impossible

## 38. An Impossible Weight

set-up. And the suffering that the human object brings upon himself by taking on the role of Subject is in fact imaginary, and unnecessary.

It's a massive case of confused and mistaken identity. The whole idea that there is such a thing as an individual, a self, a person, a human being, is simply a small, innocent mistake. There seems to be all this activity, thoughts, emotions, what writers call a 'stream of consciousness,' which gives the illusion of a certain continuity. It is this apparent continuity of brain activity which you think of as your'self,' but in fact it doesn't exist, there's no'thing' there.

Who you think you are, a human being, is actually much less; a dream character, an apparent body/mind organism functioning as a pass-through mechanism in the expression of Consciousness.

But who You really are is actually immeasurably more; and all of this, including the life of the mind/body thing you think you are, is in truth unfolding perfectly, flawlessly in the pure choiceless Awareness that You truly are.

## II

*IF THE DREAM IS THE RESULT of "divine hypnosis," why isn't the hypnosis complete? Why does anyone wake up?*

The Understanding is total grace, complete gift. That it should happen at all, that any should awaken in the dream, is a great mystery. The ego does not get put aside without a struggle; we do not give up our lives easily. The truth is that left to our own devices we would not give it up at all. What does it take to realize that the 'self' that we have constructed since we were 'born' is not real, does not exist? Sometimes it takes some pretty drastic measures. Intense physical and mental distress, often to the edge of bodily death seems to frequently be a factor in accounts of awakening. Not that that's much help, I suppose. But after awakening occurs, all this is seen in a kind of inverse way. "Whatever it takes to break your heart *open* and wake you up, that is grace." Here you are, and it all is what it is. It unfolds perfectly.

*Does psychology or therapy have any place in this process of waking up?*

It's interesting that you use that word, because that's the difference. Therapy is a process, something the dream characters go through here in the dream. Process and growth and becoming only happen in duality; such is the nature of duality. Awakening is not a process, it is popping out of the context of process, out of duality.

But in retrospect it can be seen that psychotherapy can certainly serve a purpose in stabilizing a sense of self to the point where it becomes safe or even possible to let it go. A very insecure and defensive ego, with very low self esteem, or full of fear and anxiety, will only be further affronted or hurt by being told that it doesn't really exist, that it is only a 'false imagination,' a mistaken idea that needs to be annihilated. Ironically, it takes a fairly strong ego to be able to hear this message and entertain the idea.

But dragging back and forth over the emotional coals of past events in therapy can be a pretty rugged ordeal, and after a point completely counterproductive if you get to

## 38. An Impossible Weight

taking it too seriously. From the present perspective, it's clear that it is futile to try to know or 'find out' who one is: that's just chasing after wind. The individual self which psychotherapy is designed to help in fact is an illusion, and that is the whole problem. The crucial insight is in seeing who or what one is not, and psychotherapy is not likely to take you there.

But before awakening or after awakening, the body/mind organism continues to operate as it is programmed and conditioned: and so it is always helpful to know where one's psychological blind spots are. Simply learning what and where these are, without trying to 'fix' them, can be extremely helpful; but beyond that there's not much point working on the ego (or for that matter, working to diminish the ego), since it is only a hologram or illusion which doesn't actually exist on its own merits.

Throughout Ramana Maharshi's teaching is the theme that since the ego has no real existence of its own, it disappears or vanishes when the light of inquiry is brought to it. What you are left with when the falseness of the ego vanishes, is truth. It's that simple. That's what waking up is. "Reality is simply loss of the ego."

*It just seems like a lot of people are unhappy, and therapy, different kinds of therapy, can help that.*

Well, sure. That's what's available: dream characters are unhappy, so they go to therapy in the dream so they feel happier in the dream. It's a closed system. There are also other ways in the dream to feel happier. But essentially, in case you haven't noticed, unhappiness is inherent in the dream. It's how duality works, and there will be relative happiness and relative unhappiness as long as there is 'bondage' to the terms of the dream.

In practical terms, nine tenths or more of the perceived problem, this so-called 'bondage,' or more practically, unhappiness, has to do with the concept of responsibility. People do love the concept of free will, go to the block for it, believe life isn't worth living without it. But a consistent examination reveals that it is only an idea, not your actual experience at any point. 'Causation' is so complex that there is no way you can truly say 'free will' has any meaningful input into any action performed by the mind/body you call yourself. Can you actually find one action which you can be sure, which you can prove was yours alone, or yours significantly, or even yours at all and not the result of the interconnected net of influences of genetics, environment, training, culture, conditioning, historical 'accident', 'chance' encounter, and so on? Ultimately, you cannot.

Once this is understood, it is possible to see that what we think of as individuals are not subjects, not points of origin, but are objects, instruments through which Consciousness, 'cosmic force,' 'divine energy' works or flows. The concept of 'responsibility' then pretty much relaxes and goes away. 'You' are no more responsible for what occurs through the mind/body you call your'self' than the flute is responsible for the music played on it by the musician.

And then there is the realization that this is also true of any other mind/body. And so, of course, responsibility's spawn; guilt, sin, shame, pride, arrogance, malice, all pretty much go out the window. 'You' don't 'do' things; nor does anyone else; events happen, and they happen through mind/body organisms as instruments, including the one you call yourself.

## 38. An Impossible Weight

*I'm not sure I can really accept that there's no personal responsibility, but I can see that what you're describing would be a big relief.*

It's an impossible weight for the object, the instrument, to try to take on the load of being the determiner, the subject, the one responsible, the one apparently screwing up and making a mess of things: it's essentially crazy-making, as you can see by looking at the world. The only reasonably happy and sane people are the ones who embrace some version of acceptance of what is, as the unfolding in Consciousness; even if it takes the form of a somewhat simple faith such as "let go and let God." The folks who are convinced they can, and have to, determine things for themselves, with all the attendant implications of personal responsibility, are the ones who dig themselves in pretty deep.

And yes, of course, taking personal responsibility is a more mature understanding than faulting and blaming everyone else, and so it is taught as a useful strategy for societies and for individuals in the dream. But ultimately this too is seen to be as empty a concept as the concept of the individual on which it's based.

*There's a lot of letting go in this.*

The core, central, irreducible teaching, said in some form by any teacher worth listening to, is also contained in the one line from Hebrew scripture, "Be still and know I am God." There is nothing really to teach; if one would only be still, all that can be known is here. All else is dream stuff, all else is just making noise, all else is bondage.

*But even letting go, or being still, seems like something I struggle with trying to do, and the teaching I've heard is that you can't do anything.*

The idea of non-doership is essentially a fairly simple one, but nevertheless it is difficult to talk or even think about it clearly at first because our language and concepts aren't set up for it. The Chinese have a phrase, *wei wu wei*. *Wei* is action. *Wu* is the negative, so *wu wei* is non-action. That gives the basic duality; action or not action. But then there's this experienced alternative of *wei wu wei*, which is "action which is not action." Neither sitting doing nothing nor running around trying to accomplish things, but the experience of the necessary action happening. The key is in the idea of who is doing the acting. Nobody is. The acting is happening without a doer. This is what our language and concepts have trouble with.

*My mind has trouble wrapping itself around it.*

Whose mind? What mind? The 'you' that you think has a mind is an illusion; an idea that we were all taught to believe in, but which turns out to have no basis and no reality. This becomes clear. When you look at it, there isn't really any 'mind.' What is the mind? There's no such separate thing.

What there is, what we all experience, is an apparently more-or-less continuous stream of thoughts. This is what we then call 'mind,' believing that this stream of thoughts is generated from inside our skulls. This is what we have been taught to believe since day one; but look at your own experience. Actually, you know that 'your' thoughts come from elsewhere. Sometimes we say, "I wonder where that

## 38. An Impossible Weight

idea came from!" Where they all come from; Consciousness, Source. The human mind/body instruments are not points of origin. They are not transmitters. They are only relay stations, pass-through mechanisms for Consciousness. Which is where the teaching, 'you are not the doer,' comes from: 'you' cannot be a doer of anything: things happen through the body/mind organism you think of as 'you.'

*If I'm not the doer of any action, who is?*

If you need to, you can think about things as being done by Consciousness, through the instruments of the body/mind organisms. But ultimately that too is a projection of 'Consciousness' as a being, an entity like 'God,' who does things. Often it is said that it is Consciousness, or Presence, or Love, or the Beloved, doing or thinking or experiencing. It can be comforting or inspiring to talk this way, but this is a poetic use of language and concepts. Ultimately the idea of any doer is let go of.

Finally, there is no doer and no thing done, only the doing. No experiencer and no experience, only the experiencing. And that is what Consciousness *is:* Consciousness doesn't *do* anything; it *is* everything. It is all thoroughly and completely *im*personal, both in terms of there being any person here as a 'me' and in terms of there being any divine person.

This is the essence of non-duality. There is only All That Is. That is what I Am. There is nothing other than this, either a 'me' here or a 'god' somewhere else. All is I.

Here, listen to Wei Wu Wei:

"All said and done:
Everything is I
and I am no thing.
All phenomena are objective manifestations.
What I am objectively is the totality of phenomenal manifestation.
What I am subjectively is all that all phenomena *are*.
Nothing personal about it anywhere or at any stage.
The personal notion is not inherent
and is the *whole trouble!*"

# 39.

## A Splinter...

> "The crows assert that a single crow
> could destroy the heavens.
> This is certainly true, but it proves nothing
> against the heavens,
> because 'heaven' means precisely:
> the impossibility of crows."
> – Franz Kafka

### I

A FEW LINES OF DIALOG from the movie, *The Matrix*:

'Morpheus:' I imagine that right now, you're feeling a bit like Alice; tumbling down the rabbit hole?

'Neo:' You could say that.

M: I can see it in your eyes. You have the look of a man who accepts what he sees because he is expecting to wake up. Ironically, this is not far from the truth.

*Do you believe in fate, Neo?*

N: No.

M: Why not?

N: Because I don't like the idea that I'm not in control of my life.

M: I know exactly what you mean!
Let me tell you why you're here. You're here because you know something. What you know, you can't explain, but you feel it. You've felt it your entire life. That there's something wrong with the world. You don't know what it is. But it's there, like a splinter in your mind, driving you mad. It is this feeling that has brought you to me. Do you know what I'm talking about?

N: The Matrix?

M: Do you want to know what it is?
The Matrix is everywhere. It is all around us. Even now in this very room. You can see it when you look out your window or when you turn on your television. You can feel it when you go to work, when you go to church, when you pay your taxes.
It is the world that has been pulled over your eyes to blind you from the truth.

N: What truth?

M: That you are a slave, Neo. Like everyone else you were born into bondage. Born into a prison that you cannot smell or taste or touch. A prison for your mind.

## 39. A Splinter...

*Unfortunately, no one can be told what the Matrix is. You have to see it for yourself.*

*Remember; all I'm offering is the truth. Nothing more.*

...

*M: Have you ever had a dream Neo, that you were so sure was real? What if you were unable to wake from that dream? How would you know the difference between the dream world and the real world?*

...

*N: This... this isn't real?*

*M: What is 'real'? How do you define 'real'? If you're talking about what you can feel, what you can smell, what you can taste and see, then 'real' is simply electrical signals interpreted by your brain.*

...

*N: I know what you're trying to do.*

*M: I'm trying to free your mind, Neo. But I can only show you the door. You're the one who has to walk through it.*

### II

For the past few years, I'd been going around telling friends, acquaintances, people I came across in my shamanic travels, even my therapist (which was a little dangerous), that reality was not what it pretended to be. I said that the whole structure of reality seemed very fishy to me; like it was phony, rigged, set up. I would have moments when I would stop in my tracks, whatever I was doing, the feeling was so strong. *What you know, you can't explain, but you feel it. You've felt it your entire life. That there's something wrong with the world. Like a feeling of deja vu,* except that this was a feeling that I almost saw something: almost saw through the hologram, the pretense, of what we called the real world. There was a frustration, because it never quite happened: it remained elusive, a splinter in my mind.

This feeling came most strongly when I read about some new scientific discovery. A new galaxy out there, where they had looked before and had never seen anything; the astronomer interviewed said they "must have overlooked it" before. Or a new sub-atomic particle to join the mesons and gluons and quarks; somehow these things just kept appearing. I couldn't help but feel, "Yeah, right." Too convenient.

What I told my shrink was that I was becoming convinced that somehow we were making it all up as we went along. I couldn't explain how or why, but the whole thing just did not make sense, did not add up, did not stand up to skeptical scrutiny. Too many exceptions to every rule, too many unexplained events and effects that everyone, scientists and doctors and theologians and teachers and sales clerks and carpet salesmen alike all tried to disregard and shrug off and feebly explain away.

It was this splinter in my mind that had me dabbling around in shamanism, doing weird things in the company of tribal medicine men in the middle of the Amazon rainforest, playing around on those edges of *"how do you define 'real'"*... when I fell off. When I finally saw what I had been seeing.

The truth, Who you Are, what 'really' Is, is always here; has always been here. It is not something new you have to learn. It is actually completely and totally familiar to us,

## 39. A Splinter...

even though we are not conscious of realizing it. This is the shock of recognition when it occurs: complete familiarity. Of course, this has always been! More than familiar. This truth is what is most intimate to you: more familiar and intimate than anything that you think or believe or 'know' about yourself. Because these things turn out to be constructs, beliefs, an added layer, outside the most intimate truth, which you have convinced yourself that you don't know. But you do. Go back. It is your own Self.

Once when I was in Bombay I found myself one afternoon in a remarkable little hole-in-the-wall shop in the old Fort section of the city. Dark, dingy, ancient, the shop specialized in all types of Indian handcrafts. The owner met me at the door with the classic eastern hospitality of a merchant for a prospective customer. I was offered a seat, a cup of hot *chai,* and he and his assistants proceeded to bring out and parade before me sandalwood carvings, bronze castings, statues, rugs, silk scarves, jewelry, furniture, boxes, chests, figurines, paintings, gods, goddesses, buddhas.

A particular specialty of the house was the carved wooden screens that are used as room dividers. Composed of several panels, each about a foot and a half wide by six feet high, four or five of these panels hinged together. One after another, these carved teakwood screens were unfolded in front of me, and they were dazzling. Every inch of every panel was intricately carved; and it was pierced carving, cutting right through the inch-thick wood so that the air could pass through the panels, which of course is why they are called 'screens.'

As I examined the carving on one screen, I found that the closer I looked the more I saw. It was amazing. There were elephant caravans, the palace of the Raj, tigers in the jungle, the great River Ganga, *sadhus*, temples, naked women, processions, the whole life of the Buddha, the myth of Lord Ganesha, Prince Arjuna in battle, more naked women, Shiva dancing the world into existence, and on and on, the whole history of India, of the world, of the universe. The carving was marvelous: the fringe on the carpets on the elephants' backs was detailed. The naked women were... detailed. No individual image on the screen was more than a couple inches high, and this went on for several square feet.

The carved screen had my complete and undivided attention for some time. Eventually, around the edges of that concentration, I started to become aware of something else. Something going on, that I had on some level been aware of but had not been paying attention to. The shop owner and his helpers were still at work, running around, hauling out stuff: "And also we have..." "For you, special price..." "Please sir, if you would look at this..." I was sitting on the chair, still holding half a cup of sweet tea, leaning forward toward the screen standing a couple of feet in front of me, scanning the marvelous carved landscape, when...

Pop. My focus changed, and I was suddenly looking *through* the screen. In fact, the screen and its carved universe which had occupied all my attention was suddenly vague and fuzzy, semi-transparent: I was seeing through it, past it, to...

...well, here the analogy breaks down, because what I was seeing through to was the rest of the shop, with its enthusiastic staff piling up rosewood elephants and brass engravings.

## 39. A Splinter...

But nevertheless. Pop. A very simple thing, a very ordinary thing. The suddenness of seeing through the veil. To the background, the substrate. To what is always there, and ultimately 'real' and true, but not perceived because our focus has been on the propped-up artificial screen, on *the world that has been pulled over your eyes to blind you from the truth... A prison for your mind.*

What is always there, What Is, Who you truly Are, is precisely the background, the *milieu*, in which the phony hologram, the matrix, the *maya*, exists.

Back when I was in seminary studying theology, there was a Christian theologian, Paul Tillich perhaps, who was rocking the boat by pointing toward 'God' not in personal terms but in terms of 'the ground of our being.' The background, the substrate, Teillard de Chardin's *milieu divin*, in which all this other stuff, including science and philosophy and gods and trees and thoughts and people and mountains, all appear to exist.

*You have the look of a man who accepts what he sees because he is expecting to wake up. Ironically, this is not far from the truth.* Who you really are *knows* you are asleep and *is* expecting to wake up.

But no amount of teaching or learning or talking or listening or trying or practicing can bring this about. This is the teaching of all the masters and my experience as well: *no one can be told what the Matrix is. You have to see it for yourself.* The 'pop' of the change of focus cannot be taught; it cannot even be *done:* it has to *happen.*

This is the consistent message of mystics from all traditions:

one can storm the gates of heaven, but there is no guarantee, no formula, no practice that will ensure that they will open. For that there is only unearned grace, and a willingness to be surprised by joy, to be gifted with utter emptiness of self, with the Being Consciousness Bliss that you already Are.

## III

*L*ISTEN. AMONG HUMAN BEINGS, it is said that any individual human being can attain enlightenment. Now, within the context in which it is said, this is undoubtedly true. However, it tells you absolutely nothing about enlightenment – because 'enlightenment' means precisely: the impossibility of the existence of any individual human being.

# 40.

---

## STILL EXPANSE

*"It is utter stillness.
Such is the form and shape of your original mind.
Your own nature is essentially pure
and utterly still."*
*- Hui Hai*

—

*"Mind is Buddha.
No Mind. No Buddha!"*
*- Basho*

THE ULTIMATE UNDERSTANDING is a seeing and a knowing
rather than a comprehending.
And it does satisfy all questions,
though not answer them.
Answers become as irrelevant
as the questions themselves;
both cease in the seeing.

Do not judge the questioning or the longing,
the seeking or the sadness,

the impatience or the resistance,
the opening or the letting go.
It is all the perfect unfolding as it is:
only watch it and know you are not that.
You are Loving Awareness in which all this arises.
You are Quiet Compassionate Space in which the life
that you think of as 'yourself'
unfolds.

This Still Expanse of Acceptance between the thoughts
is All That Is.
That is What You Are.
Let the Love that is this Stillness that You Are
Embrace you,
Overcome you.
*Svaha!*

# 41.

## Peripheral Vision

*"When someone asks me who they are
or what God is
I smile inside and whisper to the Light:
'There you go again pretending.'"*
*– Adyashanti*

PERHAPS A REASON THAT the Understanding is not a more common occurrence is that it is too simple, too close to home, too subtle. All the seeking is in the other direction, toward something other, something grander. Consider this: a common response when the Understanding happens is laughter. A common response is, "Oh, that!" Right here, that which is most familiar to you, but overlooked because the looking has been for something else, something beyond. That's why the finding is in stopping, in stillness. "Be still and know I am God." Your natural state. Subtle. It is lost, overlooked if there is positive movement, direct searching, active thinking, anything but profound stillness.

A metaphor. In the retina of your eye there are two kinds

of cells: cone cells and rod cells. The cones are clustered toward the center of the retina; what is in the center of your field of view is focused on them, and they register shades of light and, especially, color. The rods are more numerous around the edge of the retina, and they pick up what is on the edge of your field of view, in your peripheral vision. They do not distinguish color, can discern only black and white, but pick out contrast better than the cones. This is why the rod cells are important for night vision, and explains an odd phenomenon; that night vision is better in your peripheral vision.

Walking in the Vermont woods at night, I learned at a young age that what you could make out in the darkness, what you could see, depended on how you looked. Repeatedly, you would see a movement in your peripheral vision and turn to look directly at it, to see only darkness. Eventually, one learns not to turn, not to look directly, but to keep it just in your peripheral vision, just at the point where you are almost not looking at it at all. That is when you can see it best.

Subtle. It is lost, overlooked if there is positive movement, direct searching, active thinking, anything but profound stillness. Focus on it, and it is gone. All of the talking, all of the asking questions, reading books, meditating, thinking, focusing, seeking, is all counterproductive because it is pushing in the wrong direction, creating activity and turbulence and noise. Just as there is *wei wu wei*, the action which is not action, action which is not willed, is not volitional but witnessed as spontaneously happening: so too there is a seeing which is not seeing, a seeing which happens without trying, without looking.

## 41. Peripheral Vision

Asleep in the dream, the everyday activity is to look without truly seeing. What is called for is seeing without looking, the seeing happening without there being one who looks.

The poetry of Rumi and Hafiz, of Kabir and Tagore, is all about this, this sideways seeing, creating a still quiet openness where the subtleness which would be missed in direct seeking can present itself.

> "Don't wish for union!
> There's a closeness beyond that...
> Fall in love in such a way
> that it frees you from any connecting.
> Love is the soul's light, the taste of morning;
> no me, no we, no claim of being...
> As eyes in silence, tears, face:
> love cannot be said." (Rumi)

Cannot be said, because saying is looking directly. It's the Observer Principle in reverse. Your true nature, What Is, is pure Subjective Awareness. So become an observer to try to find it, try to look at it, try to turn it into an object, and you will not see it anywhere because as an object it is not. Pure Awareness in which everything arises is what you already are: how can it possibly be found? In stillness this is known.

The sheer enormity of the misperception, the misunderstanding, is staggering. That's why the laughter when there finally is seeing: it's not like we're even close. Almost the entire human endeavor, from daily life, daily thought and actions, to philosophy and theology, psychology and sociology, biology, physics, history and politics, is all based on a completely erroneous premise and is headed wildly, blithely, obliviously off in the wrong direction.

Only in non-action can anything meaningful happen. This is the meaning of Krishna's admonition in the *Bhagavad Gita* to "be awake to what the world is asleep to, and asleep to what the world is awake to." Being quiet in stillness, doing nothing, aware, is the only thing that is not wasting time.

*Wait. How about the unconscious?*

The unconscious what?

*What is called the unconscious. The unconscious mind, the unconscious self.*

This is what I mean by everything being based on a mistaken premise. Once you accept the widely held but unfounded belief in an individual self and an individual mind, you can then go to work and subdivide that mind into any number of conscious and subconscious and unconscious and superconscious parts and develop whole sciences to deal with each of them. But you're heading pell-mell down a dead-end road with all that. It'll keep you and everyone you know occupied in the dream for many generations, but it will never lead anywhere.

*But when I work to uncover the unconscious reasons why I do the things I do or feel the way I feel, this seems to be getting in touch with a level that is more real and more meaningful, the unconscious level, which is what drives and motivates this more superficial conscious level.*

Sure. And doing this kind of work can lead to a higher level of functioning of the body/mind organism, once the forces that are at work are understood?

## 41. Peripheral Vision

*Yes, definitely.*

Yes. But this is all within the dream, within the construct of mind in which these phenomena of body/mind organisms, and individual self, and mind divided into various levels, all have apparent reality. In this dream there are things experienced as pleasant and there are things experienced as painful. If there is a disturbed childhood in one of the dream characters, much of the later so-called life of that character may be unhappy. If there is going through successful therapy, maybe some of the rest of that life will be happier. There are many things in the dream which, if they happen, can make a part of the dream less unpleasant. If the character takes a cooking class, it may have the opportunity to enjoy better tasting foods than canned beans. If it takes a seminar and learns a new strategy or a new way of thinking or acting, the dream will be experienced in a new way that the dream character may like better. The world is full of ways to improve your experience of the dream, from the trivial to the deeply valuable and useful.

But none have anything whatever to do with what we are talking about here. We are not talking about improving your experience of the dream. We are talking about seeing the dream for what it is: as a mental construct, a mind-generated-fantasy, a projection of what is called the 'mind,' but which in fact does not exist, either conscious or unconscious.

*What do you mean, the mind doesn't exist?*

What mind? What is it that you are calling your 'mind?'

*Well, I would probably agree that there isn't a 'thing' called a mind. It's not an organ because I think it is throughout the body and not just in the brain, but it's the mind part of the body/mind organism.*

So instead of a 'thing,' would you call the mind a function?

*Okay, the thinking function, the reasoning function, and more than that; there are intuitive and other things that happen subconsciously, those are the mind too.*

I agree that there is functioning in these body/mind organisms. There is physical functioning and there is mental functioning. Physical functioning is experienced as bodily activity of various kinds. Mental functioning is experienced as thoughts and mental activity. And it is because of these activities, what the Buddhist tradition calls the *skandhas*, the thought processes, sensory perceptions, and so on, the functioning of the body/mind organism, that there is an assumption made that there is something, someone, here doing these things. But that's an unfounded assumption. To perceive that the *skandhas* are empty of an individual self doing them, is to awaken. All there is, is Consciousness. There is the apparent functioning of Consciousness in and through these apparent body/mind organisms, but they do not exist as separate entities as such.

That's why we call this the dream; everything, including the body/mind organism you call yourself, does not exist as something separate in itself, but only as an apparent functioning in Consciousness. There is no separate self or mind, only dream characters in Self or Consciousness. There is only thinking happening in this apparent organism, in these dream characters. We experience this. We experience

## 41. Peripheral Vision

thoughts happening; but the assumption that they originate inside these heads in something we call a mind is an unwarranted leap. It's the basic misperception from which everything else, all of dualism, all of the illusion of separation, all *samsara*, follows.

*So this... (pause) Wait. What I'm saying right now, I'm not saying, it isn't coming from this mind?*

Exactly.

*( pause)... Okay, you keep calling this a dream. I understand the analogy, it's a simple one really, but I don't see how it applies.*

The value of the dream analogy is that it gives a sense for how it is that physical reality, all of consensus reality, is basically not real, but is also in a sense real. The analogy is to how we think of our sleeping dreams. If you dreamed something at night when you were asleep, when you woke up you wouldn't say that what happened in the dream 'really' happened; it was only a dream. On the other hand, it was a 'real' dream; if you are telling someone about a dream you actually had, you aren't lying or making it up, you really did have this dream. What we mean by saying that the dream isn't real in the sense that consensus reality is real, is that the dream does not exist independently on its own the way it is believed other objects do: it only exists as a dream of the one who dreamt it.

What I'm telling you is that this is the case for all of what you think of as reality, what we are calling consensus reality, what humanity generally agrees is real. It is not real like you think it is: it exists only as a dream in

Consciousness. It has a certain reality to it, yes, it exists in a certain way. All there is is Consciousness, and this exists in Consciousness as an expression of Consciousness, so it does have a certain existence. But it does not exist on its own, independently; it is only here as an expression, a projection in Consciousness, the ultimate dreamer; it does not have any existence other than that.

Another similar analogy which hasn't been around as long is the hologram. A hologram is really only an illusion created by projecting a beam of coherent light. Yet a very sophisticated hologram would have the potential to look and sound and otherwise seem very 'real,' as real as physical reality, so that you could interact with a hologram of a person as if there were a 'real' person there, which of course there wouldn't be.

*Yes, but a hologram wouldn't really seem real, because it isn't substantial; you could put your hand through it or walk through it, for example. But that's why I say I don't see how it applies; I don't think you or that wall are dreams or holograms, because they are very substantial; I can't walk through you.*

Exactly. So I ask you, under what circumstances would a hologram seem very substantial? Or put it another way, to whom would a hologram appear solid?

*Another hologram...*

Exactly.

*I... (long pause)...*

## 41. Peripheral Vision

Take your time.

*The... (pause) I'm sorry, I seem to have lost my train of thought.*

Just stay with that for a while. Relax, don't try to struggle with it, just be still for a minute... (pause) Can you tell me what we were talking about?

*Umm... Advaita, non-duality.*

What was the last thing that was said before you lost your train of thought?

*I'm afraid I've sort of blanked out here.*

That's fine. A little disoriented?

*Yeah. I'm okay, but that was definitely strange.*

"Then as a stranger, bid it welcome!" Just stay with that disorientation a little before it slips away. Savor it, get the feel of it. This is very beautiful. This is actually what you are looking for, without realizing it.

The last thing that you said before blanking out was to recognize the possibility that all of this seems real only because 'you' yourself aren't real either. You said that only another hologram would see holograms as substantial or 'real.' The idea occurred to you that maybe 'you' are only a hologram.

*Oh, yeah.*

Now, if you didn't really take that as a serious possibility, that would have seemed like just an interesting idea and you would have breezed through it without any problem. But because of what's happening here, the ego, that constructed, built-up sense of an individual self, was faced with the real possibility that what you have always thought of as 'you,' this mind/body apparatus operating in the world, does not exist in any true sense as anything real but only as a hologram, a projection, a dream; and the ego is not able to deal with that, so it checks out.

This is the difference between the intellectual understanding, in which these ideas are tossed around and argued about, and the Understanding going deeper; it goes to another level, where the ego, the sense of individual self, gets exploded, annihilated. No doubt that would be experienced as a bit disorienting, yes? The ego sense of self spends all its time trying to stay in control, and that means trying to keep you away from these moments of disorientation when the bottom drops out and it doesn't know what to do.

This is so beautiful. This is what I mean when I talk about asking the dangerous question, the question that may end your life. This idea that this 'you' is not real, is only a thought, a projection, stopped you. That's why I said to savor that feeling of disorientation. Get to know it, to not fear it, to welcome it. You'll be back there again. That place where the ego is completely disoriented is what you're looking for. The Zen practice of meditating on unsolvable *koans*, for example, is designed to get the ego/mind to that place where it can't cope, and blanks out. One day, instead of bouncing back from it, going back there to the familiar, you won't. You'll stay here, fall deeper, break through to the

## 41. Peripheral Vision

other side. Then you won't go back. Then you won't be there anymore. It'll be perfectly obvious that there isn't any mind, isn't any self, isn't any 'you,' isn't any this side or other side, anything to go back to. That's what's called awakening.

Of course, please don't go around trying to disorient yourself. There's the prescriptive/descriptive fallacy again. This is just describing what happens, not something you can do. You can't cause it. Just welcome it when it comes.

*It sounds a little scary, actually, like I might lose my mind.*

You don't have a mind to lose. You'll just lose the mistaken idea that you have one. But scary, yes. That's the ego, the sense of being an individual self, reasserting itself and not wanting to go where it isn't in charge any more. That's why I say sometimes that left to our own devices, no one would choose this. The ego can't choose its own annihilation. Fortunately, it's not up to you.

We've all been conditioned to get scared at this point and worry about going insane. When you step beyond the boundaries of the almost universally accepted parameters of the dream, of consensus reality, and thoughts happen that are really 'outside the box,' outside of Plato's cave, then it is quite possible there may be some experience of psychological pain or turbulence. And also, everyone else still in the dream is going to think you are pretty weird. But trust me, the place that is really insane is where you are now, believing you are separate; not knowing your own true nature, thinking you are this thing, not realizing You are All That Is, the pure choiceless Awareness in which all this appears; Being Consciousness Bliss, Outpouring.

# 42.

## Dreams Within Dreams

*"Nothing you can explain exists."*
*- Robert Adams*

*"Consciousness is a singular
of which the plural is unknown."*
*- Erwin Schroedinger*

IN THESE PAGES there is much use made of the analogy of the dream. To say that waking consciousness, and the world that appears as 'real' in waking consciousness, is actually more like a dream, is to use a metaphor. It goes hand in hand with the metaphor of awakening, and both are used to point toward the Understanding. But when taken literally these images can take on a life of their own and lead to thoughts and questions about how one can wake up from the dream, which are nothing but an extended and rather pointless detour.

In traditional Advaita, there is a conceptual distinction made between three states or levels of consciousness, and then the Consciousness which is above or beyond or prior to the other three and which witnesses the three states of consciousness. The three states are the waking state, which is considered to be the least conscious state or the deepest stupor; the dreaming state; and the consciousness which is there in deep sleep which, ironically to most westerners, is considered to be clearest, the purest, the most 'awake' of the three. Then, there is Consciousness which perceives and experiences all three of these states, the Consciousness in which all these three states, waking, dreaming, and deep sleep, arise.

There is an inverse awareness here; the deeper one goes into what the West calls 'unconsciousness,' the Advaita model sees as more conscious. What the West calls waking up, Advaita sees as becoming more *un*conscious.

The western model is so programmed into our thinking, the waking state is given such priority and value, that the other states are valued only when they are interpreted in the context of waking consciousness. Thus the western psychological model is to make 'unconscious' processes 'conscious;' that is, recognized and interpreted by the waking consciousness. And the thought patterns that occur in dreaming consciousness are endlessly interpreted by the waking mind. The Advaita model would see this process as backwards, as dumbing-down the 'higher' levels of consciousness in a way that is amenable to the 'lowest' level.

This Advaita model of consciousness is examined by James Carse in *Breakfast at the Victory: The Mysticism of Ordinary Experience*. (Carse is professor of religion at New York University and, as far as I know, no relation. But with

## 42. Dreams Within Dreams

a name like that, who knows? Who Carse?) In speaking of the Consciousness in which waking, dreaming, and deep sleep all arise, Carse points out that

> "...while this deepest state is not directly known to the other levels of consciousness, each of those levels is perfectly known to it. In other words, self-knowledge is not knowing who or what the true self is; it is being known by that true self."

Dreams, and also other messages from what is called the unconscious or subconscious, often seem very strange to the waking consciousness, precisely because they do not fit into waking 'reality.' Waking consciousness then must interpret the dream to make sense of it in light of what it accepts as 'reality.'

> "This way the dream becomes the property of the waking I, and the deeper consciousness that was at work in it goes back into hiding.
>
> "The usual way of interpreting a dream is to translate its content into terms familiar with the waking I. If we followed the Hindus' insight into levels of consciousness, we would reverse this process. We would ask ourselves what the dreaming I knows about the waking I that the waking I cannot know about itself."

Please notice here that it is evident that Carse is thinking of the three levels of 'consciousness' as 'states' belonging to an individual 'self,' and is interpreting the 'Hindu' or Advaita tradition accordingly. He even seems to refer to ultimate Consciousness, All That Is, as a fourth, 'deepest state' of individual consciousness. Somewhat ironically, this is exactly the kind of analysis the 'waking state' engages in, to bring what seems like a strange but intriguing teaching into alignment with the waking state's beliefs; in this case the belief in separate individuals, each with their own levels of 'consciousness.'

Nevertheless, the point of all this is that, *mutatis mutandis*, there is a useful insight here. Remember Maharaj; "The very idea of going beyond the dream is illusory." It is not for the waking consciousness to go anywhere; the waking consciousness is the dream character. It belongs in the dream.

"The dream is not your problem." Who you truly are is not the dream character, not waking consciousness, not a state, not even a 'higher self' of deeper but still individual consciousness. Rather, who you truly are is All That Is, Consciousness, the Absolute; in which the sleeping dream, and the waking dream, and the dreamlessness all appear.

Consciousness, All That Is, cannot be directly known by the waking consciousness you call yourself because it cannot be translated, it cannot "become the property" of this dream character. But you, the 'you' that you think you are, is perfectly known to it. It is what You are.

# 43.

## TRINITY

*"I am Presence;
not, I am present or you are present
or he is present.
When one sees the situation as it really is,
that no individual is involved,
that what is present is Presence as a whole,
then the moment this is perceived
there is liberation."*
*– Nisargadatta Maharaj*

WOULD YOU SAY THAT any feeling or emotion is Consciousness appearing as that feeling (for example anxiety or calmness) or is it simply these feelings appearing in Consciousness? The same question applies to thoughts. As I see it, anger or compassion is in essence no different than the pen I am using... is this true?

In a sense it depends on how fine you want to split the atom, as it were. On the most basic or 'truest' level, nothing is. Ramana Maharshi said, "Whatever is not there in deep sleep, does not exist." All that is there in deep sleep is that original primal Awareness that is not even aware of its own awareness. What Maharaj refers to as your "natural state." The Zen *koan* about "what was your original face before you were born?" points to this. Before the body is born, (and identified consciousness arises) and again after it dies, you are unidentified Consciousness (Awareness, Presence.) Even during the so-called life of the body, you are not other than that, although the identification makes this hard to see. There is nothing other than this Awareness. Thoughts occur in this awareness, automobiles occur in this awareness, nebulae occur, dreams occur, memories occur, accidents occur, emotions occur. When asked if the gods of Hindu mythology were real, Ramana Maharshi said, they are as real as this world. Myth and the physical world are equally 'real.' Feelings, thoughts and pens have the same 'reality' – the same 'unreality.'

The physicists tell us that when you look closely enough, physical 'reality' is not material at all, but immaterial energy. The concept I sometimes try to express is that the basic 'building block' of what we experience around us, including ourselves and the worlds of material things and energies and thoughts, is what is referred to as *Ananda* in the Hindu expression *Sat Chit Ananda*. The Sanskrit word *Ananda* is most usually translated 'bliss', so people get a funny idea about it. But there is something much 'bigger' happening with this, and sometimes there are attempts to talk about this but it is extremely difficult to have it come out making any sense.

In the concept of *Sat Chit Ananda*, there is a parallel with the Christian mystical theology of the Trinity. Both agree that first is the origin, the unmoved Source, Being itself,

## 43. Trinity

Consciousness at rest (Awareness; Being; *Sat*; 'the Father.') Then, in some inexpressible way, there is a stirring, a movement, a breath, a turning, a reflecting, something of this sense, within this original unmoved All-That-Is. This is the *Logos*, Consciousness reflected, which is itself not other than the same Awareness. It is Consciousness now aware of itself, yet not other than or separate from pure Awareness: *Chit*, 'the Son.' It is perhaps the Intelligence, Awakeness, aspect of Awareness. The beginning of John's Gospel, ("In the beginning was the Word (*Logos*), and the Word was with God, and the Word was God; It was there in the beginning with God...") is struggling with this same inexpressible.

So there's that. But then there's something else, even more inexpressible. Both Hindu and Christian traditions see that there is somehow something (conceptually) more. In Christianity, this 'more' is called 'the Spirit' of God, which is sometimes described or defined as 'the Love between the Father and the Son'. So, not something really separate, but the Love that occurs in this movement, Breath, stirring, of Awareness; a Love so complete that it is itself not other than God.

This is pure Love; neutral, unidentified. The nature of this Love is that it cannot be contained and it pours out of itself in itself. What I call the Outpouring. It spills out, overflows, as it were. This Love is unimaginable and there is hesitation to refer to it even as love. It is fierce, power, intensity, peace, glory, burning Brilliance. Completely and totally overwhelming to the human experience and the human capacity to comprehend. *Ananda* is as pathetically inadequate a word as 'love'. And both the Christian and the Hindu traditions are quite clear that this *Ananda* or Spirit or Love is not something other than God, Being, Consciousness. God or *Brahman* is One: Father, Son, Spirit, or *Sat, Chit, Ananda* are just three concepts being thrown together in an attempt to triangulate on What Is. All of this is conceptual, the mind struggling and stretching to comprehend; there is no absolute 'truth' in these concepts and expressions; they are only, perhaps, useful pointers.

When Maharaj made his cryptic comment about everything being made out of love, the whole manifestation existing and being sustained by and in and as this primal absolute Love, this is what he was saying. This outpouring of *Ananda* God bliss beauty love gratitude intensity power Spirit Stillness Perfection Brilliance is 'energy:' the only Energy there is. It is All there is. It is the energy the physicists are detecting when they look at the subatomic particles and detect not matter but an energetic explosion. Part of the vision in the jungle was the seeing of this Energy as Outpouring from Source (and even this is concept, a glimpse at the inexpressible) and streaming, showering, as THIS, what is experienced here as this world; thoughts and diesel engines and anxiety and frogs and smoke and daydreams and sidewalks. This is what I'm trying to express here: 'God' or 'Love' or *Ananda* or 'Spirit' is precisely the 'stuff' that all of this is 'made out of:' which is why 'this' is not other than 'that;' it IS that, it is made of that.

Another way to think of the *Sat Chit Ananda* Trinity is to realize that all there is, is Consciousness, *Chit*. Consciousness at rest, in stillness, is *Sat*. Consciousness in motion, in activity, outpouring, is *Ananda*. It's all the same, it's all one.

So this is your 'essence' or 'All that is.' It can only be All

## 43. Trinity

That Is if it is all there is: if all there is, is it. So anything which looks like something else, isn't; it's it. So there's Tony Parsons, for example, pointing to a cushion thrown on the floor and saying 'this is it.' That's the whole message.

The Buddhist concept of 'all sentient beings' is meant to be inclusive; honoring all sentient beings, working for the deliverance of all sentient beings... But in fact it is incomplete and exclusive. It's anthropocentric: we honor sentient beings because we recognize that in their sentience they are like 'us.' What of trees, blades of grass, specks of dust, molecules of water, this bit of mud, dirt, stone, steel, petroleum, plastic? "It has already long been everything and always is everything."

When there's talking about *samsara* or illusion, it's not that there's nothing there. There's all-there-is, there! The illusion is in perceiving it as separate material stuff, which it isn't. It's God. Love. *Ananda*. It just looks like stuff, anger pen cat prayer solstice hummingbird death scrambled eggs, to identified consciousness (the body/ mind organisms) who think they are somebody living a life in a world.

This is what's going on in the Christian mystical tradition when there's all the talk about the love of God being this fierce 'refiner's fire' that burns everything away. This is misunderstood as some vengeful-God thing, but those who originally saw it saw this: when the Outpouring is apperceived, in-seen, 'Understood,' nothing of this human experience can stand it: everything is burned up, gone. None of this is: only that Love which is All-that-is Outpouring Presence, is. It looks like slush spraying off the wheels of a car in the city in January; it looks like a husband being sent to serve in Afghanistan; it looks like a friend's cancer or failing heart, or a mother hugging her child or my old sneakers or your ballpoint, but here it obviously isn't. Nobody sees it, but it's obviously perfect Brilliant Stillness, Outpouring.

Finally, interestingly enough, both the Christian and Hindu traditions recognize that neither *Sat Chit Ananda* nor Father, Son and Spirit are the Absolute. Both are only as far as the human mind can stretch, as close as it can come to comprehending what cannot be comprehended. *Sat Chit Ananda* is an attempt to describe *Brahman*, which itself arises from *Parabrahman*, that which is beyond *Brahman*. Father, Son and Spirit describe the Triune God which arises from 'the Godhead' beyond God. All in all it's a remarkable parallel, an element of the 'perennial wisdom' at work in two very different traditions.

Okay, so there's that. But so what? You can't talk about what cannot be comprehended, you can't teach burned up. As long as it has not been apperceived, it makes no sense, or at best it's only concepts, more ideas. When it is apperceived, there is no need. So there's a valid argument (and there are teachers saying) that there's no point in splitting the atom so fine. So: all there is, is God. But how does that help the average person, or the average seeker? It doesn't seem to; they're frustrated. So there is often the developing of a teaching to help them live this dream better.

Osho, Da Free John, Ramesh, Robert Adams come to mind as only a few of the well-meaning teachers who start out with a radical message but over time dilute it into 'principles' and 'stages' and 'practices' and in some cases even insipid little inspirational 'daily reminders' when people don't understand or respond to the pure simple teaching.

## 43. Trinity

And of course the Buddhist tradition as a whole, beautiful as it is, is infamous for institutionalizing this kind of thing. Ken Wilber has even given a theoretical basis for this, saying that those in whom there is clear seeing and knowing of What Is actually have an *obligation* to come up with a less radical version that the typical seeker can comprehend.

Here, it's different. There are (are now, always have been, always will be) plenty of versions and variations, readily available, of methods for living, for how to improve your 'self,' how to raise the level of functioning of the separate self, how to feel better in daily life. There are millions of teachers able and willing to teach these methods.

On the other hand, there are apparently few who see What Is. There is arguably some benefit in having the few who do see, say what only they can say. How can there be concern about how many can understand this or even comprehend or appreciate it? That is not the point, not the purpose. Help in daily living is available in many flavors and varieties. That is not the functioning here. Does the expression of this understanding help individuals or confuse them? There is no knowing, and there is little energy spent agonizing over the question. That is being taken care of, in ways we cannot know. That, like everything else in the dream, is not 'my' problem. There is no 'intention' here. All that can be done here is to say what is known.

Things are not as they seem. None of this matters. There is no 'you,' no 'me.' There are no individuals as separate entities; there is no 'one' home. Always everywhere perfect Brilliant Stillness, and no-thing, which has no name (love and compassion and bliss are inadequate shadow-words) Outpouring constantly. Clear, perfect Love. Infinite

Presence. And seen here now always: not seen as from this mind/body thing, but as from that same Stillness, that Presence which is All that is, perhaps 'through' or 'as' this mind/body instrument. For this Stillness, this Presence, is what 'I' is.

Amen. Svaha!

# Seven

*You will realize
that it has
always been
closer to you
than any thing
you thought
you knew.*

# 44.

## How Can This Be Said?

*"The mind has to know that it can't grasp
what I'm about to describe.
The Vastness is perceiving itself out of itself
at every moment, within every particle of itself
everywhere simultaneously."*
— Suzanne Segal

—

*"When I say the word 'you'
I mean a hundred universes."*
— Rumi

How can this be said? It is seen so clearly, but with that peripheral vision: when one turns toward it to grasp it in a concept, to express it in language, it is gone. All the teachers, the ancient masters, dance around this: it brings a smile every time I come across a reference pointing sideways at this. Yet it cannot be said. It's genius. Beyond genius: absolute, staggering Brilliance. The 'divine hypnosis' is Self hypnosis.

Have you ever tried to play a game of hide and seek with yourself? Not much fun: you always know where to look, and pretending you don't isn't very convincing. Where can I hide myself from myself so that I can't find myself... until I do? You know the answer. You just don't know you know it.

You know there's something wrong with the world, with the whole set-up. It's like that splinter in your mind. It just doesn't add up; something's wrong with this picture, but you just can't for the life of you figure what. You seek and search and struggle and try and hope and pray and listen and learn and every time you feel like you're getting it, it slips away. And you realize that that's part of what's wrong; it's crazy, it shouldn't be that hard. Then, suddenly, you're given what you want; and you realize, it shouldn't be that easy. That's not what you really wanted. And you're off again, seeking and searching and struggling.

Never realizing that that is it.

Not only do you have a lifetime of your own personal history working against you, all your experiences and thoughts and memories and hurts and wounds and loves and victories and what you think you have learned and gained and lost. But even greater is the inherited weight and momentum of this whole marvelous experiment, billions of body/minds like you but different, all hell-bent in the same direction and lending encouragement and support and shared common wisdom and reassurance to coax you along from cradle to grave. Whether you join the revolution or the Republican Party or Harley Owners Group or the Catholic Church or the Islamic Jihad or a Zen monastery or NOW or AA or the AAA or the devotees of Sri Ram or the local soccer team or Weight Watchers or the hospice volunteers or

## 44. How Can This Be Said?

Greenpeace or the Marines, they're all the same. They will all encourage you to do what they do and think the way they think, and you'd like to believe them but on some level you know they're all full of shit.

You're right about that part. The whole premise is wrong. The basis on which all the working assumptions about life, the universe and everything are made, is 180 degrees off target. What is believed and taught and supported and rewarded as natural and normal, right, healthy and sane, good and true, valuable, helpful and caring, even sacred and holy, will if followed lead you right down the garden path, valiantly doing the best you can but remaining thoroughly asleep in the dream.

One of the really amazing things about all this is the realization that the whole human tradition and history and movement and tendency toward 'spirituality' and 'the holy' and 'sacredness' is entirely off track. It is totally misguided. There is nothing holy or spiritual or sacred or divine about All That Is. It is entirely a-theistic. It is completely and thoroughly impersonal from start to finish. The human tendency toward awe and mystery and the numinous is just that: a tendency, part of the programming of the body/mind organisms.

There's nothing *wrong* with it, nothing to be shunned or avoided or corrected. This particular body/mind, with both Native American and Roman Catholic backgrounds, has it in spades: that devotional, *bhakti* tendency that brings tears to the eyes when we sing *bhajans* or read Rumi; and as you may have noticed it tends to express itself accordingly. It's a wonderfully endearing quality of these body/mind things in the dream, and in fact it can be quite beautiful.

But it's only a matter of their functioning, only a matter of perspective. There's nothing inherently spiritual or holy in realizing that the one that thinks it feels spiritual or holy does not exist. It's just What Is.

> "You see, the search takes you away from yourself; it is in the opposite direction; it has absolutely no relation. The search is always in the wrong direction, so all that you consider very profound, all that you consider sacred, is a contamination in that consciousness. You may not like the word 'contamination,' but all that you consider sacred, holy and profound is a contamination." (U.G. Krishnamurti)

The Truth is the opposite of everything you have learned. Things are not as they seem nor as you have been led to believe. Thinking is not your normal state. Personal involvement is not your natural state. Even something as 'sacred' and elevated as what you call 'love' is not your natural state. Trying, caring, longing, desiring, having beliefs, having opinions, needing to defend those positions, needing anything at all; none of these are your original nature, your true being. All these are learned, conditioned behaviors, hypnosis to keep you asleep in the dream. The conditioning goes so deep you think it is your true nature, but I assure you it is not. Go back. Your Self is prior to everything that you think you know is true or real.

And when Self, this Truth, the no-thing-ness of your original nature, explodes and annihilates your dream awareness, you will realize that it has always been closer to you than any thing you thought you knew.

> "I've told you all that constitutes the very core of Truth: there is no you, no me, no Superior Being, no disciple, and no guru." (Dattatreya)

## 44. How Can This Be Said?

Nihilism? You call this nihilism? This is so far beyond nihilism you have no idea. Are we getting anywhere here? Am I saying what cannot be said? Of course not.

> "The world's existence is like the dream world of a dreamer. We sense the world to be real because we feel our body to be real, and vice-versa. This is the primordial illusion. People think that the world is ancient. Actually, it arises with your consciousness.
>
> "That which is seen is the reflection of your own consciousness.
>
> "You see yourself in the world while I see the world in myself. To you, you get born and die; while to me, the world appears and disappears."
> (Nisargadatta Maharaj)

You see? A glimpse, maybe, a glimmer; but this is pointless, because you know the unspeakable as well as I do. You are I. Here we go again.

There's only ever one thing happening here. I know, I'm always saying there's nothing happening. Same thing. It looks amazingly, infinitely complex, zillions of things interacting and intricately interrelated; but it isn't. It's completely simple. You know this. There is only ever always one thing going on, one dance, "the only dance there is," and I is dancing. And that dance is Stillness.

I once spent an afternoon listening to a teacher explaining reality like this: Say you have spent your whole life looking at a photograph of a tree. Beautiful, full color, fine resolution. So you think that's all there is; that beautiful photograph of a tree is what you think of as reality. But I'm here, he said, to take you back a step, before the photograph. (He had read Maharaj.) So I show you the negative from which the photograph was made. (This was before digital cameras.) Suddenly, you realize your whole reality has a flip side. Here in duality, everything has its opposite, which exists along with it. Now, if you place the negative over the photograph, you can see they cancel each other out. Where there is dark in the photograph, there is light in the negative, and vice versa. Even the colors are the opposite of each other. So what you get when you hold them together is: precisely nothing. The positive cancels the negative and vice versa so there is neither positive nor negative, there is nothing. Void. And that is what reality truly is. Not what you have always thought it is, and not its opposite, but the simultaneous existence and non-existence of both. Finally, I got up and walked out.

What he was saying of course is perfectly accurate. What then? What's the problem?

The tree, you fool! My god, man, go back a step yourself! There's a tree outside, in the rain and sun, roots in the dirt, leaves in the wind, which somebody pointed a camera at to make that negative and photograph. And the living truth of that tree is so far from the whole belabored logic of the photograph and its negative and the nothing of the two of them combined that you can't even guess it. Talk about Plato's cave! Wake up! All this talk is useless. The truth of What Is is so far beyond what you perceive and think and theorize that it's all really quite useless.

But you know this too.

## 44. How Can This Be Said?

"This we have now
is not imagination.
This is not grief,
or joy, not a judging state,
or an elation, or a sadness.
Those come and go.
This is Presence
that doesn't.

What else could anyone want?

This we are now
created the body, cell by cell;
the universe, star by star.
The body and the whole universe
grew from this;
this did not grow
from anything."
(Rumi)

# 45.

## Most Peculiar

*"You have to understand, most of these people are not ready to be unplugged. And many of them are so inured, so hopelessly dependent on the system that they will fight to protect it."*
— 'Morpheus' in The Matrix

—

*"Nobody told me there'd be days like these. Strange days indeed."*
— John Lennon

"A STRANGER IN A STRANGE LAND:" that's what most of the experiencing of this world amounts to since the jungle. The Brilliance, All That Is, knowing that there is no 'david,' only Consciousness streaming here; there has been some adaptation to this and so living continues through this dream character, with always everywhere perfect Brilliant Stillness, outpouring constantly and seen; now, always, not as from this mind/body thing.

The dream characters are what they are; ordinary folk going about life, the dream humming along and the dream characters playing the parts scripted, oblivious to the True and thinking their 'selves' are real. Unaware of the Brilliance that 'they' are. Most not very happy much of the time, but they do have moments; and in any case the interactions are the relatively straightforward interactions between dream characters within the parameters of the dream.

Yes, there are times when it seems comprehension breaks down and there is only severe bafflement and an inability to communicate. And yes, there is a certain unfiltered rawness to the experiencing of life, and the severe limitations of the mind/body apparatus at times become very evident. Even so, from this perspective it is all amazing and beautiful and always completely impersonal. Just seeing what arises; what will today's script bring?

It's a little surreal: here is Consciousness streaming, somehow pretending it has forgotten who it is, when here it is quite obvious who it is. The dream lacks conviction, credibility, and there's a sense of constant amazement that no one sees how phony and propped-up this whole illusion really is. It's actually full of holes, full of clues. It carries all the inconsistencies and missing bits that any dream does. Many times a day there are moments that are giveaways, when the dream cover is blown: but nobody sees this because they are all conditioned to patch in for what would otherwise bring down the whole house of cards. "Did you see that? No, I didn't either." "What was that? Oh, right, nothing. Couldn't have been." It's crazy really, but there's a certain consistency to it and it's kind of endearing.

## 45. Most Peculiar

The difference between awake and not awake is so incredibly thin it hardly can be said to exist. It's as if, to use an admittedly strange image, all that is needed is a very tiny shift in your mind, to shift your mind metaphorically to one side of where it is, by an almost imperceptible amount; and that shift, that pop would be sufficient to change the perspective enough so that all would be seen as it is. Tiny; so tiny that almost nothing is needed. I call it a 'phase shift,' probably from watching too much *Star Trek;* everything remains as it is, it's just that the perceiving is brought into phase with What Is. What has changed? Nothing; that's how tiny a shift is needed.

Another analogy. Say you had a dream or a vision and in the vision everything is streaming light. That's all there is, just light streaming. And part of the light streaming shapes itself into a chair, so you sit down. And then the light streaming over there shapes itself into a person who says, "I want to be able to wake up and see the light." You look at this streaming light formed into a person-shape and say, "But what you are is obviously streaming light." The streaming light says, "No, I don't think so, I don't experience that. I feel very dark and alone and am in so much pain. Show me how I can see this light you are talking about." Meanwhile the streaming light formed into a person-shape is practically blinding you with their beauty and brilliance, and all you can really think is, what the hell is up with this?

When things are seen like this, it's hard at times to keep in mind that from the point of view of the dream characters the gap is not so tiny as to be infinitesimal, it's so huge as to be infinite. But what you can see is that there's no reason, no need for this.

It's like, say you've just stepped into heaven. Perfection, beauty, wonder, freedom, bliss, abundance, love, everything you can think of. Astonishing. Your heart sings. Then over in the corner you notice a miserable little character curled up tight with his hand over his eyes, clutching his few dirty broken belongings, muttering to himself. You go over and try to talk to him; "Hey friend, hey, open your eyes, look around, see where you are." He curses at you, turns away, clutches his coat around him, muttering. You try again; "Hey come on man, look, everything's okay! Look, let go of that stuff, you don't need it, everything is provided here, beautiful things, anything you want." He lashes out at you, screams, "Leave me alone, don't take my stuff!" This isn't endearing, this is pathetic.

The odd thing about the 'spiritual seeker' characters, the ones that talk about wanting to wake up, is that while they are saying that they are simultaneously, and completely without realizing it, spending most of their time and energy actively doing whatever they can to prevent that from happening. Seriously. You think I'm exaggerating with all this, but I'm not. Seekers talk about waking up, about enlightenment, but almost none have any idea what they are talking about. They talk about it as something they can get, something they can come to, 'attain,' that will change them and how they experience life. It's apparent that somewhere along the line these dream characters have absorbed some dream idea of 'waking up' that apparently means some shift in the dream but quite clearly does not involve actually waking up, which would necessarily mean that the dream, and they, would cease to exist as such.

> "Seeking begins with the individual and ends in the annihilation of the individual." (Ramesh)

## 45. Most Peculiar

'Annihilation' here isn't referring to some party game. It is a total and radical thing, often bloody and brutal, called annihilation; wiping out of existence; ceasing to be; death. Not death of the body; nothing dies when the body dies. Real death; the only real death, as real as death gets: the death of an individual person/self.

Spiritual seeking is the art of walking in very small circles. This does two things: it creates the illusion of motion, of getting somewhere; and it prevents one from stopping, from becoming still, which is when one would look around and see the futility of it all. Most of all, it's not very challenging to the ego, that sense of individual self. Working on being 'spiritual' reinforces that sense of self, pretty much the opposite of doing anything that might damage it in any way, let alone lead to its death.

The streaming light is already streaming light. The little guy in the corner is already in heaven. There's literally nothing they have to do to get anywhere or become anything. The only thing that's keeping you from seeing it is this blasted insistence on hanging on to the broken little possession which you think is all you have; the idea that you are somebody. This belief, this story, that there is a person in there, with deeply cherished memories and wounds and dreams and hopes and aspirations and attributes and thoughts and theories; that is the thing that you are clutching so tightly to your chest as you engage in all this seeking, which prevents you from finding anything, from seeing where and what You are.

What would it take to get that little character hunched in the corner of heaven to get up and open his eyes and see where he is? Think about that; because what that would take, is what it would take for any seeker to awaken, to "enter the kingdom of heaven."

> "Many people do think they don't 'see' it, but I think one has to see it first before one can reject it; we see it so briefly but unconsciously reject it immediately. I think it is impossible not to see it."
> (Douglas Harding)

It's like the armchair traveler who loves the travel books and magazines but won't actually go anywhere because he doesn't want to risk traveling. Seekers talk about awakening, and read all the spiritual books and magazines, and even do all the practices, retreats and meditation and service and devotion, but only so long as it only amounts to spinning their prayer wheels and doesn't actually entail being annihilated in the process.

You really gotta let that go. It's that simple. No waking up can possibly happen as long as that hanging on to a 'me' is there. Going to *satsang* and asking all kinds of questions about the spiritual theory you're working on, or about healing the injured self, or about gaining more insight, is all quite useless, and from this perspective incomprehensible.

> "So-called self-realization is the discovery for yourself and by yourself that there is no self to discover. That will be a very shocking thing – 'Why the hell have I wasted all my life?' It's a shocking thing because it's going to destroy every nerve, every cell, even the cells in the marrow of your bones. I tell you, it's not going to be an easy thing.... You have to become completely disillusioned, then the truth begins to express itself in its own way."
> (U.G. Krishnamurti)

## 45. Most Peculiar

If you're going to do anything, do this. First, figure out whether this waking up, this enlightenment is really something you want. Do you really want to die? Do you really want for 'you' not to exist; and for living to continue, if it does, not as who you know and love as yourself but as a hollow husk with impersonal Consciousness blowing through it? If this is what you want (how can you possibly?) then you are talking about waking up from the false dream of individuality, and then you can proceed. Your thinking, your praying, your meditating, your asking questions at *satsang*, whatever you 'do,' will be with the realization that what you think you are is illusory, and with the intent of exploding, obliterating, that illusion called 'you.'

Can you 'do' this? Of course not; 'you' is a dream character following its role in the dream. But who knows what that role calls for? If that role calls for this character to wake up, then it has to start somewhere, and the character may find itself engaging in things that will ultimately bring about its own death. Not physical death. These are disposable containers; look around, they're being recycled constantly. Rather, real death, as real as death gets. Death of the one who cares.

If you decide that what you really want is something other than this complete and ultimate 'waking up,' then bless you. Have a wonderful life; enjoy the incredible edible banquet of material and spiritual and psychological and New Age goodies that are out there. Grow and expand and change and develop and improve your life immeasurably; evolve and become more mature and deeper and wiser and more beautiful. Discover your higher self and your higher purpose and fulfill them. I mean this absolutely sincerely; and even, I notice, with a touch of delicious wistfulness from what's left of the david thing. This is not in any way some kind of second class status; there is no such thing. Take what the dream has to offer; that's what the dream's there for, to be enjoyed. Consciousness only enjoys it, only perceives it at all, through the dream characters, and there have to be some through which can be experienced enjoyment of the whole panoply of the spiritual marketplace.

But in that case don't come here talking about waking up; that just doesn't make any sense at all.

# 46.

## Eternal Unborn

*"You will come in due course to realize
that your true glory lies
where you cease to exist."*
— Ramana Maharshi

*"You poor sad thing thinking death is real
all by itself."*
— Ikkyu

As for the death of the body, so-called physical death, it should be clear that a question or difficulty can only arise if there is identification as the body. Thus identified, you see bodies die; you assume that the discreet individual who was that body died with it; and you conclude that one day you yourself will die.

The ego sense of individual self tries to generate hope in an afterlife, or a rebirth, or some kind of second chance, but the evidence for these is sketchy at best and so panic and dread set in because physical death sure looks pretty final.

Most of the world religions teach some form of immortality, but you don't believe them; if you did you would not fear the annihilation of death. It has been said that fear of death is the basic, primal fear that generates all other fear, and is the underlying psychological factor shaping all of life.

All of this is illusion, and all based on the essential misconception that you are an individual, inseparably associated with the body that apparently dies.

What is unborn cannot die. You are the unborn. This is basic to the Understanding: how can there be any concern over the apparent death of these body/mind organisms, these characters in the dream, when it is known that what 'I' is, what the 'I' is that animates all such organisms, is All That Is; eternal, unbound, unborn.

> "What is real does not die. What is unreal never lived.
>
> "Once you know that death happens to the body and not to you, you just watch your body falling off like a discarded garment.
>
> "The real you is timeless and beyond life and death. The body will survive as long as it is needed. It is not important that it should live long."
> (Nisargadatta Maharaj)

After the death of the body, 'I' is the same timeless, unborn impersonal Presence which 'I' is before the birth of the body. The identification as a body/mind is a transient phase and does not effect what 'I' is.

But there is more to this. Even within the dream, even if there is identification as the body/mind you call yourself, still the fear of death is misguided and unnecessary. Our cultures

## 46. Eternal Unborn

have done us a disservice, created a bogeyman out of death that does not hold up to scrutiny. The western medical model is that death is failure; and as such it must be denied, avoided, postponed as much as possible. This belief runs deep in our culture, but it is only conditioning, and is not shared by many other cultures. Indeed, once again, a little reflection reveals it to be insane thinking. Once the body is born, its death is inevitable, absolutely, certainly; a natural consequence of birth. In what reasonable way can it possibly be seen as failure, as something to be avoided?

No one ever experiences their own death. No one ever will. By definition, it is not possible. The most widely accepted definition of physical death is 'brain death;' flatline; no sensory perceptions, and no processing of perceptions; no thought, emotion, memory, no internal activity of any kind; therefore, what we call no experience. Death is the ceasing of experience in that body/mind. Therefore, if there is no experiencing in that body/mind, there can be no experiencing of death in that body/mind.

It's similar to falling asleep. In all the times you have fallen asleep during your life, you have never experienced it. You experience being drowsy, you experience lying down, getting sleepier... next thing you know you are waking up and postulating that at some point you must have fallen asleep, but you do not have a direct experience of that because the one who would have experienced falling asleep, had it been awake, had fallen asleep!

So it is with death. There is perceiving and experiencing up until death, then the experiencing stops and we say that the body/mind has died. Simple. Death is never experienced, because experiencing stops. How can one possibly fear that which one will never experience?

Certainly, it is a possibility that there may be pain or suffering in the body/mind before death, before the experiencing ceases. And this may be feared, or at the very least not looked forward to. This is a natural response in the body/mind. So, we can be clear: it is old age, or sickness, or a specific disease, which may be feared. But death itself does not exist as something to be experienced; it is merely the word we give to the cessation of experiencing.

Much fear of death arises from misinformation, based on the segregation and active avoidance of death in our cultures. In fact, the body is well designed to die, and it is rare that physical death itself is accompanied by intense suffering. It does happen, yes, but most commonly pain or suffering comes before, during the sickness, and when the time for death arrives the physical and mental functionings naturally draw back and shut down gradually. Death is usually much easier and gentler than the popular imagination holds. This is confirmed by those who work regularly with the dying.

At bodily death, then, Consciousness no longer experiences the dream in or through that body/mind organism. The animating force of Consciousness ceases functioning in that body, and so the body no longer appears animated, is no longer sentient, no longer is what we call 'alive,' and it rapidly disintegrates, decays into its constituent elements. But there can be no direct experience of this because the experiencing has, by definition, ceased already. And Consciousness, which is what I is, what You are, which is All That Is, continues; is unborn, never dies, is eternal. Was never limited to that body/mind in any case.

## 46. Eternal Unborn

So we return to the concept that the only true death is not the death of the body but the death, the annihilation, of the sense of individual self. It is this death, this annihilation of self, that the ego fears and is busy constructing morbid, gruesome fantasies about. It is this death that generates the fear of physical death. And it is this death that is actually worth investigating.

There is an image frequently encountered in dreams: an open door, darkness beyond; stepping through, falling into empty space. The ego would have you wake up at this point in a sweat, fear of death making your heart pound.

But this reaction is only a matter of conditioning, of belief; a matter of identification as the body. In fact, the imagery is very appropriate. Nearly every spiritual tradition advocates stepping off the edge into Void. The ego sense of individual self will necessarily interpret its own negation as Void; that which it is not, that where it cannot go.

Please see that this next bit is very rational and quite simple, but transformative if truly understood. It is rare to find anyone to whom this concept has even occurred, let alone one who truly understands it. It is the secret of life and death, and the certain knowing inherent in awakening:

If 'this,' the world of things and ideas,
is seen as what is real, as true, as 'reality,'
then That which is completely and radically 'not-this,'
for which there are no words or ideas within 'this,'
will necessarily be seen as no thing, as unreal, as Void.
Thus it may be feared, dreaded, denied.

It is only when 'this,' this so-called 'reality'
is completely understood to be dreamlike illusion
that what is 'not-this'
will, at the same time, be seen to be What Is.

Void, then, is not your enemy, but your true Self;
and it is the function of the nonexistent, false sense of
individual self to hide this from you.
The fear and avoidance is seen to be misplaced;
in fact it is now impossible; it disappears, and
the heart turns from the illusion of 'this'
and opens to What Is.
Knowing that its true glory lies where it ceases to exist.

There is much to be said for dying now and not waiting until the body dies; things might be a little rushed then, and one might find it hard to concentrate. Now, in the midst of what you take to be your life, there can be, if needed, a 'positive' practice of building up and strengthening the sense of individual self until it is strong enough to undergo the 'negative' process of realizing that it is a sham, unreal after all, never did exist; and then perhaps it can be let go, let die, let fall away.

Then there can be a liberation from that ego that haunted and plagued us all our lives with fears of its own demise, for it turns out not to be anything real, nothing even to struggle against or try to defeat. The ego, and the death it has convinced you is your greatest fear, is only a tired tape recording in an empty room, which from outside you thought was a powerful and fearful enemy; but now the plug is pulled and the voice slurs to a stop.

This is what it is to 'die before you die;' to step through the gateless gate into Void, and to walk the universe alone.

## 47.

## Magical World

*"The world is illusory.
Brahman alone is real.
Brahman is the world."*
*- Ramana Maharshi*

*"The whole world in all ten directions
is a single bright jewel.
What's it got to do with understanding?"*
*- Gensha*

### I

ALL IS AS IT IS.
It's a magical world; it's all done with mirrors.
If this dream has any rules,
one seems to be that if you turn away from something
you will be facing it again.
What you turn away from
what you turn toward
is yourSelf.

Only the one who sees their true face
without a mirror
knows the Self.
Then the magic bubble is burst
and all projection ceases
for there is but one
without a second.

There is no separation or distance
because there is nothing to be separate or distant.
That which is seeing
through the eyes of a loved one,
through the eyes of a stranger,
(the eyes of the mouse, the hawk,
the brightest star, this stone;)
is that which is seeing through
what you call 'your' eyes.

And on some 'level' all know this.
This is the whisper, the haunting, the sensing,
(so often misunderstood)
like a splinter in your mind:
That which is seeing is All.
And All is as it is.

## II

*I*N HIS REMARKABLE LITTLE BOOK, *Gifts of Unknown Things*, biologist Lyall Watson mentions, among many other things, ocean squid. From a biologist's point of view there are some odd facts about squid, which add up rather strangely, if they add up at all.

## 47. Magical World

The squid has an eye which is astonishing to find in a mollusc such as itself, a fairly undeveloped unsegmented invertebrate. The eye of the squid is extraordinarily developed: an iris, a lens that can focus at variable distances, and a retina with both rod and cone cells for seeing both contrast and color. The eye of the squid is every bit as developed as the human eye and has the ability to see as well. In spite of this, the animal to which this eye is attached does not have a brain with anything close to the capacity to process the visual information provided by the amazing eye. In fact it doesn't really have a brain at all. Its nervous system has only very rudimentary nerve ganglia which serve the basic motor functions of the organism; no brain, no optic center to form images from the vast information received by the complex eye.

Also, there are literally billions of squid. They are highly mobile, and are present throughout the oceans; at every depth, every temperature gradient, in every ocean of the world, day and night.

An eye capable of the best vision on the planet. Attached to a highly mobile and ubiquitous but extremely simple and easily reproduced organism, with a rudimentary nervous system having hardly any optical processing ability.

I read the book many years ago, but I still remember being absolutely floored by the implications of the one-liner with which Watson concluded his discussion on the squid:
> "Visitors are warned that this facility is under constant closed-circuit surveillance."

I wonder now if Watson knew how close he was:

> "Seeing truly is not merely a change in the direction of seeing but a change at its very center, in which the seer himself disappears." (Ramesh)

It is clear that it is not the body/minds, not the organisms, human or squid, that are seeing.

That which is seeing
   through the squid's eye
is that which is seeing through
   what you call 'your' eyes.

That which is seeing is All.

# 48.

## ALL IS WELL

*"Oh dweller within,*
*You are the light in the heart's lotus.*
*In every heart you are.*
*And if but once only*
*the mind of the one who seeks*
*will open to receive You,*
*truly that one is free forever."*
*- Shankara*

So much worrying, so much anxiety, unrest. All the billions of body/mind organisms, trying, longing, hoping, striving, struggling. Hardly one is free of that inner crying out, that quiet fear. *Dukha*; suffering. It is the way of all the earth.

If you read *Silence of the Heart*, the transcriptions of Robert Adams' talks, you will hear him saying over and over, "all is well." His teacher (after the fact, as Ramesh was in this case) was Ramana Maharshi, who so frequently answered all manner of questions in the same way: "all is well."

Many times I say that the Understanding, this teaching, is not about comfort. Not about helping the ego feel safe and comfortable. Self realization is annihilation, pure and simple. The truth is that you are not; there can be no question of the 'you' being comforted. And that is true; this is not about comfort, but about truth. If truth is to be known, the individual self is not to be comforted, but totally lost, annihilated, dissolved. There is no other way: there is no way to wake up while staying comfortably asleep. Comforting, stabilizing, strengthening the sense of individual self can only lead to prolonging the suffering. The sense of individual self, looking for comfort, must always be frustrated, always come up empty, for it is not.

And yet. Yet if only once, only for a moment, there could be letting go, if there could be that pop of the shift in focus and the individual self seen beyond, seen for what it is, "an echo, a rainbow, a phantom, and a dream," then there is something. Then the individual self is gone, and needs no comforting. The individual self was simply a thought, an idea; a 'false imagination' that cried out for comforting. When the true nature of things is seen, apperceived, then there comes something far beyond comfort, though there is nothing any longer that needs it.

It is seen that what one is is All That Is, and That is the constant outpouring of Love beyond love, Beauty beyond beauty, compassion bliss gratitude glory wonder perfection; streaming, outpouring, beyond comprehension.

All that is, is described as *Sat Chit Ananda*. Not a being, but Being itself; existence itself, not a thing existing. This is pure Awareness, pure Consciousness. Be-ing which is Conscious-ness is absolute, perfect, knows no bounds,

## 48. All Is Well

and spills out in itself, uncontained; is always everything everywhere.

This spilling out, this outpouring of Be-ing Consciousness as itself is all of *this*. All of this universe, planet, worlds of senses and ideas, worlds of things and non-things, these bodies, these minds, these trees roads houses squirrels insects telephones.

All of this, everything everywhere, is not as it appears, as some solid separate material stuff. The physicists will tell you this: look closely enough and this body or this table are not solid substance, but are composed of molecules, then atoms, then subatomic particles which themselves are not particles at all, but moments of energy. I am telling you that this energy which everything is, is What You Are; is Consciousness, Being, outpouring itself in itself. This is what is called *Ananda*, because the very nature of Consciousness outpouring in itself is perfect love, beauty, completion. Bliss. This streaming is what is *perceived* as all this, all this crazy world, including the body/mind you think is 'you.' But in truth, when seen as it is, this is not you, this car is not a car, these groceries are not groceries; these are all pure love light consciousness bliss streaming here.

This is obvious. It is seen here always; once seen it cannot not be seen. It is inexpressible. There is no way I can communicate this without sounding like a blathering nut case or like the Dr. Bronner's bottle. But it is true. All is well. All is so incredibly well. Everyone is asleep and does not see it. And so they "lead lives of quiet desperation," lives of anxiety and fear. But those few who are awake and see it, witness life being lived in constant, total amazement.

And since everything is literally made out of pure Love beyond love, streaming; since this pure Love beyond love is the 'stuff' out of which is made everything that we perceive as creation; how then can anything, the smallest thing, not be well? Everything, the smallest thing, is God, is Self, is your own true nature and the true nature of All That Is, pure Awareness, pure Love, Outpouring as Itself.

The human race truly has no idea what love is.

I cannot give comfort to the individual self that seeks it. Perhaps in some limited way others can, telling stories here in the dream that bring some fictitious comfort to these fictitious selves.

But when there can be total letting go of that idea of being a separate self, then what is seen is the love compassion bliss that you are and that the slightest thing is.

If nothing else, trust me on this. There is no way anything at all can not be well. All is perfection, pure bliss love outpouring. Any perceptions to the contrary are simply not true. All is well. Totally.

*Svaha!*

# 49.

## A Parable: Wake Up!

*"Mind and Maya are one.*
*Maya fuses with the mind.*
*The three worlds are plunged into delusions.*
*To whom can I explain this?"*
*– Kabir*

### I

AS THIS BOOK WAS BEING PREPARED for printing, some unusual news found its way to this small corner of the universe. The winter had been spent deeply immersed in caring for both of my aging parents, and sequestered at the computer working out a final manuscript, so I was a little out of the loop; and besides, even in this digital age of internet and email, the snow-covered hills of Vermont are not exactly at the center of the world of Advaita. So some months had passed before an old-fashioned telephone call brought news to this rural outpost.

What follows is a parable. Listen well.

Some months after my last visit with Ramesh, it seems that there was a somewhat similar situation, in which many seekers were exposed to their own Beloved Teacher's strange behavior and departure from the teaching of pure non-duality. At an international seminar held on India's west coast, this Beloved Teacher apparently exhibited erratic behavior and inconsistent teaching not unlike what I had observed in my teacher, months earlier.

According to most accounts, the 150 or so ardent spiritual seekers and long-time devotees in attendance were surprised at the uncharacteristically defensive and argumentative way in which the Teacher treated questions, often answering with mundane non-sequiturs and irrelevancies; his comments impugning the moral standing of his own guru as well as other masters; his clear departure from the pure non-dual teachings of the perennial wisdom; and assertions that only his teaching was correct and all others that had come before were false.

By all accounts the gathering erupted in confusion, recriminations, accusations, and general chaos. In the midst of this, something even stranger emerged. Allegations of sexual misconduct were made against the Beloved Teacher; allegations which he first denied outright, then admitted to and briefly apologized for, only to immediately dismiss as irrelevant and unimportant. Needless to say, devoted followers of the guru, "widely regarded as the world's greatest living sage," were devastated.

Life is messy, isn't it? Who the hell's dream is this anyway? Things never quite work out the way they are 'supposed' to. You can just hear the disillusioned hopes and dreams and projections crumbling all around you. Flameouts

## 49. A Parable: Wake Up!

and meltdowns by famous and dearly loved gurus are not uncommon, of course. Occupational hazard, it would appear. The stresses set up, the expectations and projections on both sides, are immense, and inherently unstable.

Let me be clear: I do not know all the details of what happened. I do not know who else was involved or why, or what the explanations were. Frankly, I'm not interested. There is no interest in condemning the Teacher or excusing him; nor in condemning or excusing his accusers. From this perspective, there is no reason to defend him or to join the chorus of voices disparaging him. There is nothing at stake here, nothing happening. The drama of the dream unfolds. Who is it that cares what the dream characters are 'doing?'

There is so much pain and confusion around such an 'event' that investigation is made difficult. The tendency in these circumstances is to project and exteriorize even more than usual, and this only exacerbates the pain and confusion. Moments such as these are moments of *krisis*, in the original meaning of the Greek word: a moment of decision, a turning point.

There is an opportunity here, if one can but see it through the storm. There is an opportunity to see all that arises here, the disappointment, the anguish, the recriminations, the blaming, the demands for explanations or for amends, as the outward projections they are; and an invitation to turn and look within, where can be found both the root causes and their dissolution.

On the part of the Beloved Teacher's handlers and promoters, of course, anger is understandable: if you have committed yourself in good faith to marketing something, only to find out that what you are promoting is not as represented, it would be natural enough to be pissed off and feel betrayed or double-crossed. It's bad for business, damn it.

Somewhat more disheartening (though not surprising) is the speed with which ravingly loyal devotees made for the exit, hurling condemnations behind them. Illustrates the truism that here in duality, love and hate have much in common and are never far apart.

Otherwise rational but now terribly wounded devotees (*former* devotees) almost instantly began deconstructing their Beloved Teacher. 'All this calls into question whether he was ever enlightened, ever had the ultimate Understanding.' Really? Well, if he was never enlightened, what were you doing sitting listening to him all those years, getting all those deep spiritual insights? 'We were mistaken.' Well, if you were mistaken then, could you be mistaken now? How would you know? Do you have even the slightest idea what it is that you are talking about? The ego is so alarmed at having been caught with its own pants down (so to speak), having sworn devotion and gone all gooey-eyed toward the great guru who was supposed to make you one of the chosen few but who turns out to be a dirty old man (oops!) that it's backpedaling as fast as it can and making even less sense than usual. Re-writing history is the oldest form of spin control.

A sad shaking of the head; 'I could never call him *bhagwan* now.' What, are you nuts? *You* are *bhagwan*; the UPS driver is *bhagwan*; Bill Clinton and George Bush are *bhagwan*; the marauding raccoons pillaging my garden are *bhagwan*. Madonna, Britney Spears, and J.Lo's grandmother are *bhagwan*, for god's sake. Orange soda, cheese twists, and

## 49. A Parable: Wake Up!

Oreos are all *bhagwan*. How does one old geezer get an exemption?

Very well. If one were to conjure up a comment on the relative stature of this particular Beloved Teacher, I know of no one among the leading luminaries of Advaita (other than, understandably, those who were his own disciples) who would have maintained, even before this event, that he was ever of the uncompromising caliber of, for example, a Ramana Maharshi or a Nisargadatta Maharaj. The Beloved Teacher himself would not maintain any such thing, and never did. He is a classic adherent to the *jnani* tradition, an intelligent and adroit and relentless mind, who says that he considers himself lucky never to have had big spiritual or mystical experiences.

In the Maharshi there was not only such a mind, but a heart that had been completely exploded, incinerated, in the Love beyond love that is All. And when what is Understood by the mind is also known by heart, when the mind and the heart are no longer two, this inseeing in the heartmind is deeper even than Understanding. Look at their photographs; this is evident even there. The Beloved Teacher's eyes are piercing, penetrating. Insistent. This is captivating, challenging, inspiring. Ramana's eyes are infinity, Void, the total death of self in Love. This is unspeakable.

But awakened? Who can say? Who could say before this event, and who can say now? Before, there is a rush to acclaim him "undoubtedly the world's leading Teacher alive today..." Who on earth is qualified to make such a judgement? After, there is a rush to call him phony. Look within: if you thought him awakened before, and have your doubts now, you must have the integrity to realize that apparently events can prove you wrong, and you are in no position now, nor were you then, to be the judge. How deeply the Understanding of no-self permeates in the case of any body/mind is, to use the Beloved Teacher's own terminology, between that one and God.

What is the need to label anyone teacher? What is the need to label anyone fraud? Where is the expectation? Where is the disappointment? If you come to disagree with or dislike a guru, there can be staying or there can be leaving. Go somewhere else. Or not. What happens is what is in the flow of Consciousness to happen. The flow of Consciousness will take care of the guru, as it will take care of you. What is to blame?

Please see that this is not about that. Like everything in the manifestation, it is not as it appears.

## II

WELL-MEANING FRIENDS SPEAK of this 'terrible scandal' and ask, what are we to do now?

Well, let's take it from the top. This has been said here many times, but here we are in the trenches; so, once more into the breach. All there is, is Presence, Awareness. This pure Presence, pure Awareness, All That Is, appears as all this world of people and things and ideas. There are no separate persons or entities of any kind, any where. All separation and distinction into separate individual persons or entities is part of the overall shared illusion under which that which thinks of itself as the human race labors. To whom can I explain this?

## 49. A Parable: Wake Up!

You're *making this all up!* Literally. It's all projection of mind in Consciousness. Telling stories. The whole house of cards being constantly propped up and reinforced by telling itself *stories of separation*. Like this one. Can you see? Stop! Go back! Wake up!

Once this is understood, inseen, apperceived, every problem or issue which has ever been known or ever will be known goes away. Because all problems and issues are based on distinctions, on a belief in separation.

Granted, the Beloved Teacher does not talk the way Maharaj talked; always, uncompromisingly, from the single point of the Absolute. The Beloved Teacher often, and increasingly of late, says things that certainly sound very dualistic. Can it be maintained that, in the tradition of the 'crazy wisdom' of gurus, all of these are said intentionally, to steer seekers away from the trap of big dramatic thinking and back into their own hearts until they are ready to see it for themselves? Or is there perhaps some 'slippage' in the Beloved Teacher body/mind? Is this 'slippage' purely a matter of ego and lack of understanding, or is there a biological, physiological component, involving his advanced age? As long as it is viewed from the point of view of the dream characters who take themselves – and any teacher, Beloved or otherwise – as individuals, one way or another there will seem to be a problem.

But you see, so what? Here's the point. All of this is Presence, all this is happening in that Presence, that Consciousness, through apparent body/mind organisms: and once there is not identification as one of these organisms, as this body/mind, then what happens in any one of these organisms is simply not significant. When you are disturbed by the Beloved Teacher, you are not seeing that you *are* the Beloved Teacher; or more accurately: what you are, the Beloved Teacher is.

It is inevitable that the whole variety and array of possible events and behaviors and thoughts and lives will happen: even though, as is also inevitable, there will be parts of this variety that you do not 'like.' It is only ignorance, often quite self-righteous ignorance, which judges the infinite variety and finds some 'appropriate' and some not.

It is all the perfect unfolding of totality in Consciousness. The so-called sage knows this, and knows that the body and mind which others would call 'him' or 'her' is included in this understanding.

This is nowhere near politically correct, but can you see that directing anger and venom and outrage at some'one' who you erroneously see as separate from yourself, and set up as someone special on a pedestal, and who you then hold to a particular set of arbitrarily constructed rules which prevail in a particular culture at a particular time, only to then have them dis-illusion you... is absurd?

Scenario one. When the complete disidentification as a separate self – as an individual entity – occurs, all there is is awareness, no one aware. There may be witnessing a different approach to the teaching, for whatever 'reasons,' taking shape in the mind. There may be witnessing 'inappropriate' actions happening. There may or may not be witnessing some thought that these things may at some time have repercussions. There might be witnessing the general furor and reaction in the 'other' apparent body/minds when these things become known. Perhaps there is witnessing an attempt to minimize the chaos by trying to explain

## 49. A Parable: Wake Up!

the insight that none of this is, that none of this matters; or perhaps there is simply witnessing this impersonal witnessing itself being interpreted as 'denial,' 'insensitivity,' or 'cover-up.' *None* of it matters: it is all the perfect unfolding. This stuff happens all the time; why should it matter more if it is happening in 'this' body/mind rather than in another?

Scenario two. What would bring a respected spiritual teacher to repudiate the spiritual teaching for which he was respected? To contradict in his own name the received teaching of which he was custodian? *If,* perhaps, such a teacher's own awakening had consisted of an experience and an awareness somewhat less than the total annihilation of self. *If,* hypothetically, the *total* disidentification as a separate entity, which all the masters including his own guru spoke of, did not actually occur in his case. And *if,* nevertheless, his teacher had clearly said things to him that he had at least interpreted as saying that awakening had occurred. As life progressed, the ongoing experience of existing as a separate self would continue – despite the awakening having been *said* to have occurred. Would this not set up a certain amount of stress in the body/mind system? On the one hand there is the received teaching of the perennial wisdom that this awakening consists of the annihilation of any sense of a separate self. And at first there is passing this teaching on. But at the same time, there is a continued experience of actually living as a separate self. In good faith and with the best intentions, would not the received explanation of what awakening is, need to undergo interpretation and modification?

Scenario three. What would it be like, even for a sage, to have an unstable student hear you say, "you are not this body:

you are the All," and have them finally lose their moorings and tip over the edge into psychotic megalomania? Would it, perhaps, lead you to tone down the teaching, to say and do things to actively steer these high-strung seekers *away* from this crazy-making stuff, trusting in Consciousness that those who will, will find it nonetheless?

Scenario four. In any case, what part would advancing age and its effects on mind and body have in all of this?

Or, scenario five. Maybe the guy's a schmuck, a complete fraud from start to finish.

Think about it. Would you know? How would you know? Is it important to know? Who is it that thinks it's important to know?

Ah, now, finally, we're getting somewhere. Our old friend, that sense of being a separate self, the so-called ego, that propped-up hallucination, needs to continue to prop itself up.

It's all done with mirrors. You gotta realize, if there are issues about an ego out there, there are issues about an ego in here. *Regardless* of whether or not you are 'right' about the ego out there.

What do you say we let Beloved Teachers everywhere worry about Beloved Teachers? What is going on in the body/mind organism of this one? Is there remorse, regret? Is there arrogance, anger? Is there peace, bemusement? How can you know? What is happening is happening, what will happen will happen. If it is in the unfolding of totality for him to self-destruct, that will happen. If he is to emerge

## 49. A Parable: Wake Up!

from this unscathed as a great teacher, that will happen. If he is to somehow muddle along more or less as before, events will bring that about. It's all taken care of.

> "Secret retributions are always restoring the level, when disturbed, of the divine justice. It is impossible to tilt the beam... Settles forevermore the ponderous equator to its line, and man and mote, and star and sun, must range to it, or be pulverized by the recoil." (Ralph Waldo Emerson)

The Beloved Teacher has not 'done' anything to anyone. If there is making some'one' into a god and then it becomes evident that Consciousness streams here through 'flawed' instruments, well, there it is. Big surprise. Welcome to your own projections. The projections by which that false sense of self can continue to believe in itself.

### III

THE ISSUE OF SEXUAL MISBEHAVIOR is highly charged. Many may feel that this is most important, but from this perspective that assumption must be investigated.

I was recently reading that Mahatma Gandhi in his latter years was known to regularly sleep with his barely pubescent early-teenage nieces. Wow. The culture we live in would have some labels for that, no? Remember Nisargadatta Maharaj's answer to the question of whether the sage will always exhibit exemplary behavior? What are you talking about? Exemplary according to whom, according to what standard? (And can such sayings be used to justify irresponsible behavior? Sure, the devil can cite scripture for his purpose, and even "God is love" can be so misused; does that make it less true?)

Cultural moral norms vary widely according to time and place. This is hard for most to accept: we've all been trained (brow-beaten, really) to absolutize the current norms as 'natural', 'God-given,' or 'self-evident,' when in fact they are totally relative. There may be room for tolerance on some kinds of behavior, but not on *that*... whatever *that* happens to be for you. This is not even open for discussion, either in society at large or among spiritual seekers, and the penalties for disagreeing are the most severe a society can mete out.

Meanwhile, my friends the Shuar in the Amazon jungle have a highly sophisticated society, in many ways more enlightened than our own, which has functioned smoothly, joyfully, respectfully, healthily, for literally thousands of years; and it has done so on a set of sexual norms and mores and practices which would land any and all of them in a federal penitentiary, and have them all branded as perverts and listed on the internet as sex offenders, if the good people of the United States of America had anything to say about it. What are you talking about? According to whom?

At the risk of bringing down the great wrath of the politically and psychologically and spiritually correct crowd, let me say this to the women who were involved (who have stated that their involvement was willing and not in any way coerced by the Beloved Teacher) and to all those who may identify in some way with them; and also to those who were or are involved with the Beloved Teacher in a guru-devotee relationship and who are disturbed by these events. I do not know who you are, and this is not meant to offend; it is meant in thoughtfulness and compassion.

When the request, or the suggestion, was first made, why didn't you hightail it back to Sedona (or Chelsea, or

## 49. A Parable: Wake Up!

Munich...)? Or, simply walk out, go somewhere else, find another guru? Wouldn't it be fairly clear at that point, from your perspective as an identified body/mind 'person,' that something was amiss? If you don't feel it is appropriate now, how could it have been appropriate then? Stop! Investigate into this. If all this is so exploitative and manipulative and sordid, what are you doing in the middle of it?

Instead of looking outwards, look within. That need for specialness is strong, is it not?

Yes of course, the guru-disciple relationship is an unequal one, and the guru carries great responsibility. Let the guru own his part. You get to look at your part. Even if your part is one tenth his part, if you focus on his part and avoid looking intently at your own you will be forever crippled, the more so because you will always find many who will agree with you and support you in your woundedness. You can use that support to be right, to be forever a victim of a Beloved Teacher gone bad, and in so doing strengthen your identity and your sense of individual self; or, you can move toward discarding all of it and realizing who You Are. What an amazing, once in a lifetime invitation and opportunity to awaken!

So it seems you've helped to publicly discredit an old man (who, if truth be told, was doing a pretty good job of that himself, even without your help) and shame yourselves. What are *you* going to do now?

May I make a suggestion? And I offer this both to those whose main concern is with the inappropriate sexual behavior of a teacher in such a position, and to those who are more disturbed by the corruption of the Teaching. And of course you can consider this as optional. It's not up to you anyway.

Go back. Back up. Whatever place you have come to in this, whether you blame someone else or blame yourself, whether you feel vindicated or feel used, disappointed or betrayed; back up. All of this is only facade. *It is the world that has been pulled over your eyes to blind you from the truth.* You think this is real, as real as it gets; you, this life, these events. In truth all this, all that you feel is real and important, is only story, is only conditioned belief in the mind. Back up, to what is prior to this.

Go back. In this day and age, somebody tells you there is an enlightened master in India, and you can buy an air ticket and in a few hours be sitting on the carpet in front of him. The American Dream Machine has led you to believe you can short-cut a thousand lifetimes and just show up as close as you can to what you've heard is the top.

By Indian guru standards, this Beloved Teacher is very westernized and very gentle and does not talk in radical terms at all. This makes him very Beloved, but tends to disguise the simple fact that most who have shown up at his house were in way over their heads. I really don't want to hurt anyone's feelings here, but basically you've been to some seminars (maybe twenty years of seminars) with some lower-tier New Age wingdings in Santa Barbara, or on the London or Amsterdam *satsang* scene, done some meditation retreats, visited some ashrams and had some initiations, and now you figure you're ready for the big time. But it's *all dreamstuff.*

Ramana Maharshi quite likely would have simply ignored you and your questions, as he did many. Nisargadatta Maharaj would have unceremoniously thrown you out on your ear. The Beloved Teacher smiles and talks about

## 49. A Parable: Wake Up!

feeling comfortable and peaceful in everyday living, and you feel great, and you go have *chai* with the other seekers and talk about it, and it's all very rewarding and you feel you're really getting somewhere.

It doesn't make any difference: it is all projection, and none of this drama would have happened were you not completely and literally full of your*self.*

Suddenly everybody has theories about whether Beloved Teacher is in over *his* head. That's Beloved Teacher's problem. Let him worry about that. Everybody is arguing that gurus should follow the behavioral norms of the culture they are in, even if for them it's all relative and unimportant. That's not your problem! Let the gurus worry about their problems. Find out what your problem is and work with that.

Everyone who is concerned about these events has been given a gratuitous whack upside the head and you're wasting it speculating about the Beloved Teacher! The Beloved Teacher is completely irrelevant! Your problem is that you're taking the dream that *you* are projecting as real, as something outside. Stop. Go back.

This will not be fun, will not be thrilling, will not feel good or stroke your identity as an advanced spiritual seeker, the way going to India and sitting with a Beloved Teacher did. Do the work you need to do, find the help you need to find. What form this will take is not up to you. Nothing is. It will happen. If there is openness, if there is consent. If there is surrender.

Instead of looking outwards, look within. Whatever is not present in deep sleep does not exist. Gurus and teachings and various behaviors are not there in deep sleep. Nor are *satsangs* and seminars and books like this. What are you doing? Invite silence, stillness. Don't waste your time doing anything other than being silent, being still within. Anything which is your'self' is illusion, not true, does not matter. And it is this that you project outward, onto the blank screen without. Anything which is 'out there' is illusion, not true, does not matter. Let yourself be emptied of these. Let there be emptiness. Let yourself be ripped open, hollowed out, gutted.

Be aware that what form this will take is not up to you, and that it may take 'time.' It may take a lifetime, may take more than a lifetime. It doesn't matter. Let yourself be brought to a place where it doesn't matter. In stillness, find yourself asking the dangerous question, the question that the ego does not want you to think of, the question that will end your life. Let yourself be brought to a place where it is no longer necessary to find some'one' to blame, either yourself or another. Where that need for specialness no longer destroys you. Where it is no longer necessary, or possible, to turn away from yourSelf and look outside of yourSelf to label what is 'wrong' or 'right.' Where it is not possible to look outside yourSelf to see What Is.

Looking outside continues the dream. Only looking within, relentlessly deep within, past and prior to the superfluous levels – intellect and reason and emotion and feeling and psyche and subconscious – to What You Are; only this can lead to the awakening which itself has nothing to do with either without or within.

Wake up!

―――――――

"Reality is what we take to be true.
What we take to be true is what we believe.
What we believe is based on our perceptions.
What we perceive depends on what we look for.
What we look for depends on what we think.
What we think depends on what we perceive.
What we perceive determines what we believe.
What we believe determines what we take to be true.
What we take to be true is our reality."

―――――――

- David Bohm

# Epilogue: An Eckhartian Ontology

*"He who wants to understand my teaching
of releasement must himself be perfectly released."*
— Meister Eckhart

*"There is an unborn, unmade, uncreated.
Were it not for this unborn, unmade, uncreated,
there would be no release from
the born, the made, the created."*
— Buddha

## I

KEN WILBER WAS ONCE ASKED why it was that the East has had such a rich tradition of transcendent spirituality over the centuries, while one has to look much harder to find it in the Western traditions: "How could a whole civilization miss the point for so long...?"

Wilber responded,

> "Imagine if, the very day the Buddha attained his enlightenment, he was taken out and hanged precisely because of that realization. And if any of his followers claimed to have the same realization, they were also hanged. Speaking for myself, I would find this something of a disincentive...
>
> "As soon as any spiritual practitioner began to get too close to the realization... that one's own mind is intrinsically one with primordial Spirit – then frighteningly severe repercussions usually followed."

All the more amazing, then, that the teachings and writings of medieval European mystics such as Hildegard of Bingen, Mechtild of Magdebourg, John of the Cross and Teresa of Avila, Henry Suso, John Tauler, and the anonymous English author of *The Cloud of Unknowing*, among others, should have survived at all.

Meister Eckhart, a German friar of the Order of Preachers of St. Dominic, lived and taught in the years 1260 to 1327. Just how he came to the Understanding which he espoused (or which espoused him) has not been recorded: however, his writings and sermons speak of the same truth of radical non-duality that mystics and sages, East and West, have always pointed toward.

Eckhart spoke of something he called "releasement," an ultimate letting-go which amounts to a total negation and annihilation of the individual self. This releasement opens into the "breakthrough beyond God," which for all intents and purposes corresponds with what is referred to in other traditions as awakening, enlightenment, or the Understanding. What he saw, he insisted could not be understood unless and until this releasement and breakthrough occurred, when all would become obvious.

What Eckhart taught, what his releasement is a letting-go *into*, is a unity which dramatically transcended medieval Christian belief. The human and the divine, he saw, are "one unique unity without difference," because "prior to distinction into substances... the acting of God and the becoming of man join both God and man into one identical event."

Being, for Eckhart, is Presence – which is one, universal. Western philosophers from Aristotle to Thomas Aquinas had seen separate beings as entities separate from the Creator. For Eckhart this is not so: Being is God; and inasmuch as anything is, it is God, having "the identical being and the identical substance and nature... If God's nature is my nature, then the divine being is my being. Thus God is more intimately present to all creatures than the creature is to itself."

"There is a power in the mind," he said, "which touches neither time nor flesh; it emanates from spirit and remains in spirit..." Again, "There is something in the mind of such a kind that, if the mind were entirely thus, it would be uncreated."

> "When I still stood in the ground, the soil, the river, and the source of the Godhead, no one asked me where I was going and what I was doing. There was no one there to question me. But when I went out, all creatures cried out, 'God.'"

Needless to say, this sort of talk got him into very serious trouble with the Inquisition from Rome, before whose tribunal he was required to defend himself against charges of heresy – charges which, as Wilber alluded to, carried penalties of exquisitely medieval forms of torture and execution. But it is clear that Eckhart could not not see what he saw, and could not not speak of it even though it is also clear that there was more than a little frustration that none of his listeners appeared able to understand. He sometimes called those who followed the external religious practices of his time "ignorant asses;" and when the Inquisition tribunal incorrectly paraphrased his teaching he somewhat curtly replied that the statement as phrased was "insane."

At times his sermons, in the language of his day, begin to sound remarkably like the sayings of Ramana Maharshi or Nisargadatta Maharaj:

> "I beseech you for the love of God that you understand this truth if you can. But should you not understand it, do not worry yourselves because of it, for the truth I want to speak of is of such a kind that only a few good people will understand it...
>
> "My essential being is above God insofar as we comprehend God as the principle of creatures. Indeed, in God's own being, where God is raised above all being and distinctions, I was myself, I willed myself, and I knew myself to create this man that I am. Therefore I am cause of myself according to my being which is eternal, but not according to my becoming which is temporal. Therefore also I am unborn, and according to my unborn being I can never die. According to my unborn being I have always been, I am now, and shall eternally remain... In my eternal birth all things were born, and I was cause of myself as well as of all things... And if I myself were not, God would not be either: that God is God, of this I am a cause. If I were not, God would not be God. There is, however, no need to understand this...
>
> "In the breakthrough... I am above all created kind and am neither God nor creature. Rather, I am what I was and what I shall remain now and forever...

## Epilogue: An Eckhartian Ontology

> For in this breakthrough it is bestowed upon me that I and God are one. There I am what I was, and I neither diminish nor grow, for there I am an immovable cause that moves all things...
>
> "Those who cannot understand this speech should not trouble their hearts about it. For as long as man does not equal this truth, he will not understand this speech. For this is an unhidden truth that has come immediately from the heart of God."

In short: Eckhart knew, in a way beyond experience and concepts, that there was 'something' beyond 'God;' and that that 'something' is 'I.' This he was compelled to express in concepts and in a manner that would allow him – barely – to escape being killed for his trouble.

## II

Thus:

1.
Being is.
Being lets beingness be.
Beingness is presence, the experiencing of being.
Being 'gives' presence, lets presence, beingness, be.

"Being lets 'beings' be present and lets beingness be their presence." (Reiner Schurmann)

Being is 'ising': Being is all that *is*.
Thus, anything which *is*,
inasmuch as it is, is Being.

Being is Presence, capital 'P.'

Being has been called God, All That Is, *Sat Chit Ananda;*
Being, Consciousness, Outpouring.
Perfect. Brilliant. Stillness.


2.
It can be asked, What is prior to Being?
'What' lets Being be?
As it is prior to Being, this 'what' is not.
Here is Void, Nothingness, no-thing-ness.
Prior to Being, 'it' lets Being be:
That in which Being is,
Plenum, the fullness of no-thing-ness
out of which, in which, as which
Being (and hence all beingness) arises.

The paths of mysticism, *bhakti,* and *jnana*
join here and end here.
All paths can lead this far and no further.

'Being' and 'Nothing' are the last concepts,
and the last experiences, available to us.

From here there is only the open door, darkness beyond;
stepping through, falling beyond emptiness.


3.
Prior to Being and Nothingness,
which lets both Being and Nothingness be,
is inexpressible, ineffable.

Conceptually, the question can be asked;
but here thought and concepts reach a wall, an abyss.

## Epilogue: An Eckhartian Ontology

The mind cannot make the leap to an answer
*conceptually or experientially.*
However: it can be *known*, apperceived, inseen
(inheard, infelt, intasted.)
Does exist. Cannot be expressed.
Here, words and ideas can only
point in the general direction.

'Godhead:' that from which God comes;
*Parabrahman:* that from which *Brahman* arises;
but these words mean nothing,
are only superlatives added to existing concepts.

The words try to point not only beyond themselves but
beyond beyond;
beyond any ultimate that can be
thought of, conceived,
by the human mind or heart.

Yet it can be *known*
(in a way beyond knowledge)
in silence, in stillness
*in* the heart:
(in complete letting-go:
the breakthrough, the crushing flash
which incinerates all sense of separation.)
*Tat tvam asi:* I am that.
That is what 'I' is.
Outpouring in Itself Being and non-being,
beingness and nothingness,
What-Is and Void.
Unborn.
Eternal.
I.

---

*"Our original nature is, in highest truth,
devoid of any atom of objectivity.
It is void, omnipresent, silent, pure;
it is glorious and mysterious peaceful joy
and that is all.
Enter deeply into it by yourself awakening."*

---

- Huang Po

Reality's cloister
        the circumscribing barrier
   no vision can detect no thought penetrate
in one glance this beyond-which-nothing
    at a single point pierced by not-this
shatters
    into nothingness
    dissolving the fabric
              undoing the weaving of the veil

can there be any identity when there is this
    knowing, immediate irrevocable
        i am not, nor any else –
can there then be any role for the ghost
    found standing in the mist
        of that dissolved veil?

        no seer sage, no guru guide –
can there be any guiding on a journey such as this?
    a journey from here to here
    a voyage neither begun nor ended
        along no path, a billion paths
            no traveller. no returning

the only bodhisattva's vow –
simply Being this One All I Am
    no fear, no attachment
        no intention or expectation
    no separation no connection
    no identity
    uncaring
Presence
    Being
    Stillness here
and so Being be emptiness
        an opening

forever seeing I, amidst I unseeing –

All That Is – That Is All

# NOTES

The following are quotations and references not credited in the text:

page vii: "It's all words, no?..." quote from Bianca Nixdorf can be found on page 302 of Ramesh Balsekar's book, *Your Head in the Tiger's Mouth*, Blayne Bardo, ed., Redondo Beach, CA: Advaita Press, 1998.

also on page vii: "When you are very quiet..." This unusually quixotic quote from Maharaj is from *Consciousness and the Absolute: The Final Talks of Sri Nisargadatta Maharaj*, Jean Dunn, ed., Durham, NC: Acorn Press, 1994, page 76. Thank you Michael.

pages 14 and 373: "...Settles forevermore the ponderous equator to its line..." from Ralph Waldo Emerson, *Lectures and Biographical Sketches*, Honolulu, Hawaii: University Press of the Pacific, 2003.

pages 36, 64, 100, 141, and 271: "...the peace that passes all understanding..." from the Christian scriptures, *Philippians* 4:7.

pages 41, 73, and 225: "The Tao that can be spoken..." these are the famous opening lines of Lao Tzu's *Tao Te Ching*, Gia-Fu Feng & Jane English, trans. New York: Random House Vintage Books, 1989

pages 50 and 220: "...not my will but Thine be done..." from the Christian scriptures, *Gospel of Matthew* 26:39.

pages 50 and 222: "...only he who loses his life will find it..." from the Christian scriptures, *Gospel of Matthew* 10:39.

page 58: "...eye has not seen nor has ear heard nor has the human heart conceived..." from the Christian scriptures, *I Corinthians* 2:9.

page 87 and *passim*: "Dr. Bronner's" is a registered trade mark of Dr. Bronner's Magic Soaps, Inc., Escondido, CA: *www.drbronner.com*.

page 88: "I trust I make myself obscure?" is attributed to Sir Thomas More in the movie, *A Man For All Seasons*. Commentary on theological and metaphysical discussions in general.

page 102: "...a tale told by an idiot, full of sound and fury, signifying nothing..." from William Shakespeare, *Macbeth*, Act V, Scene 5.

page 113 and 164: "No Guru, No Method, No Teacher" is from Van Morrison's song *In The Garden*, on the album *No Guru, no Method, no Teacher*, Polygram Records, 1986. (Van Morrison has another song, and album, entitled *Enlightenment*, but that didn't seem relevant.)

pages 122, 135, 183, 201, and variations *passim:* "Consciousness is all there is." This concept was a mainstay of Ramesh Balsekar's early teaching, and will be familiar to anyone who has read his earlier books or listened to his talks in the period prior to around the year 2000. An example among many too numerous to cite: *Consciousness Speaks,* Redondo Beach, CA: Advaita Press, 1992, page 22. Needless to say perhaps: if Consciousness is all there is, there is no thing else.

page 181: "We dance 'round in a ring and suppose..." and "When we understand, we are at the center..." My appreciation to Stephen Mitchell, who juxtaposed these two texts in the Foreword to his book, *The Enlightened Heart,* New York: Harper Collins, 1989.

page 185: "...we are such stuff as dreams are made on..." from William Shakespeare, *The Tempest,* Act IV, Scene 1.

page 207: "...Robert Adams once suggested..." See Catherine Asche's 'Editor's Note' in Wayne Liquorman's *Acceptance of What Is,* Redondo Beach, CA: Advaita Press, 2000, page vii. As near as I can make out, the original basis for this may come from Robert Adams, *Silence of the Heart,* Atlanta GA: Acropolis Books, 1999, page 193.

pages 236 and 335: "...life, the universe, and everything..." is, of course, a reference to Douglas Adams' *Hitchhiker's Guide to the Galaxy* 'five-volume trilogy.' Vol. 1-4: New York: Simon & Schuster Pocket Books, 1979-1987. Sorry, but I couldn't resist. While we're here, allow me to quote the principles Adams lays out on the flyleaves of the fifth volume of the series, *Mostly Harmless,* New York: Harmony Books, 1992:
> "Anything that happens, happens.
> Anything that, in happening, causes something else to happen, causes something else to happen.
> Anything that, in happening, causes itself to happen again, happens again.
> It doesn't necessarily do it in chronological order, however."

With an appreciation for the import of the last line, is it possible to find anything in this which is inconsistent with the profound teaching of the perennial wisdom?

page 243: "...a voice of one crying out in the wilderness..." from the Hebrew scriptures, *Isaiah 40:3.*

page 245: "My skin is not my own." from Frank Herbert, *Children of Dune,* New York: Penguin Books, 1987. Herbert's *Dune* series is an allegorical tale of awakening if ever there was: "The sleeper must awaken." As in *The Matrix,* the fanciful concepts of what it is that is awakened *to* are useless, but that's not surprising. It is the metaphor of waking up that is well illustrated in both.

page 249: "...as in a glass, darkly..." from the Christian scriptures, *I Corinthians* 13:12.

page 256: "...greater love than this, no man hath..." from the Christian scriptures, *Gospel of John* 15:13.

page 259: *"per omnia saecula saeculorum."* from the Roman Catholic tradition, a commonly used ending for prayers, occurring frequently in the Latin mass. Its usual translation was "world without end," which not only misses the original sense but also introduces a bizarre concept, as the Catholic church in fact explicitly teaches that the world will come to an end. A more faithful translation might be "through all ages of ages," or "throughout all eternities, eternally," which comes closer to the sense of timelessness in which it is used here. (There are no ex-Catholics, only recovering Catholics.)

page 290: variation on "Whatever it takes to break your heart and wake you up..." from Mark Matousek, *Sex, Death, Enlightenment*, New York: Riverhead Books, 1996.

page 315: "Then as a stranger, bid it welcome..." from William Shakespeare, *Hamlet*, Act I, Scene 5.

page 327: "It has already long been everything and always is everything." from Hermann Hesse, *Siddhartha*, New York: Bantam Books, 1971, page 145

page 341: "A stranger in a strange land." from the title of Robert Heinlein's *Stranger in a Strange Land*, New York: Penguin Books, 1987. Originally from the Hebrew scriptures, *Exodus* 2:22.

page 346: "...enter the kingdom of heaven..." from the Christian scriptures, *Gospel of Matthew* 19:23.

page 361: "...lead lives of quiet desperation..." from Henry David Thoreau, *Walden*, New York: Penguin Books, 1986.

page 373: "...the devil can cite Scripture..." from William Shakespeare, *The Merchant of Venice*, Act I, Scene 2.

page 381: "Ken Wilber was once asked...." This is from an interview with *Shambhala Sun* magazine, and appeared in the September 1996 issue. It can also be found in Ken Wilber, *One Taste: Daily Reflections on Integral Spirituality*, Boston: Shambhala Publications, 2000, page 325.

# READINGS

(A partial listing)

Abbott, Edwin
    *Flatland*
    New York: Dover Publications, 1992

Adams, Robert
    *Silence of the Heart*
    Atlanta, GA: Acropolis Books, 1999

Adyashanti
    *The Impact of Awakening*
    Los Gatos, CA: Open Gate Publishing, 2000

—    *My Secret is Silence*
    Los Gatos, CA: Open Gate Publishing, 2003

—    *Emptiness Dancing*
    Los Gatos, CA: Open Gate Publishing, 2004

Avery, Samuel
    *The Dimensional Structure of Consciousness:*
    *A Physical Basis for Immaterialism*
    Lexington, KY: Compari, 1995

Balsekar, Ramesh
    *Pointers From Nisargadatta Maharaj*
    Durham, NC: Acorn Press, 1982

—    *Experience of Immortality*
    Mumbai, India: Chetana, 1984

—    *Explorations Into the Eternal*
    Durham, NC: Acorn Press, 1987

—    *A Duet of One: The Ashtavakra Gita Dialogue*
    Redondo Beach, CA: Advaita Press, 1989

—    *The Final Truth: A Guide to Ultimate Understanding*
    Redondo Beach, CA: Advaita Press, 1989

—    *Consciousness Speaks*
    Wayne Liquorman, ed.
    Redondo Beach, CA: Advaita Press, 1992

—    *A Net of Jewels*
    Gary Starbuck, ed.
    Redondo Beach, CA: Advaita Press, 1996

—    *Your Head in the Tiger's Mouth*
    Blayne Bardo, ed.
    Redondo Beach, CA: Advaita Press, 1998

—— *Who Cares?*
Blayne Bardo, ed.
Redondo Beach, CA: Advaita Press, 1999

—— *Advaita, The Buddha, and the Unbroken Whole*
Susan Waterman, ed.
Mumbai, India: Zen Publications, 2000

—— *Sin & Guilt: Monstrosity of Mind*
Susan Waterman, ed.
Mumbai, India: Zen Publications, 2000

—— *The Ultimate Understanding*
Susan Waterman, ed.
London: Watkins Publishers, 2002

—— *Consciousness Writes*
Mumbai, India: Zen Publications, 2003

—— *The Wisdom of Balsekar*
Alan Jacobs, ed.
London: Watkins Publishers, 2004

Barks, Coleman, & Michael Green
*The Illuminated Prayer: The Five Times Prayer of the Sufis*
New York: Ballantine Books, 2000

Brunton, Paul
*A Search in Secret India*
New Delhi, India: Cosmo Publications, 2004

Caplan, Mariana
*Halfway Up The Mountain: The Error of Premature Claims to Enlightenment*
Prescott, AZ: Hohm Press, 1999

Carse, James P.
*Breakfast at the Victory: The Mysticism of Ordinary Experience*
New York: HarperCollins, 1994

Chuang Tzu
*The Complete Works of Chuang Tzu*
Burton Watson, trans.
New York: Columbia University Press, 1968

—— *The Way of Chuang Tzu*
Thomas Merton, ed.
New York: New Directions Publishing, 1969

*The Cloud of Unknowing*
William Johnston, ed.
New York: Doubleday Image Books, 1973

DeMello, Anthony
*The Heart of the Enlightened: A Book of Story-Meditations*
New York: Doubleday, 1989

—   *Awareness: The Perils and Opportunities of Reality*
    New York: Doubleday, 1990

—   *The Way to Love*
    New York: Doubleday, 1992

*The Diamond Sutra*
    Mu Soeng, ed.
    Somerville, MA, Wisdom Publications, 2000

Eckhart
    *Wandering Joy: Meister Eckhart's Mystical Philosophy*
    Reiner Schurmann, trans. & ed.
    Great Barrington, MA: Lindisfarne Books, 2001

—   *Meister Eckhart, Volume 1: Teacher and Preacher*
    Bernard McGinn, trans. & ed.
    Mahwah, NJ: Paulist Press, 1986

—   *Meister Eckhart, Volume 2: The Essential Sermons, Commentaries, Treatises, and Defense*
    Edmund Colledge & Bernard McGinn, trans. & eds.
    Mahwah, NJ: Paulist Press, 1981

Eliott, T. S
    *Four Quartets*
    New York: Harcourt Brace Javanovich, 1971

Feuerstein, Georg
    *Holy Madness: The Shock Tactics and Radical Teachings of Crazy-Wise Adepts, Holy Fools, and Rascal Gurus*
    New York: Paragon House, 1990

Gangaji
    *You Are That: Volumes 1,2*
    Ashland, OR: The Gangaji Foundation, 1995 & 1996

*The Gospel of Thomas: The Hidden Sayings of Jesus*
    Marvin Meyer, trans. & ed.
    New York: HarperSanFrancisco, 1992

*The Gospel of Thomas: Annotated & Explained*
    Stevan Davies, trans. & ed.
    Woodstock, VT: Skylight Paths Publishing, 2002

Goswami, Amit
    *Physics of the Soul*
    Charlottesville, VA: Hampton Roads Publishing, 2001

Hafiz
    *The Gift*
    Daniel Ladinsky, trans.
    New York: Penguin Books, 1999

— *The Subject Tonight is Love*
Daniel Ladinsky, trans.
New York: Penguin Books, 2003

Han-Shan
*Cold Mountain: 100 Poems by the T'ang Poet Han-Shan*
Burton Watson, trans.
New York: Columbia University Press, 1970

— *The Collected Songs of Cold Mountain*
Red Pine, trans.
Port Townsend, WA: Copper Canyon Press, 2000

Harding, Douglas
*On Having No Head: Zen and the Rediscovery of the Obvious*
Carlsbad, CA: Inner Directions, 2002

— *Look For Yourself*
Carlsbad, CA: Inner Directions, 2002

Huang Po
*The Zen Teaching of Huang Po on the Transmission of Mind*
John Blofeld, trans.
New York: Grove Press, 1958

Hui Hai
*Zen Teaching of Instantaneous Awakening*
John Blofeld, trans.
Ashprington, UK: Buddhist Publishing Group, 1987

Hui-Neng
*The Sutra of Hui-Neng, Grand Master of Zen*
Thomas Cleary, trans.
Boston: Shambhala Publications, 1998

Ikkyu
*Wild Ways: Zen Poems of Ikkyu*
John Stevens, trans.
Boston: Shambhala Publications, 1995

— *Crow With No Mouth: Fifteenth Century Zen Master Ikkyu*
Stephen Berg, trans.
Port Townsend, WA: Copper Canyon Press, 1989

Kabir
*Songs of Kabir*
Rabindranath Tagore, trans.
Boston: Weiser Books, 2002

— *The Weaver's Songs*
Vinay Dharwadker, trans.
New Delhi: Penguin Books India, 2003

— *Kabir: Ecstatic Poems: Versions by Robert Bly*
Robert Bly, ed.
Boston: Beacon Press, 2004

Kapleau Roshi, Philip
*Awakening to Zen: The Teachings of Philip Kapleau Roshi*
Polly Young-Eisendrath and Rafe Martin, eds.
Boston: Shambhala Publications, 2001

Katie, Byron
*Loving What Is: Four Questions That Can Change Your Life*
New York: Three Rivers Press, 2002

Kersschot, Jan
*This Is It: Dialogues on the Nature of Oneness*
London: Watkins Publishing, 2004

Krishnamurti, Jiddu
*Freedom From the Known*
New York: HarperCollins, 1969

Krishnamurti, U.G.
*The Courage to Stand Alone*
New York: Plover Press, 1997

— *Thought is Your Enemy*
New Delhi, India: Smriti Books, 2001

— *The Mystique of Enlightenment*
Boulder, CO: Sentient Publications, 2002

*The Lankavatara Sutra*
D.T. Suzuki, trans.
New Delhi, India, Munshiram Manoharlal, 1999

*The Lankavatara Sutra: An Epitomized Version*
D.T. Suzuki, trans., and Dwight Goddard, ed.
Rhinebeck, NY: Monkfish Book Publishing, 1932

Lao Tsu (Lao Tzu)
*Tao Te Ching*
Gia-Fu Feng & Jane English, trans.
New York: Random House Vintage Books, 1989

Le Guin, Ursula
*The Pathways of Desire*, a short story
in the collection, *The Compass Rose*
New York: Harper Paperbacks, 1982

Levine, Steven
*Healing Into Life and Death*
New York: Doubleday Anchor, 1984

— *Who Dies? An Investigation of Conscious Living and Conscious Dying*
New York: Doubleday Anchor, 1982

Lin-chi
> *The Zen Teachings of Master Lin-chi*
> Burton Watson, trans.
> New York: Columbia University Press, 1999

Liquorman, Wayne
> *Acceptance of What Is*
> Redondo Beach, CA: Advaita Press, 2000

— (as Ram Tzu)
> *No Way: for the Spiritually "Advanced"*
> Redondo Beach, CA: Advaita Press, 1990

McKenna, Jed
> *Spiritual Enlightenment: The Damnedest Thing*
> www.WisefoolPress.com: Wisefool Press, 2002

— *Spiritually Incorrect Enlightenment*
> www.WisefoolPress.com: Wisefool Press, 2004

Marvelly, Paula,
> *Teachers of One: Living Advaita; Conversations on the Nature of Non-Duality*
> London: Watkins Publishing, 2002

Mitchell, Stephen, ed.
> *The Enlightened Heart: An Anthology of Sacred Poetry*
> New York: HarperCollins, 1993

— *The Enlightened Mind: An Anthology of Sacred Prose*
> New York: HarperCollins, 1993

Nisargadatta Maharaj
> *I Am That*
> Maurice Frydman, trans.
> Durham, NC: Acorn Press, 1973

— *Consciousness and the Absolute: The Final Talks of Sri Nisargadatta Maharaj*
> Jean Dunn, ed.
> Durham, NC: Acorn Press, 1994

— *Prior To Consciousness*
> Jean Dunn, ed.
> Durham, NC: Acorn Press, 1997

— *Seeds of Consciousness*
> Jean Dunn, ed.
> Durham, NC: Acorn Press, 1982

— *The Ultimate Medicine*
> Robert Powell, ed.
> San Diego, CA: Blue Dove Press, 2001

— *The Nectar of Immortality*
Robert Powell, ed.
San Diego, CA: Blue Dove Press, 2001

— *The Experience of Nothingness*
Robert Powell, ed.
San Diego, CA: Blue Dove Press, 2001

— *The Wisdom Teaching of Nisargadatta Maharaj*
Carlsbad, CA: Inner Directions, 2003

Nisker, Wes
*The Essential Crazy Wisdom*
Berkely, CA: Ten Speed Press, 1998

Osho (Rajneesh)
*Autobiography of a Spiritually Incorrect Mystic*
New York: St. Martin's Press, 2001

— *Love, Freedom, and Aloneness*
New York: St. Martin's Press, 2001

Parker, John W.
*Dialogues With Emerging Spiritual Teachers*
Fort Collins, CO: Sagewood Press, 2000

Parsons, Tony
*As It Is: The Open Secret of Spiritual Awakening*
Carlsbad, CA: Inner Directions, 2002

— *All There Is*
Shaftesbury, Dorset, UK: Open Secret Publishing, 2003

— *Invitation to Awaken: Embracing Our Natural State of Presence*
Carlsbad, CA: Inner Directions, 2004

Poonja, H.W.L.
*Nothing Ever Happened, Volumes 1,2,3*
David Godman, ed.
Boulder, CO: Avadhuta Foundation, 1998

— *The Truth Is*
York Beach, ME: Samuel Weiser Inc, 2000

Ramana Maharshi
*Be As You Are: The Teachings of Ramana Maharshi*
David Godman, ed.
New York: Penguin Arkana, 1985

— *The Collected Works of Ramana Maharshi*
Arthur Osborne, ed.
Boston: Weiser Books, 1997

— *The Power of the Presence: Transforming Encounters With Sri Ramana Maharshi: Volumes 1, 2, 3*
David Godman, ed
Pondicherry, India: All India Press, 2000

— *The Essential Teachings of Ramana Maharshi*
Carlsbad, CA: Inner Directions, 2001

— *Talks With Ramana Maharshi: On Realizing Abiding Peace and Happiness*
Carlsbad, CA: Inner Directions, 2001

— *Ramana, Shankara, and the Forty Verses: The Essential Teachings of Advaita*
Alan Jacobs, ed.
London: Watkins Publishing, 2002

Ram Das
*Be Here Now*
Three Rivers, MI: Three Rivers Press, 1971

— *The Only Dance There Is*
New York: Doubleday, 1974

Rumi, Jalaluddin
*The Essential Rumi*
Coleman Barks, trans.
New York: HarperCollins, 1996

— *The Glance*
Coleman Barks, trans.
New York: Penguin Books, 1999

— *Hidden Music*
Maryam Mafi & Azima Melita Kolin, trans.
London: HarperCollins, 2001

Segal, Suzanne
*Collision With The Infinite*
San Diego, CA: Blue Dove Press, 1998

Seng-Ts'an
*Hsin-Hsin Ming*
Richard B. Clarke, trans.
Buffalo, NY: White Pine Press, 2001

Shankara
*Shankara's Crest-Jewel of Discrimination*
Swami Prabhavananda & Christopher Isherwood, trans.
Hollywood, CA: Vedanta Press, 1978

Sobottka, Stanley
*A Course in Consciousness*
http://faculty.virginia.edu/consciousness/home.html: 2004

Suzuki, D. T.
    *Essays in Zen Buddhism*
    New York: Grove Press, 1961

Tagore, Rabindranath
    *Gitanjali*
    New Delhi, India: Rupa Co., 2002

——    *Fireflies*
    New Delhi, India: Rupa Co., 2002

Teillard de Chardin, Pierre
    *Le Milieu Divin*
    London: William Collins & Sons, 1962

Tung-shan
    *The Record of Tung-shan*
    William F. Powell, trans.
    Honolulu, Hawaii: University of Hawaii Press, 1986

Vaughan-Lee, Llewellyn
    *The Bond With the Beloved*
    Inverness, CA: The Golden Sufi Center, 1993

——    *The Face Before I Was Born*
    Inverness, CA: The Golden Sufi Center, 1998

Wachowski, Andy, and Larry Wachowski, Directors
    *The Matrix*
    Warner Studios Video, VHS format, 2004

Waite, Dennis
    *The Book of One: The Spiritual Path of Advaita*
    New York: O Books, 2003

Walsh, Roger
    *Essential Spirituality*
    New York: John Wiley & Sons, 1999

Watson, Lyall
    *Gifts of Unknown Things*
    New York: Bantam Books, 1978

Wei Wu Wei
    *Posthumous Pieces*
    Hong Kong: Hong Kong University Press, 1968

——    *The Tenth Man*
    Hong Kong: Hong Kong University Press, 1971

——    *Open Secret*
    Hong Kong: Hong Kong University Press, 1971

——    *All Else Is Bondage: Non-Volitional Living*
    Fairfield, IA: Sunstar Publishing, 1999

— *Ask The Awakened: The Negative Way*
  Boulder, CO: Sentient Publications, 2002

— *Fingers Pointing Toward the Moon: Reflections of
  a Pilgrim on the Way*
  Boulder, CO: Sentient Publications, 2003

— *Why Lazarus Laughed: The Essential Doctrine;
  Zen-Advaita-Tantra*
  Boulder, CO: Sentient Publications, 2003

— *Unworldly Wise: As the Owl Remarked to the Rabbit*
  Boulder, CO: Sentient Publications, 2004

Wilber, Ken
 *Grace and Grit: Spirituality and Healing in the Life and Death
 of Treya Killam Wilber*
 Boston: Shambhala Publications, 1991

— *The Essential Ken Wilber: An Introductory Reader*
  Boston: Shambhala Publications, 1998

— *One Taste: Daily Reflections on Integral Spirituality*
  Boston: Shambhala Publications, 2000

— *No Boundary: Eastern and Western Approaches to
  Personal Growth*
  Boston: Shambhala Publications, 2001

— *The Simple Feeling of Being: Embracing Your True Nature*
  Boston: Shambhala Publications, 2004

Wu Men
 *The Gateless Barrier: The Wu-men kuan (Mumonkan)*
 Robert Aitken, trans.
 New York: North Point Press, 1991

— *The Gateless Barrier: Zen Comments on the Mumonkan*
  Zenkei Shibayama
  Boston: Shambhala Publications, 2000

david carse lives in vermont
where he continues to work as a carpenter.
he does not teach.